TELEGRAM

A COLLECTION OF 27 ISSUES

DISCARD

By Maranda Elizabeth

Telegram
A Collection of 27 Issues
Maranda Elizabeth

Published by Mend My Dress Press, Tacoma, WA
MendMyDress@gmail.com
MendMyDress.com

Library of Congress Cataloging-in-publication data availible upon request

Elizabeth/ Maranda
        Telegram/ Maranda Elizabeth
        ISBN-13 978-0-9850131-6-5 (pb)
        1. Zines 2. Autobiography 3. Mental Health
        4. Gender 5. Title

Manufactured in the United States of America

TELEGRAM

A COLLECTION OF 27 ISSUES

By Maranda Elizabeth

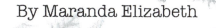

Contents

Issue 21 was written before issue 20 and therefore appears before issue 20

This Zine-Book is Dedicated To:

Weirdos & loners & misfits & freaks everywhere! We all need to have our own voices, and use them, and know that our stories & feelings & experiences are real & valid, and we are allowed to share them, and to feel both vulnerable and safe when we do. We can be quiet when we want/need to be and noisy when we want/need to be. We are working to create spaces in our hearts, homes, towns, and worlds, where it is okay to be, to breathe, to exist, and to take care of ourselves and each other in any way we need to. We are learning about all these processes and more, we are finding and befriending one another, we are creating magical times & spaces, we are surviving & living & thriving. Dancing, hugging, laughing, cuddling, crying, running, making, destroying, growing, learning, collecting, writing, singing, playing, building, everything...

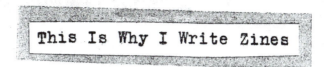

This Is Why I Write Zines

The questions I get asked the most are, 'What is a zine?', 'Why do you make zines?', and 'How do you share such personal stuff with friends / acquaintances / strangers / everyone?'

The reason I write is this:

I have always written. As children, my sister and I learned how to write before we were in school; we were the first kids who could write our names and write full sentences. I loved paper and pens and office supplies, and on days when our mom had to go to work and there was no one to take care of us, my sister and I would go to her office with her, where we were given stacks of scrap paper, and we would pretend we were also working, writing important notes on all the papers. I've kept a diary from the age of five, and have been writing stories for almost as long. When I was really young, I would invent my own characters, and set them right down in the middles of the universes of *The Baby-Sitters' Club* and *Sailor Moon*. In Grade Seven, I got the highest mark in class for an assignment to make a children's book. I wrote a story about three cats who decide to become vegetarian ("Let's befriend the fish instead of eating them!" they exclaim, as they play by the pond.) I cut & pasted the cats out of felt, and wrote the text with a gold gel pen. We would turn tissue paper boxes and cereal boxes into mailboxes, and tape them to our bedroom doors. We would design the covers of fake magazines, dream up fake articles, subscribe to one another's titles.

Zines are also how I learned to write. A decade-long and continuing practice/process… It was a long time before I felt like I could truly be honest in my zines. Years. And even now, there is always something I am holding back. Something must remain mine entirely. I am often asked how I learned such honesty. I don't know if there are words for that kind of learning process; it just happened, eventually. I knew that if I wasn't honest, if I didn't write the things that scared me, I would die. It wasn't until after my first suicide attempt, shortly after I'd turned twenty-one, that I realized how badly I needed to tell my stories and share my secrets.

I didn't know anyone who was writing about mental health at the time, so I started writing about it myself. I was afraid, of course, of so many things, but there was nothing else I could do but write. And still, it's the only thing I can do, the only thing I *want* to do. I write out of necessity.

Another reason I write is this:

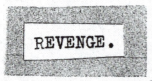

My not-so-secret wish, especially when I am feeling particularly bitter, is that everybody who ever treated me like shit in the past is gonna stumble into a bookstore and see my name and my words on the bookshelves, or search my name online and see that I am doing all these wonderful magical things and my life has gotten so much better since they disappeared. I want to give a real fuck-you-I-made-it-and-you-didn't angry-grateful middle-finger-&-autograph to everyone who was mean to me, everyone who bullied me and threw garbage at me and yelled from the windows of their cars at me in my small hometown, even though that's not my general attitude in my daily life (anymore). If success is the best revenge, if living well is the best revenge, then my zines and this book and my life are revenge, I am revenge, and this is enough for me to know that it was all worth it.

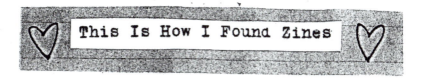

This Is How I Found Zines

I encountered and re-encountered zines a few times before I started making my own. In Grade School, between the ages of nine and twelve (!), the school library had a small collection of music fanzines. It was a half-size black & white zine, stapled in the middle. I forget the title, but I remember reading interviews with Hole, Bikini Kill, Nirvana, and Sonic Youth. At the same time, there was a boy in our class who would make mix tapes for my sister and I; they were mostly filled with Nirvana songs, and we were lucky enough to have teachers who occasionally let us listen to the tapes on those indestructible little brown tape recorders found in classrooms all over Canada.

I found zines again when I was thirteen. Two girls at our school had begun making a compilation zine, which anyone could contribute to, and they would hand out free copies around school hallways, coffeeshops (well, the one coffeeshop we had in our town, which would go out of business every year or two, only to return with a new name and new management, cycling like this for a decade or so), and sidewalks. The zine was called HEY (sometimes the acronym meant Helping Encourage Youth, sometimes it meant whatever you wanted it to mean), and was filled with rants, poetry, sketches, crosswords, short stories, and so on, all written by local teenagers. Although I read every issue (and desperately wish I had held onto them!), I was too shy to contribute anything of my own.

My sister and I started making zines when we were sixteen. We worked on a zine about nothing & everything for a little while, but soon found we would rather make our own perzines (personal zines), rather than compile our writing together. So I started making *Telegram*, and she started making *Culture Slut*.

We shared a bedroom at the time. We were going through our glam phase, obsessed with David Bowie, T. Rex in the 70's, Robin Black & the Intergalactic Rock Stars, Rachel Stamp, in the 2000's, and the movie *Velvet Goldmine*. Our walls were painted hot pink and we draped feather boas over our furniture. I would sit on my bed, she would sit on hers, and together, we would listen to mix tapes from our pen pals and make zines.

I can't say this enough: Zines are not a quirky thing I do for fun! Zines are something I do for survival. With zines, I have found friends, communities, feminists, radicals, queers, weirdos, new ideas, new ways of thinking; I've found guts & courage & honesty; with zines, I have learned critical-thinking skills, anti-oppression tools and strategies, histories & herstories & hirstories, politics (and how the personal is political & the political is personal), intersectionality, ways to share & learn & create... so much more than I could ever say. Zines have saved my life, over and over.

A Note About the Title, & Why I'm Not Re-Sharing All the Pages.

Telegram borrows its name from a T.Rex song called *Telegram Sam*. My zine was originally called *Telegram Ma'am*, so that is the name that appears on older covers, but not a name I use anymore. When I started making this zine, I was going through my glam phase and also getting into feminism and riot grrrl, and I chose a title that I felt reflected & embraced those aspects of my life (as well as my love of snail mail). Eventually, I realized that although I am still a raging feminist, I no longer identify as female, and writing under a gendered title made me feel uncomfortable and alienated/alienating. Altering the title has helped me feel more free, open, and in control.

I'm just gonna say it: Some of my old zines are really embarrassing. I think a lot of zinesters feel the same way about their old zines. I've evolved as a feminist, a writer, and a weirdo, and I just don't think all those words are worth sharing again. I would rather let them go and share more important things. My writing and my politics have been and continue to be processes. I want to move on, continue learning & living & creating.

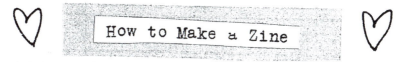

How to Make a Zine

Anybody can make a zine. You need paper, a pen, scissors, glue, staples, and access to a photocopier. You can handwrite your zine, type it on a junk store typewriter, or choose a font and print the text from your computer. You can write about *anything*. I started by writing small, maybe not terribly important, things, and gradually became more honest and open and started writing about my real life and what was really going on. I dared myself to write about things that scare me, things that scare me to share, and I dared myself to photocopy them and share them. This has saved my life. I am not exaggerating.

What do you want to write about? You could go out on a walk and tell me about the things you saw and the thoughts you thought. Tell me what your home is like, what your family is like, what you've been learning lately, what you'd like to learn. Tell me about projects you're working on, places and spaces you like to spend your time.

```
You can write about...

Flowers, coffee, dancing, depress-
ion, tattoos, painting, bicycles,
trees, apartments, cats, sex,
food, confusion, sewing, emotions,
adventures, graffiti, traveling,
community, fear...

Seriously, anything!
```

Once you've written your zine, it's time to cut&paste it all together, and share it (if you want to)! I like to put my zines together on my bedroom floor, but you can make yours wherever you want; maybe not outside, unless you want your words to blow away in the wind. Then again, those words could then be encountered by strangers who would then be inspired to make their own zine, so maybe you do want to make them outside. When everything is just how you want it, and the glue is dry, it's time to make a trip to your nearest or cheapest photocopier. Most towns have copy shops, but those places can get pricey, and good copy scams are getting harder to find. Ask around. If you find a place that still goes by the honour system, you're in luck. You can lie and save money. If you have friends or family who work in offices, ask if you can use their photocopier. Sometimes you can scam copies at university campuses, too. Libraries have photocopiers, but my local library recently upgraded their technology to count copies and prints, with a machine that makes you pay before you print, so they're not the place to go for copies. But don't worry; you'll find a trusty photocopier, and your zine will be complete!

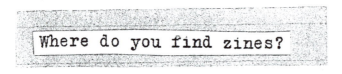

Zines are everywhere. You just have to be looking for them. Sometimes I think the best way to find zines is to make zines, just like the best way to get a letter in the mail is to send a letter in the mail. There are zinesters who write & share locally, and there are zinesters who write & share internationally. That means you can find zines in your own town (yes, even if you haven't met them yet, there are probably other zinesters in your town!), or you can go online and find zinesters everywhere else. People sell their own zines individually on sites like Etsy.com and various messageboards, and there are also a lot of distros, where you can get lots of different zines from lots of different people sent to you via snail mail in one magical package.

♡ ♡ ♡

Where do you find people who will read your zines?

Again, people who will read your zines are everywhere! They are in your town (unless you don't want to share your zines locally right now, and that is okay) and they are all over the world. Zines usually cost around $1 - $3 each, or can be traded for zines, mix tapes, whatever. The best way to get people to read your zines is to read their zines; ask to trade with other zinesters you meet in person and online, get zines from distros and write to the creators and send them your own zine; bring your zine to shows and other gatherings and events; leave your zines in libraries and bookstores and bathrooms and wherever else you feel like it. Also, there are zine fairs and zine readings being organized all over the place, all the time. Search for events in your area. You can also rent a P.O. box at your local post office if you don't want to give out your home address, but they cost a pretty penny, so take time to figure out if that's what you wanna do. And you can use a fake name, but talk to a postal worker first to make sure mail sent to that name will be delivered; sometimes there are problems with this, especially if you receive a package in the mail and need to show ID to pick it up. As long as you've got zines on your minds and in your hearts and in your hands, you will connect with other zinesters, I promise!

♡ ♡ ♡

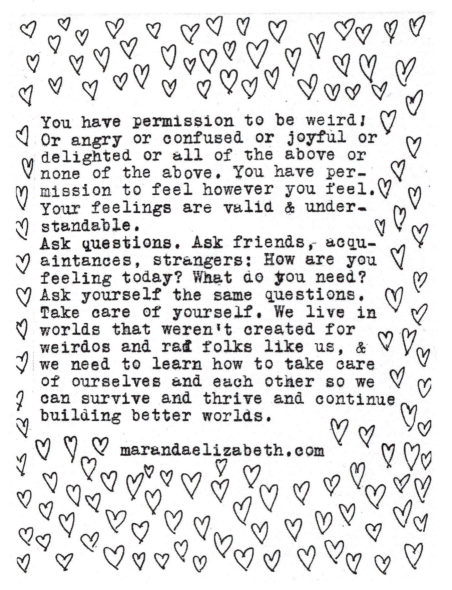

You have permission to be weird!
Or angry or confused or joyful or
delighted or all of the above or
none of the above. You have permission to feel however you feel.
Your feelings are valid & under-
standable.
Ask questions. Ask friends, acquaintances, strangers: How are you
feeling today? What do you need?
Ask yourself the same questions.
Take care of yourself. We live in
worlds that weren't created for
weirdos and rad folks like us, &
we need to learn how to take care
of ourselves and each other so we
can survive and thrive and continue
building better worlds.

marandaelizabeth.com

♡ ♡ ♡

A Sort Of Continuation of the Weirdo
Manifesto / Permission to Be Weird,
which I wrote as I was trying to figure out my priorities in life & why
I write & all that, blah blah...

♡ ♡ ♡

I want to create something that embraces, encourages, and sustains the freaks, weirdos, loners, and misfits, because I've always been all of those things and I don't want to run away from it or try to hide it, and I don't want anyone else to either. I want to be the freak-weirdo-misfit-loner forever, and have the most wonderful days because of it. I dream of creating communities and projects and events that support the radical awesomeness of all of us, where we can have more control over our own worlds, and not be scared to love and talk and write and dream.

Sometimes it seems like everybody hates themselves. Everybody hates everything. Everybody complains. And it's boring. So when I'm feeling down, I start asking myself questions like, What is a healthier action I can take to feel better right now? How can I take care of myself and my friends? How can I change my current mood, my current situation? And then I try to find the energy and inspiration to seek answers and see them through.

The point is, I can't give up. The world wants me to give up; it wants all of us to give up. I refuse. I don't think I was meant to survive, but here I am, so I might as well stick around and use my weirdness and awkwardness to generate positivity all around me, to cultivate meaningful days, to encourage all the other weirdos to do the same. That has become my priority: the care and encouragement of weirdos everywhere.

♡ ♡ ♡

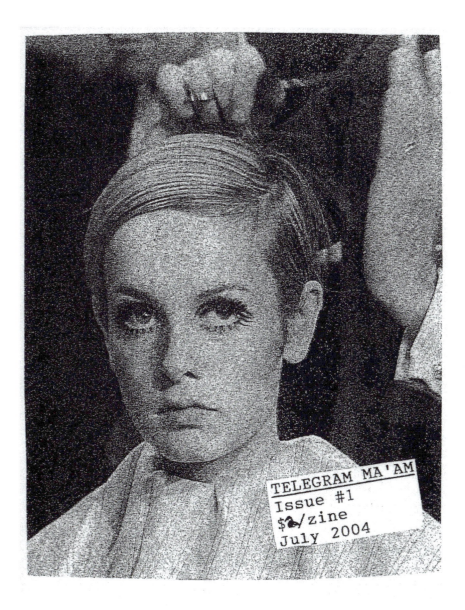

TELEGRAM MA'AM
Issue #1
$2/zine
July 2004

Welcome to issue #1 of my zine. You may already know me as the co-author of another zine called _____. Well, we've pretty much put that one to rest, so I guess you could call this my solo effort. There really is no thee to this; just a small collection of some of my thoughts, ideas, mix tapes, and other junk. I hope you enjoy reading it.

Name: Maranda
Age: 18
Birthday: October 16th, 1985
Favourite Bands: Hole, Nirvana, Pearl Jam, Placebo, One976, CJ Sleez, David Bowie, The White Stripes, T. Rex, Metric, The Sounds, The Cure, The Smiths, Bif Naked, The Raveonettes, Joan Jett, L7, Sarah Slean, Madonna, Yeah Yeah Yeahs, Peaches, Bikini Kill, The Distillers, Melissa Auf der Maur···
Interests: Writing, crafting, sewing, fashion design, reading, zines, feminism, daydreaming, DIY, old Hollywood, snail mail, notebooks, thrift stores
Favourite Magazines: Bust, Bitch, Nylon
Favourite Movies: Velvet Goldmine, Ever After, Rock 'N' Roll High School, Hedwig and the Angry Inch, Moulin Rouge, Rocky Horror Picture Show, But I'm A Cheerleader, Show Me Love, Trainspotting, Slums of Beverley Hills, Girl Interrupted, Donnie Darko, The People Vs. Larry Flynt, Reality Bites, The Seven Year Itch, Some Like It Hot, Funny Face
Favourite Quotes:
 "Life is too important to be taken seriously." — Oscar Wilde
 "Jealousy is all the fun you think they had." — Erica Jong

BOOKS I LOVE

The Torn Skirt by Rebecca Godfrey
Fanny by Erica Jong
Sophie's World by Jostein Gaarder
Cat's Eye by Margaret Atwood
Clara Callan by Richard B. Wright
Violet & Claire by Francesca Lia Block
Into the Forest by Jean Hegland
Prozac Nation by Elizabeth Wurtzel
More, Now, Again by Elizabeth Wurtzel
Disco Bloodbath by James St. James
Don't Sleep With Your Drummer by Jen Sincero
The Practice of Witchcraft by Robin Skelton
The Teenage Liberation Handbook by Grace Llewellyn
Pink Think by Lynn Peril
Perfume by Patrick Suskind
Lolita by Vladimir Nabokov

In my mind, I've been writing an epic novel. This really big book with an enchanted forest, fairies, witches, a castle, a village, magic, glitter, nature, and everything else. I've even drawn a map of the place. I've created some characters but they don't have names yet. I have the perfect descriptions, but they have yet to be put down on paper.

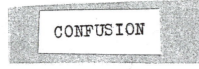

I'm tough and strong but sometimes I'm also naïve and weak. I cry very easily for what seems like no real reason, but physical pain doesn't bother me at all. I cry during certain movies, but I didn't cry when I got hit by a truck. The smallest things can really piss me off, but really big things don't affect me. I have a lot of strange problems. I think I'm agoraphobic. I can't stand leaving the house because I don't like being around people, and I'm always afraid of getting hit by a car. There are so many odd things that I don't know how to fix.

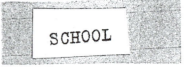

I have never been comfortable in public. I remember always feeling uncomfortable, even when I was a little kid, going to school. Always feeling homesick in the pit of my stomach and feeling like I wanted to cry. I loved when my mom picked me up at lunchtime so I could go home and macaroni & cheese, or mushroom soup, and watch *The Three Stooges*. And I hated going back. In all the years I spent going to school, I never adjusted to it, I never understood the idea of spending five days a week waking up early, then going to a big building to sit at a desk surrounded by people I didn't like. I thought I was way too smart for them, and honestly, I know that I was. I kept to myself in class, never speaking very much, always being quiet, or I would scream and yell when I was mad. and then I would get suspended. It was always one or the other, never anything in between. I get a really creepy feeling looking back on those years. So much time was wasted.

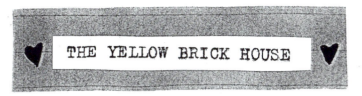

THE YELLOW BRICK HOUSE

Up until a couple years ago, I wanted to live in a square-shaped brick house, and have a coffee table in the livingroom. I realized that probably the only reason I wanted those things was because that's what I had when I was little, before my parents split up. I hadn't even realized I'd been thinking about it because I didn't think their separation bothered me. It happened so long ago that I don't even remember what it was like living with two parents, and how could I miss something I never had anyway? I just don't care. I don't like him so much, and I like living in a house with all women. I don't like the fact that we barely have enough money for groceries most of the time, but I seem to be surviving. This is why I never understand why people hurt so much when their parents get divorced. It didn't affect me emotionally, so I don't know what it's like to care about it.

STRANGER

Almost everyday, I wish I were someone else. Well, not someone else, really, just a better version of myself in a different place. I'd like to be a stranger in town, anonymous, so I can walk around unnoticed, or spend forever looking at books in the library without bumping into anyone I know. I could spend all day at the library, but I don't allow myself to do that here. Maybe I'll try.

Telegram Ma'am
Issue #2
$2/zine
September 2004

INTRO INTRO INTRO INTRO INTRO INTRO

In *Telegram*, I hope to write something that somebody cares about. There's nothing I love more than when I read a zine and it sounds like something I've already written in my diary. Hopefully you'll find something in here you can relate to, tell your friends, and make your own zine.

"Perhaps for the first time in my life I understand good manners. I understand that you must be polite to all people at all times because you never know what difficulties they might be struggling with at that precise moment, you never know how the slightest wrong thing that you say could be the last little iota it takes to send a person who is just barely holding it together into a complete breakdown. The one little mistake you make, bumping into someone as you walk busily across a crowded sidewalk, shoving a woman aside as you push your way into a crowded subway car, spilling red wine on someone else's white shirt because you weren't paying attention as you made your rounds through a cocktail party – you never know if that misguided gesture might not be the reason some poor lost soul ends up in the loony bin. Anyone can be that delicate."

Elizabeth Wurtzel, *More, Now, Again*

SELF-INDULGENCE

I think that in some ways, zines can be extremely self-indulgent. It's almost like having your journal and your deepest secrets published just because you can. Right now, I try to keep my zine from being too personal. There are some things that I just don't feel like telling everybody. In the future, I hope to be able to share more, but right now feels too soon.

I JUST DON'T KNOW WHAT TO DO WITH MYSELF

There are so many things I'd like to do with my life, but I am finding it increasingly difficult to figure out how to do it, when to do it, and how to make a living while I'm at it. I have a firm belief that everybody should be able to make a comfortable living doing what they enjoy. It's such a contradiction, though, because I know that could never be. There are a hell of a lot of things that just wouldn't get done. A lot of things wouldn't be made because people wouldn't want to work on assembly lines putting them together. Stores would close because nobody wants to be a cashier, nobody wants to work in retail. So while I think we should all be living our lives doing what we love, I know it's impossible. I'm determined to be one of the rare people who can get away with it. I used to want to be a fashion designer, photographer, musician, and painter, all sorts of things, but I mostly I just want to be a writer.

LINDSAY

Lindsay is the town I grew up in. We moved there after our parents separated, just before we turned five. I always wondered how we ended up in that particular town, and I didn't find out 'til years later that we moved there because our grandparents, our mom's mom and dad, had recently moved there as well. They were among my mom's likely very small support system at the time, and of course, grandparents provide free childcare.

Our mom was good at making sure we didn't really know how poor we were, even though we secretly knew that our grandparents were paying for our winter coats, summer dresses, and bikes, and sometimes we would go to the food bank. We had our Christmas presents donated to us from the Salvation Army one year. I always knew we had less than the other kids at school: less money, less clothes, less food. But I didn't know how much less. And I knew that our families were different. Most of my friends were living in two-parent (and two-income) homes, and even for those friends of mine whose parents were divorced or separated, they had a step-parent living with them. My sister and I just had our mom; she was raising twins on a single-income home, and we weren't getting fancy birthday presents like CD players and bicycles from our father, like some of our friends were; we weren't even always getting our basic child support, and sometimes our dad was too drunk to show up for our alternate-weekend visits. He wasn't supposed to be drinking around us, but we never saw him without a beer in his hand.

♡ ♡ ♡

My sister and I were home alone from a young age, since childcare was not always accessible and/or affordable to us. I don't remember much of what we did during the hours between the end of the school day and the time our mom came home from work, besides watching TV and eating junk food and banging our fists on the walls to tell the neighbours to shut up, but I like to think that we were able to develop our imaginations during that time, to create our own stories and adventures and games. We lived in low-income housing back then, a series of yellow brick townhouses down by the river, alongside the abandoned traintracks. We shared a room for a few years, until we were able to move two doors down to a three-bedroom place, and that was the first time we got to have our own bedrooms and choose our own paint colours, the first time since very early childhood that we did not have to live with boring white walls. Again, I didn't know that we were living in a place for poor folks, but I did know that our home was different from our friends' homes, both structurally and otherwise. I knew the stress in my mom's voice when a letter from the housing association would arrive in our mailbox.

Lindsay is a small town. Most of its residents seem to be either elderly or teenage, and there is a large class divide between a) broke folks who probably make up most of the population, and b) middle/higher-class but maybe not totally rich folks who make up the rest of the town. Lindsay is filled with fancy boutiques and many fast food chains, and has one of the highest teen pregnancy rates in the province of Ontario. There are probably a million other towns just like it all over Canada. Despite some of my bitterness and bad experiences, it still holds a dear place in my heart. I secretly like going back now and then and seeing what changes have taken place, even if those changes usually upset me: another demolished building, another fire, another out-of-business sign.

♡ ♡ ♡

Telegram Ma'am

Issue #3

November 2004

$2 / zine

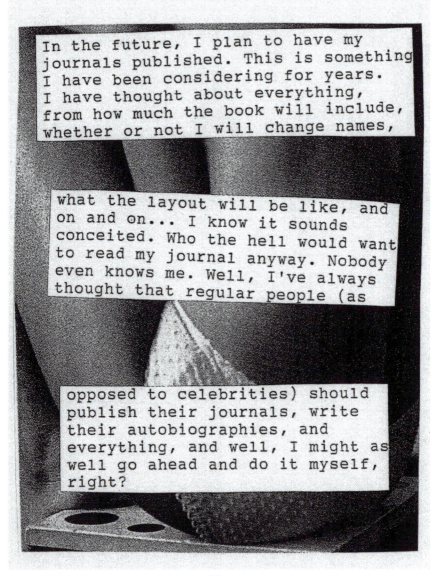

In the future, I plan to have my journals published. This is something I have been considering for years. I have thought about everything, from how much the book will include, whether or not I will change names,

what the layout will be like, and on and on... I know it sounds conceited. Who the hell would want to read my journal anyway. Nobody even knows me. Well, I've always thought that regular people (as

opposed to celebrities) should publish their journals, write their autobiographies, and everything, and well, I might as well go ahead and do it myself, right?

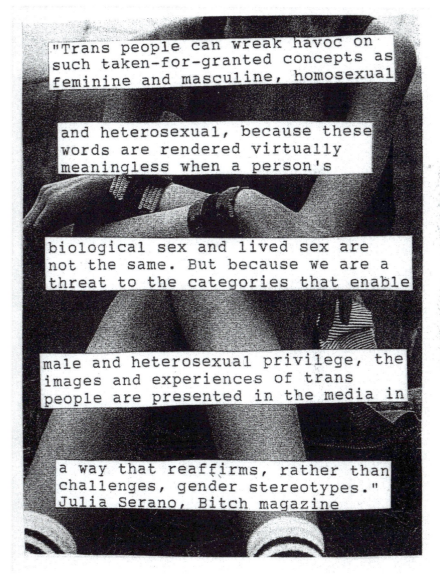

"Trans people can wreak havoc on such taken-for-granted concepts as feminine and masculine, homosexual

and heterosexual, because these words are rendered virtually meaningless when a person's

biological sex and lived sex are not the same. But because we are a threat to the categories that enable

male and heterosexual privilege, the images and experiences of trans people are presented in the media in

a way that reaffirms, rather than challenges, gender stereotypes." Julia Serano, Bitch magazine

"Do leave a corner of your garden
wild, and leave it for the fairies.
All too often we forget these
things as we control our immediate
environment, lay out our gardens
with beds and lawns and don't think
of the other kingdoms who share
space with us."

Telegram Ma'am

Issue #4 April 2005 $2/trade for your zine

RIOT GRRRL IS···

BECAUSE us girls crave records and books and fanzines that speak to US that WE feel included in and can understand in our own ways.

BECAUSE we wanna make it easier for girls to see/hear each other's work so that we can share strategies and criticize-applaud each other.

BECAUSE we must take over the means of production in order to create our own meanings.

BECAUSE viewing our work as being connected to our girlfriends-politics-real lives is essential if we are gonna figure out how what we are doing impacts, reflects, perpetuates, or DISRUPTS the status quo.

BECAUSE we recognize fantasies of Instant Macho Gun Revolution as impractical lies meant to keep us simply dreaming instead of becoming our dreams AND THUS seek create revolution in our own ways every single day by envisioning and creating alternatives to the bullshit Christian capitalist way of doing things.

BECAUSE we want and need to encourage and be encouraged in the face of all our own insecurities, in the face of beergurboyrock that tells us we can't play our instruments, in the face of "authorities" who say our bands/zines/etc are the worst in the US and...

BECAUSE we don't wanna assimilate to someone else's (boy) standards of what is or isn't.

BECAUSE we are unwilling to falter under claims that we are reactionary "reverse sexists" AND NOT THE TRUEPUNKROCKSOULCRUSADERS THAT WE KNOW we really are.

BECAUSE we know that life is much more than physical survival and are patently aware that the punk rock "you can do anything" idea is crucial to the coming angry grrrl rock revolution which seeks to save the psychic and cultural lives of girls and women everywhere, according to their own terms, not ours.

BECAUSE we are interested in creating non-hierarchical ways of being AND making music, friends, and scenes based on communication + understanding, instead of competition + good/bad categorizations.

BECAUSE doing/reading/seeing/hearing cool things that validate and challenge us can help us gain the strength and sense of community that we need in order to figure out how bullshit like racism, anle-bodieism, ageism, speciesism, classism, thinism, sexism, anti-semitism and heterosexism figures in our own lives.

BECAUSE we see fostering and supporting girl scenes and girl artists of all kinds as integral to this process.

BECAUSE we hate capitalism in all its forms and see our main goal as sharing information and staying alive, instead of making profits and being cool according to traditional standards.

BECAUSE we are angry at a society that tells us Girl=Dumb, Girl=Bad, Girl=Weak.

BECAUSE we are unwilling to let our real and valid anger be diffused and/or turned against us via the internalization of sexism as witnessed in girl/girl jealousism and self defeating girltype behaviours.

BECAUSE I believe with my wholeheartmindbody that girls constitute a revolutionary soul force that can, and will change the world for real.

"We had just gotten off tour with Mudhoney, and I decided to stage-dive. I was wearing a dress and I didn't realize what I was engendering in the audience. It was a huge audience and they were kind of going ape-shit. So I just dove off the stage, and suddenly, it was like my dress was being torn off of me, my underwear was being torn off of me, people were putting their fingers inside of me and grabbing my breasts really hard, screaming things in my ears like "pussy-whore-cunt". When I got back onstage I was naked. I felt like Karen Finley. But the worst thing of all was that I saw a photograph of it later. Someone took a picture of me right when this was happening, and I had this big smile on my face like I was pretending it wasn't happening. So later I wrote a song called "Asking For It" based on the whole experience. I can't compare it to rape because it's not the same. But in a way it was. I was raped by an audience, figuratively, literally, and yet, was I asking for it?" Courtney Love

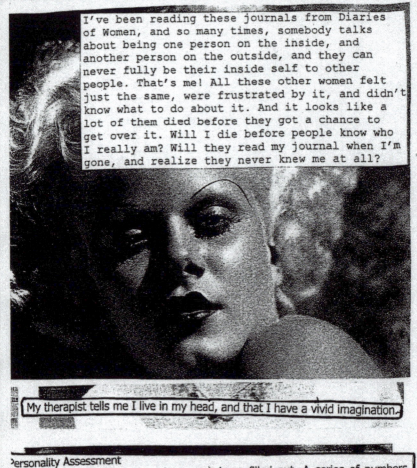

I've been reading these journals from Diaries of Women, and so many times, somebody talks about being one person on the inside, and another person on the outside, and they can never fully be their inside self to other people. That's me! All these other women felt just the same, were frustrated by it, and didn't know what to do about it. And it looks like a lot of them died before they got a chance to get over it. Will I die before people know who I really am? Will they read my journal when I'm gone, and realize they never knew me at all?

My therapist tells me I live in my head, and that I have a vivid imagination.

Personality Assessment
My questionnaires for therapy have now been filled out. A series of numbers, letters, and dots. I'm afraid they're going to tell me I'm depressed and slightly insane. I remember the last time I did these questionnaires; they never told me my results. Or, if they did, I don't remember.

Issue #5

July 2005

$2 Canada & US

$3 Elsewhere

or trade for your zine

Telegram Ma'am

About a girl who likes to write when she has nothing to write about, procrastinate when she has things to do, watch movies until she has them memorized, highlight the best parts in her books, listen to music as though it were the only thing that ever mattered, paint her nails to feel fabulous when she's all alone, walk in the rain because she feels like it creates a wall around her that hides her from the rest of the world, read by the river, laugh until she cries, dance around her house when no one else is home, daydreams when she rides in cars, daydreams when writes, daydreams when she reads, daydreams when she pretends to listen, daydreams when she breathes, applies make-up meticulously for nothing but a trip to the grocery store, wishes she was a pin up girl, does not like to be seen or noticed, intimidates strangers and such, loves her glasses more than she should, takes forever to respond to emails, enjoys taking photos of herself and her cat, is quiet when others are around and loud when she's by herself, plans her funeral, wants to live in Europe one day, needs to travel the world, collects snow globes and fortunes from fortune cookies, intentionally creates situations where she will have butterflies in her tummy, checks the time every five minutes when she knows exactly what time it is, tends to be naïve, wishes she had the guts to live out of a suitcase, wants to fall in love but fears commitment, gets giddy when she receives mail, fantasizes about a Pearl Jam cover band that consists of nothing but her and a xylophone, wishes she could play bass but doesn't particularly want to play in a band, is terrible at saving money, worships at the alter of Courtney Love, makes sure to write in her journal almost every single day, tries to remember each and every conversation she's involved in, wants to be invisible, has had sex dreams involving just about everyone she's ever met, loves and trusts pen pals more than real life pals, dislikes all things pertaining to keys and locks, idolizes Marilyn Monroe and Bettie Page, secretly likes models, eats chocolate as often as possible, enjoys forming words from the 3-4 letters in license plates, feels ill when she watches TV, is attempting to get over her fear of telephones and public places, is on Effexor XR for depression, anxiety, and social phobia, desperately wants a teaset, has anorexic tendencies, enjoys spending time at her grandparents' house, does not plan on ever getting her license, is scared of the future, enjoys the months of May and October, dislikes being cold, doesn't know what else to say.

It's finally happened. I'm on antidepressants. I'd known for years that it I needed to have them prescribed to me (again), but was too afraid to say anything until a couple of months ago when things started to get really bad. To put it in a nutshell, I felt completely hopeless, and could barely stand to get out of bed. I felt like I had nothing to look forward to, and everything to continue living my life would be utterly pointless. I expressed these sentiments to my therapist (who I was/am seeing for different reasons), and she recommended I make an appointment with my doctor, and let him know about it. With my permission, she called him as well, and told him everything I had told her.

A couple of weeks later, after talking to my doctor, he prescribed me a pill called Celexa. It turned out to have terrible side effects that made me feel even worse than I did when I was on nothing at all. I was tired all the time, but I couldn't sleep, I always had a sore throat and a headache, I had no energy, I could not get out of bed at all, and I could not stop thinking about suicide. So I went back, and was taken off Celexa, and put on another pill called Effexor XR. This was a much better choice for me because it is not only for depression, but for anxiety and social phobia as well. As of this writing, I have only been on Effexor XR for a month or so, but I already feel like a completely different person than I was just a couple of months ago. I've been getting out of the house more, have been more productive, don't feel as uncomfortably as I used to when I'm talking to people, have hope for the future, and am generally a happier person.

The trouble with antidepressants is it can take a long time to find the right one, and this is obviously quite frustrating. When I hear people say not to go on pills because they will turn you into a zombie, I can't help but feel like they have lazy doctors who don't know them well enough to prescribe them the proper medication, so instead they've been stuck on pills that are probably doing more harm than good. But even after going through all these bad experiences, it is still worth taking the time and effort to find the right pill because given the chance, it could change and/or save your life.

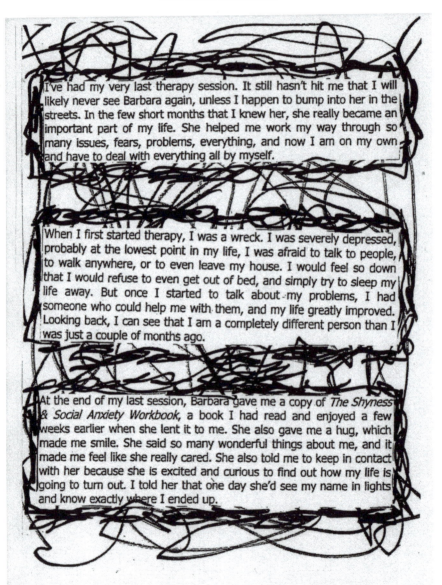

I've had my very last therapy session. It still hasn't hit me that I will likely never see Barbara again, unless I happen to bump into her in the streets. In the few short months that I knew her, she really became an important part of my life. She helped me work my way through so many issues, fears, problems, everything, and now I am on my own and have to deal with everything all by myself.

When I first started therapy, I was a wreck. I was severely depressed, probably at the lowest point in my life, I was afraid to talk to people, to walk anywhere, or to even leave my house. I would feel so down that I would refuse to even get out of bed, and simply try to sleep my life away. But once I started to talk about my problems, I had someone who could help me with them, and my life greatly improved. Looking back, I can see that I am a completely different person than I was just a couple of months ago.

At the end of my last session, Barbara gave me a copy of *The Shyness & Social Anxiety Workbook*, a book I had read and enjoyed a few weeks earlier when she lent it to me. She also gave me a hug, which made me smile. She said so many wonderful things about me, and it made me feel like she really cared. She also told me to keep in contact with her because she is excited and curious to find out how my life is going to turn out. I told her that one day she'd see my name in lights and know exactly where I ended up.

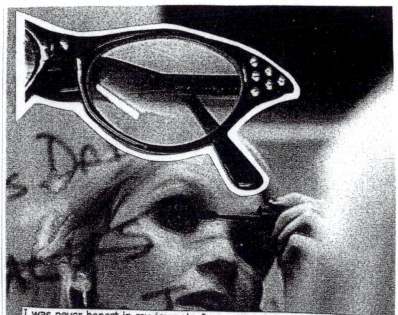

I was never honest in my journals. I was never honest with myself. I used to not name names, I used to not name feelings, I used to lie and lie and lie. Pretending nothing happened, pretending I didn't care, pretending it didn't matter, got me nowhere. My journals were supposed to be my innermost thoughts and feelings, and they turned out to be a whole lot of nothing. Moments and feelings that should've been precious to me have been completely forgotten, left behind in the past, never to be experienced again. It was only last year that I started being completely honest in my journals. I didn't care what anybody thought anymore, I didn't care if anybody found my journals and read them to themselves or to the world. I wrote everything the way it happened, the way I felt, every moment, every feeling, every conversation, every smile, every frown, every day, every everything... I recorded it all. And life got better.

or trade for your zine

$3 International

$2 Canada and US

January 2006

Issue #6

TELEGRAM MA'AM

self-portrait

INTRO INTRO INTRO INTRO INTRO INTRO

photo: Cottingley fairies

Much has changed since the last issue of *Telegram*. I've fallen in love. I've acquired two jobs: one as a crossing guard, the other as Blockbuster employee. I celebrated my 20th birthday. I've become less of an introvert. I've gotten over many of my fears, including my fear of public places, fear of telephones, and fear of falling in love. I've become a happier, more outgoing person. I feel like a completely new person. I'm still me, though; I still start all my sentences with 'I'.

Most of my time is now spent divided between two jobs, visiting the boyfriend whenever I can, writing in my journal, reading many books, daydreaming, attempting to plan a successful future, and working on the zine. I've become a busy bee. Sometimes I miss having no life at all. Most times I don't.

I am finally content with who I am and where my life is going.

Ladies and Gentlemen, I have become what is commonly known as a *happy person*. If you've read past of issues of *Telegram Ma'am*, then perhaps you know a little bit about my history with antidepressants. If you haven't, then here is a short recap:

When I was 12 years old, I was prescribed an antidepressant called Luvox. I was given very little information about this pill, in fact, probably none at all. I was told nothing about effects or side effects. I was simply told I must take them in order to get better. However, I was a stubborn little girl, and caused dramatic scenes in which I raged and raged some more about useless they were before emptying the plastic orange bottle into the garbage can. By the age of 13 ½, I was simply refusing to take them at all, so the doctor stopped writing prescriptions for me.

I soldiered on through my teenage years, being expelled from high school before the end of Grade Nine, and spending a lot of time at the library and the bookstore before becoming a total recluse, spending my days reading, watching movies, writing in my journal, and, of course, cutting myself. Mind you, I was still depressed, though now I was going untreated.

At the age of 19, after suffering much too long with agoraphobia, social anxiety, and depression, I finally started seeing a therapist in a nearby city who went by the name of Barbara. To make a long story short (this is just a recap, remember), Barbara pretty much changed my life entirely.

During our appointments, she would take me out for walks around the city so I get used to being around people. Traffic, and busy, crowded places again. These walks, at first, were somewhat disastrous to me. I would anxiety attacks so bad that I would find it difficult to breathe, and my legs would shake so much that I would have to sit down immediately and take a break because I could no longer hold myself upright. Eventually, though, week by week, being out in public got a little easier, and discussing my issues with Barbara helped immensely. After seeing her for some time, we decided it would be a smart idea to see about getting me back on prescription antidepressants. So of to the doctor I went.

My family doctor started me off with a prescription of a pill called Celexa. However, I started suffering from side effects such as nausea, headaches, sleepiness, insomnia, and so on almost immediately, so after only two weeks, I was take off Celexa, and prescribed another pill; Effexor XR. This one proved to be best for me, as it was not only an antidepressant, but a medication prescribed for social phobia and anxiety as well. My dream pill! Effexor XR made me feel better almost right away, and the only side effect I suffered (and continue to suffer) is lack of appetite. In my six months on this pill (which I am still taking today), my life has greatly improved in many aspects. I am no longer afraid of public places, meeting new people, and running simple errands like going to the post office or the drugstore, which I could not do on my own before. I was finally feeling positive, and becoming more at ease with

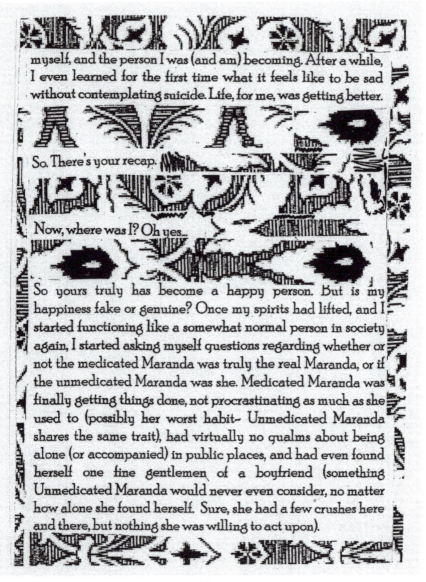

myself, and the person I was (and am) becoming. After a while, I even learned for the first time what it feels like to be sad without contemplating suicide. Life, for me, was getting better.

So. There's your recap.

Now, where was I? Oh yes...

So yours truly has become a happy person. But is my happiness fake or genuine? Once my spirits had lifted, and I started functioning like a somewhat normal person in society again, I started asking myself questions regarding whether or not the medicated Maranda was truly the real Maranda, or if the unmedicated Maranda was she. Medicated Maranda was finally getting things done, not procrastinating as much as she used to (possibly her worst habit- Unmedicated Maranda shares the same trait), had virtually no qualms about being alone (or accompanied) in public places, and had even found herself one fine gentlemen of a boyfriend (something Unmedicated Maranda would never even consider, no matter how alone she found herself. Sure, she had a few crushes here and there, but nothing she was willing to act upon).

After months and months of deep contemplation, and asking myself questions that seemed like they might never be answered, I finally came to the conclusion that *this*, the Medicated Maranda, is the real me. When I am not taking something to help the chemical imbalance in my brain, my head is just way too foggy to be able to think straight, and to make intelligent, educated decisions for myself. I simply get stuck in a rut, and wile away the hours (days, even) curled up under a blanket in my bed, waiting for the world to disappear. I have had several incidents where I forgot to take my pill, and I can't function without it. I find myself crying uncontrollably for seemingly no reason at all, losing my balance and coordination, contemplating suicide, and unable to do simple tasks like pour myself a drink, read a book. Or tidy my bedroom. However, once the medication is running through my system again, I feel one hundred times better, and am able to function again without a problem. The pills seem to clear the clouds and fog in my mind and let me see my life for what it really is, which, of course, is not worth giving up.

You are the 1920s.

Flappers, Fitzgerald, free-flowing money. The Jazz Age is your era!

Boys passing notes with ratings of fellow classmates, girls only. Boys I used to be friends with, boys I never liked, boys I never knew. My best friend's rating: 10. My close friend's rating: 8. My rating: 0. Imagine how I felt... I wonder now if they realize how much they've scarred me. I want to say that it is all in the past and that it doesn't matter anymore, and I know that that's true, but I just can't get it off my mind. I wonder if they know how much they made me hate myself, and my body, and how distrustful they made me of men. I wonder if they know how uncomfortable they made me feel with every relationship I ever had, and every kiss, and every glance. I wonder if they know that it is because of them that I could not, for the longest time, let anyone get close to me, physically or emotionally, because I was afraid they would hate what they saw. Hiding my face with my hair, hiding my body with baggy clothes, hiding my personality with silence. The walls I built around myself were hard to break down, and some still remain. Every insecurity of mine was preyed upon; I could never be pretty enough, I could never be loved, I would always be alone. I had the brains, but not the beauty. I'm too smart for this.

For the longest time, I dreamed of a bicycle, nothing modern, something classic, vintage. I wanted a pretty little thing with a basket on the handlebars where I could set my purse as I peddled my way around town, sometimes running errands or visiting friends and family, sometimes just taking a stroll for a bit of fresh air and exercise. Upon mentioning this bicycle dream of mine at my grandparents' dinner table one Sunday evening, my nana told me to have a look in the shed and take my pick. Excitement! So I went to the shed at the back of their house, and chose a beauty; the classic blue and white bicycle with chrome details. My poppa fixed her up for me, filled the tires, made sure she was safe, and I called everyone out of the house to watch me take a ride. Peddling up and down the street, I decided my new friend would need a name. From then on, she was called Lulu. My Lulu does not have a basket yet, but she is a dainty, wonderful thing, and we shall have a ball together come Springtime.

Lulu, My One and Only

TELEGRAM MA'AM

Issue #7 June 2006
$2 Canada and US
$3 International
or trade for your zine

HEART
© Maranda

001; The young girl with the fiery, wavy hair, pale skin, and freckles is dancing, twirling, shrieking with delight [*Dance with me. Tell me you adore me.*] as her taffeta skirt in all its immaculate ruffles flows around her thin, nubile body, surrounding her in a delicate cloud of white. She bundles taffeta in her soft, clean hands, playfully lifting her precious skirt for an audience of one, feeling warm and safe in the affection that shows in his eyes. [*Sweetheart, I know you admire me, I know you envy me. Don't let me make you cry; I couldn't bear it.*]

002; The young woman with the crimson, messy hair, iridescent skin, and powder covering her freckles is jumping, cartwheeling, screaming with pleasure [*Tell me you want me. Tell me you need me. Tell me you own me.*] as her taffeta skirt in all its stained ruffles shreds around her weak, fragile body in a fog of white, grey and brown. She clenches taffeta in her pallid, shaking fists, eagerly lifting her treasured skirt for an audience of one, anxious yet liberated in the concern that shows in his eyes. [*Darling, I know you're scared and worrisome. Your tears reddened your eyes.*]

003; The dying woman with the red, tangled, unkempt hair is limping, falling, finally being dragged, moaning with exhaustion [*Take me. Help me. Save me.*] as her taffeta skirt trails behind her in all its tattered ruffles of dirt and blood. She caresses her cherished taffeta with her elongated, skeletal fingers for the last time, slowly parting a tear in her skirt for an audience of one as she cries and loses herself in the indifference that shows in his eyes. [*Valentine, I know it's over, but please, please, let me be wrong. I can see your tears staining your cheeks.*]

ARRIVALS AND DEPARTURES
© Maranda

FRIDAY NIGHT

5:30 p.m.

She is standing in line at the local bus station that has grown so familiar, it feels like her second home. Little snowflakes collect on the ground and the lenses of her glasses, blurring her view as though her eyes have welled with tears. The sun will be setting soon, chilling the evening air, and she shivers as she thinks of this. Sneaking glances at the other soon-to-be passengers, she sees girls with brown and blonde hair, dressed in tweed coats, rolled up jeans, tall boots, and carrying sequined purses; boys with shaggy hair, dressed in black jackets, baggy pants, and sneakers; she, with long, black hair, dressed in faux fur coat, corduroy skirt, and black boots, carrying a white purse; everybody handling luggage of various sizes, styles, and colours. The snowflakes settle on each person's luggage for a moment before melting or being blown away. Two of the most essential items are held in this girl's purse: her ticket and her book. The cold wind picks up, blowing her hair in her eyes, blocking her view. She brushes the strands away with her mittened hand, and glances at her watch.

5:35 p.m.

The bus's engine starts, alerting the crowd of their upcoming departure, and the bus driver begins taking tickets, and helping passengers load the undercarriage luggage compartments. The line is moving, and the girl moves along with it, handing her ticket to the bus driver, and climbing onto the bus, keeping her bags with her. She spots an empty seat near the back by the window, and takes it, setting her backpack on the seat beside her in hopes of remaining alone for the journey. This time, she is lucky. The bus begins the long drive before a stranger can approach with, "Is this seat taken?"

5:45 p.m.

She stares out the large window, watching the grey city buildings pass by, and the bare tree branches sway in the snowy wind until the bus leaves town for the highway. Once she grows tired of the mundane view, she unzips her purse, and pulls out her book, where her bus ticket receipt is being used as a bookmark. The words leap up from the pages, dancing around her eyes and mind, passing the time before she must disembark and transfer at the next station.

7:25 p.m.

This bus has reached its final destination: a busier station in a larger city. Her fellow passengers stretch a bit as they stand up from their seats and gather their belongings, making their way out to the aisle and to the door where they will meet their loved ones, catch another bus, or continue to where they are headed on their own. Slipping her receipt back into her book and her book back into her purse, the girl straps on her backpack, makes her way out into the aisle with the others, and lugs these weighty bags of hers over to another line-up, this one containing more unfamiliar faces in fashionable clothing. She wonders if they feel the same way she feels: eager about their upcoming arrival, yet already disheartened at the thought of their subsequent departure.

8:00 p.m.

Another exodus, and she is on her way to reunite with her love for a weekend visit. It is dark now, and the city lights glow and glisten, though the girl pays them no mind. Once the bus gets moving, her nose is once again buried in her book.

9:15 p.m.

Finally, the journey is over. She has arrived in the city her love resides in, and her book is tucked back into her purse, where it will remain untouched until it is time to make the return trip on Sunday night. When she delicately steps off the bus and onto the pavement, she glances about her, looking through the crowd until she spots her love, who is leaning against the brick wall of the bus station. He spots her at the same time, and they share a moment of recognition as their hearts quicken their pace before they rush to each other, and cling in a sea of kisses and hugs and caresses and smiles. "I've missed you."

10:00 p.m.

After a short walk through the city with their fingers interlaced, in the cold, dark night that is filled with young people heading out to the bars to celebrate the onset of another weekend, they have arrived at his house, her bags have been dropped to the floor, and she has collapsed in his warm bed at the mere touch of his hands to her hips and his lips to her neck. The girl and the boy will remain like this for two days and two nights; two creatures with bodies entwined into one complete being. Each moment is another to make last as long as possible before being absorbed into their memories forever. Three and a half hours on a bus pass so slowly, yet two days and two nights in each other's arms seem to pass faster than the speed of light.

SUNDAY NIGHT

4:30 p.m.

The girl and her love hold hands, squeezing tightly, fingers interlaced like the night they first met, as they walk back to the bus station in a light snow to end a perfect weekend at the very place where it began. At first, they fight to hold back their tears, a lump gathering in their throats, but once the station is in sight, and the bus's engine can be heard, their tears are suddenly freed, and they run down one another's faces like so many April showers. Soon they are clinging to each other once again, she not wanting to go home, and he not wanting to let her go. So they stand by the dull, grey building among others who are saying their goodbyes, arms wrapped around one another until the time for the girl to leave her boy inevitably arrives.

4:55 p.m.

They share one last kiss, one last "I'll miss you," one last "I love you," before she once again hands her ticket to the bus driver, and boards the bus for her journey home. Once seated, she waves to her love from the window, and he blows her a kiss. The bus pulls out, and she loses sight of him in the distance, walking away.

5:15 p.m.

Her tears have finally stopped pouring, so she decides to take out her book, not to pass the hours this time, but to distract herself from the anguish of leaving the place that feels like home, and the love that feels like eternity. Five pages in, she realizes she does not know what is going on in the story; she cannot concentrate, so she decides to take a nap.

6:40 p.m.

Arriving, once again, in the larger city bus station to transfer, the girl carries her bags and her book, which have been held in her hands as the slept, into the bus station, where she will finally be able to focus as she waits to board her next bus. People of varying age, nationalities, and statures are milling about, hands full with luggage, books, and snacks. She double checks the time of her bus's departure before finding a seat in which she rereads the five pages she missed earlier, and continues to read two or three chapters. Announcements of other departures, and bus station rules can be heard over the loudspeakers, but she ignores them, having memorized them long ago. Soon she is taking her place in line again.

7:30 p.m.

Another bus, another window seat, another long stretch of highway. "Is this seat taken?" The girl looks up from her book to see a middle-aged man standing before her, obviously frustrated at the filled-to-capacity bus. She silently moves her backpack from the seat beside her, and allows the man to sit. Immediately, his leg is pressing against hers, and no matter how much she wiggles, he just doesn't take the hint, and she cannot get comfortable. The time passes slowly as she tries to ignore him, and lose herself in a story.

9:00 p.m.

It is snowing again, each unique snowflake floating in the glow of the streetlights, alone until they reach the ground to lay with the others that have gathered throughout the evening. The girl's book is placed back in her purse as the bus arrives at the station where her journey began. When she steps off the bus, the wind whips her hair into her eyes, and she brushes it away with her mittened hand, just like the last time she was here. Also, the little snowflakes wet the lenses of her glasses, but this time it doesn't matter; her view is already marred by tears. *I am home-sweet-home*, she thinks to herself, leaving the parking lot of the bus station with a vacant air to her step.

TELEGRAM
MA'AM

Issue #8

October 2006

$2 Canada and U.S.

$3 International

or trade for your zine

It's funny how you think that a change of location comes with a change of self as well; new personality, new memories, new social skills... Apparently, it does not work that way. I may be in a different city, surrounded with new people and buildings and scenery and shopping, but I am still the same-old Maranda, complete with my usual insecurities and social and otherwise tendencies and habits. I still haven't even gone for a walk by myself yet, but I swear, I have good intentions. It's okay that I'm not a different person, though. I just should have known better.

rage

I hate that I live in a world that makes me feel like I am inadequate and ugly and worthless and a damned inconvenience to those around me, when I know that isn't true. I hate the way that I am made to feel like I am supposed to have bigger breasts, longer legs, fuller lips, and smoother skin. I hate that because I am a woman, my entire life is supposed to revolve around what *somebody else's* (re: MAN'S) ideas of what I should be. I hate that say things like, "I hate being a girl" when I know that I should love it. I hate that I am being told to avoid situations in which I could be raped, when MEN ARE NOT BEING TOLD TO STOP RAPING WOMEN. I hate being spoken to like I am a child. I hate not being able to function without pills. I hate having to get drunk to feel comfortable. I hate my apologetic nature. I hate feeling FEMINIST GUILT over my actions and inactions. I hate the way I keep my mouth shut. I hate the way I look at other girls and women as *competition*. I hate not having the guts to throw my make-up in the garbage. I hate feeling unintelligent. I hate feeling hateful. I hate not knowing what to do about it.

I have a lot of online friends, and this summer, I was able to visit one of my online friends in the States. She's someone I felt an immediate connection with the moment we found each other. I've known her for almost two years now, but we'd probably known each other for only a few months before the idea of meeting in person was mentioned.

Whenever I told someone I was planning on traveling to the States to meet Brittany, they'd act shocked and worried. What is she wasn't who she said she was? I met Brittany on Hole.com, and I knew she was the girl she said she was. The only thing I was worried about was that we might not get along as well in person as we do online, and that meeting each other wouldn't have been such a great decision.

After an exhausting fifteen-hour Greyhound trip from Guelph, Ontario, to Pittsburgh, Pennsylvania, Brittany and I were finally able to give each other real hugs. One of the first things I thought, and told her, was that having her arms around me was so much better than seeing *hugs <3* typed on my screen.

We ate lunch together, and were feeling shy, even though we know so much about each other; it was just strange to hear one another's voices instead of reading emails and chats and LiveJournal entries. It didn't take long, though, for us to feel more comfortable, and to start having fun together. We spent a week hanging out, taking pictures, watching movies, exploring the spaces around us, eating so much we thought our stomachs would burst, and enjoying the novelty of being able to say "I love you" in person. She introduced me to *My Summer of Love* and I introduced her to *Velvet Goldmine*. We spent every moment together, and even when we slept, we had weird dream about each other.

One thing my week with Brittany made me realize is that I truly do wish I had more 'real life' friends. To be honest, I have *none*. Before moving to Guelph, I merely had acquaintances, workmates, and my cat. Upon moving to Guelph, I still have my cat, and my boyfriend, but that is all. I'm not really complaining. I love my life. Sometimes I just wish I had some girl friends to hang out with, talk to, drink with, *something*. Brittany and I aren't just friends; we're sisters. We may not share the same blood, but we're sisters nonetheless. So it's difficult to have only a limited time together before going back to typing our conversations. I want friends who I can see and hug and dance with whenever I please.

On my last day with Brittany, it was so hard to leave her behind. She stood in line with me as I waited for the bus, as we hugged as many times as possible while taking our last photos together. It's hard to take photos when you're feeling glum, but I wanted our last day together to be documented. We stayed right beside each other until we absolutely had to separate, and the guy in front of us purposely moved his luggage slowly so we could share one last hug. Eventually, I had to board the bus alone and make the fifteen-hour journey to my home. Even if we can't be together as often as I'd like, I am still so grateful to have Brittany in my life. I've never had a friend as marvellous as her before, and I don't expect to find anyone else quite like her.

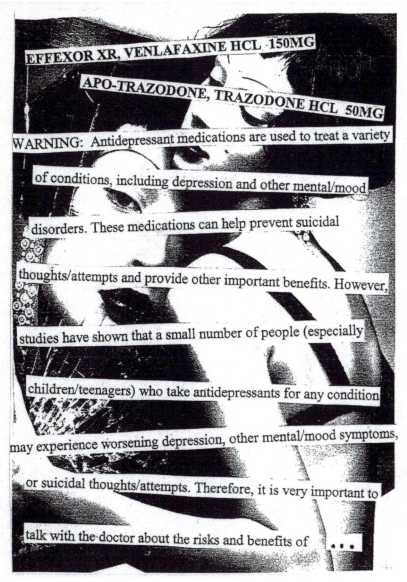

EFFEXOR XR, VENLAFAXINE HCL 150MG

APO-TRAZODONE, TRAZODONE HCL 50MG

WARNING: Antidepressant medications are used to treat a variety of conditions, including depression and other mental/mood disorders. These medications can help prevent suicidal thoughts/attempts and provide other important benefits. However, studies have shown that a small number of people (especially children/teenagers) who take antidepressants for any condition may experience worsening depression, other mental/mood symptoms, or suicidal thoughts/attempts. Therefore, it is very important to talk with the doctor about the risks and benefits of ...

TELEGRAM MA'AM

Issue #9

April 2007

$2 Canada and US

$3 International

or trade for your zine

The rest of the zine was so hard for me to read again, because those times were so painful, and also because I was so fucking naïve back then. I don't remember feeling hopeful back then, so I think maybe I was lying when I wrote that, just to give myself a reason to keep on living – but then, if I was still trying to stay alive, there must have been some kind of hope there, right?

♡ INTRO INTRO INTRO ♡

In the past few months, I have gone from living in my first apartment with my partner, to spending time in emergency rooms, mental hospitals, one homeless shelter, my mom's tiny apartment, and now I am on my own again, renting a room from an old lady, with just enough space for my cat and I. It's hard to explain just how all of this happened, and sometimes I still feel confused.

It was after my first hospital stay that I lost my job and my partner broke up with me. Looking back, the winter months have become a strange blur of tears, screaming, failure, and madness, to finally hope and determination. I have done some awful things as of late, but I am working towards becoming a better person (again), regaining my health, and fighting for my life as hard as I can. Most of the things I have written for this issue were painful to relive, and much of what has been going on will remain a secret because a) it is none of your business, and b) it would be hurtful to share details that involve others. I wanted to share as much as I could, though, because I think I have a story worth telling, and I think there are many people out there who need to hear it. I feel as though I have come out of a long, dark tunnel, and I can finally look back not only with relief that the worst of it is over, but with the insight that comes with recovery.

♡ DYING ♡

At first I kept busy. Not wanting to leave behind a mess, I tidied my art and mail supplies; I fed the cat and filled her water dish. I took more and more pills, washing them down with straight liquor. Then I decided to go to bed. He was still drifting and I curled up with him. I loved him. My eyes felt sewn shut. My mind wandered. Then it raced. Then my head spun. When I opened my eyes, everything was blurry. I closed them again. Now I was drifting. My body was relaxed, but I could hear and feel my heart pounding, faster and faster. I thought it would soon beat out of my chest. I thought it would beat faster and faster until it stopped. I can't keep a secret. I told him what I had done. Shock and panic and anger and guilt. 911. At the hospital, I was informed that I could have died with a much smaller dose.

ESCAPE

Losing myself in daydreams is what I do best. Sometimes I daydream so intensely that I fall asleep, slowing my subconscious to take over completely. In reality, I may be sitting on a bed that is not mine, scratching at dry skin, but in my mind I am wandering a sidewalk covered in delicate pink blossoms meeting a new friend; I am transported to the past, naked in the backseat of my ex-lover's car a kilometre or two away from some forgotten movie on the screen at the drive-in; or I am in my imaginary bed of the future, cuddling my cat and drinking a homemade fruit smoothie.

Most of the books I read involve escape in one way or another: *The Torn Skirt* by Rebecca Godfrey, in which the main character, Sara Shaw, escapes her home, her school, her comfort zone and finds herself downtown, on rooftops, and in detention centres and group homes with young hookers, sleazy men, social workers, and girls more fucked up than her. In the end, she escapes it all, pretending to know what to do next. In *Banana Kiss* by Bonnie Rozanski, Robin Farber lives in a psychiatric institution where nothing exists until she observes it, she escapes the hospital, her home, her group home, her sister's wedding, her job, yet no matter where she ends up, she is always somehow free, creating her own world.

Insanity, to me, is a kind of freedom, a kind of escapism. When I am able to let myself go totally, to scream nonsense as loud as I can, to throw things and destroy things and lunge at the throats of the people I am angry with, and pray for the courage to have revenge, to fall to the floor when I have run out of strength, this is when I escape what most of us accept as the real world to become whoever my mind has chosen to be for the moment.

As long as I can remember, I dreamed of escaping the town of Lindsay, finding some wonderful city where I could start over and become a new person with a new life. I could have an apartment with thrift store furniture and little plants, I could learn my way around the mysterious sidewalks, discover quaint little coffeehouses, one-of-a-kind shops, and bookstores that feel like second and third homes.

When the darker part of my mind took over, I needed to find a safer place, a place where I could take a break and get some help. To get to that sort of place, I had to hurt myself. Convincing myself it was the only option, I found myself in an emergency room hooked up to machines and drinking liquid charcoal. I had escaped, but at a great cost to my personal life, my emotions, and my usual well-being. Soon I was out, but everything had gone wrong, turned sour, fallen apart, died. All the good things were lost. I failed over and over again. There was nothing left.

Just as I thought it was all over, it dawned on me: I have a future. As cliché as it is, I have so many things to look forward to and be excited about. By cleaning up my mess, I can escape the darkness and make myself pure again, I can make all the bad things good, and dedicate my life to keeping it that way. All of my daydreams have potential, all of that power is within me plotting its escape from my mind to the real world.

I had *escape* tattooed on my arm today.

♥ THE FIRST TIME AROUND ♥

In November 2006, I was taken by ambulance to an emergency room following an overdose of sleeping pills, painkillers, and liquor. Paramedics asked me ten thousand questions, not just to gain useful information, but to keep me awake so they wouldn't lose me. I was strapped down to the stretcher, blood was taken, an IV was hooked up, and tubes were put up my nose to give me oxygen.

I felt tired and drunk, almost unable to keep my eyes open or speak, but I was repeatedly told to do just that. I don't remember every detail.

Eventually, I was lying in a hospital bed where I was made to drink a large cup of liquid charcoal, which would help clear my stomach of the toxins I had ingested. No one who hasn't been through this could ever comprehend just how sickening it is. Thinking about it still makes me feel ill. I was given half an hour to drink the charcoal. Six hours later, I was only half finished, and had endured many threats to have it forcibly fed to me through tubes. I slept off and on, and the cup disappeared from my tray, unfinished.

Many doctors, nurses, and psychiatrists spoke with me, all wanting to know exactly what had happened and why. *I* wasn't even entirely sure what had happened or why. Yet I had to continually explain myself. I told them this was not a suicide attempt; I just needed to take a break from life and this was the only way.

I was nauseous for days. I cried and cried. After spending a night or two at the hospital, I was brought to a place down the road called Homewood. It is primarily known as a rehab centre, and there are also wards for treating patients with depression, eating disorders, and post-traumatic stress disorder. I was admitted and shown to my bedroom, shared with a woman who was afraid of the dark and told me she had invented the Nintendo Game Boy.

For a while, I stayed in my room at all times, emerging only for meals and meds. Once I had been granted privileges, I spent time wandering the halls, visiting the library, and eating in the cafeteria. I snuck my camera in and took pictures of my bedroom.

It was only a few days later that I was released as an outpatient, promising to attend group therapy twice a week for social anxiety disorder. I thought my life would get better after this, but it got much, much worse.

♥ THE SECOND TIME AROUND ♥

Day One: Wednesday, January 31st, 2007

After a trip to Ottawa to visit my sister, I arrived at the Peterborough Greyhound station where my mom picked me up. Once we were halfway back to Lindsay, she let me in on her little secret: we were not on our way to her home. Instead, we were on our way to the emergency room. I was upset that she hadn't told me this right away and wouldn't give me a chance to at least visit my cat before checking in.

When we got there, a nurse took my blood pressure and asked me what was wrong. I briefly explained to him that I was feeling suicidal and I needed help. After filling out some forms, he had me move down to the next desk to show another staff my health card and to affix my yellow plastic bracelet. Then I went to the waiting room.

An hour and a half passed by, and I preoccupied myself with a used copy of *White Oleander* by Janet Fitch until I could no longer take the sounds of bratty, sick children and exasperated parents, and took a seat farther down the hall. After a few minutes, a nurse brought me into another room, a room where they put casts on patients, and I waited some more to see a doctor. There was plaster dust on the floor and dirt on the bedsheets.

A doctor came in to see me. I cried and raged. I was brought to yet another room, this one empty but for a bed and a chair. I sat on the floor. A nurse came in and sent me off to the bathroom with a plastic cup to pee in. When I came back, she took a sample of blood from my arm. "Once the test results are back," she told me, "you can be admitted to the second floor." The Mental Health Ward.

I waited. The nurse came back and searched my purse. She took away a bottle of vodka, my digital camera, and a nail file. The next time she returned, a security guard accompanied her. He led me past the waiting room and into an elevator. People stared. We emerged on the second floor. He left me there with another nurse who brought me into an interview room to fill out more forms. Afterward, I was shown to my bedroom, number 2238, and given some pamphlets about the hospital. A wide door with a narrow window opened into a large room with blue and white walls, salmon-pink floor, a bed in one corner, desk and chair in another, and a spectacular view of the police station and dentist's office across the street. My new home. I went straight to bed, exhausted from traveling and crying.

Day Two: Thursday, February 1st, 2007

My mom brought me some clothes, books, toiletries, and my blanket. Being with the other patients made me feel small and weak. I got into the routine of eating scheduled meals and attending required "meetings," spending my spare time in my bedroom either reading a book, writing in my journal, or writing letters to friends. Sometimes a nurse would come in and ask how I was feeling, and try to talk to me about thinking positively and setting goals. My goal is to find a home and keep it.

Later, the same nurse told me she thinks mental health is much more important than physical health. "It is much more difficult to walk around with a broken heart than it is to walk with a limp," she said.

That night, I had trouble sleeping, even though I was fairly tired. There was too much on my mind. Around midnight, another nurse came in to talk to me, noticing I was still up. She told me she used to be a library technician. "Think of all the books out there waiting to be read by you," she said. I told her that thought was often what kept me alive.

Day Three: February 2nd, 2007

More of the same. I wake up, take my pill, eat breakfast, retreat to my room to immerse myself in words. I underlined sentences in the book I was reading: "Not all of what they say is meant for me." "He was just scared of my behaviour." Patients have come and gone, having their names erased from the markerboard.

Day Four: February 3rd, 2007

The night-time was bad. My head was spinning so fast I could not sleep no matter how much I wanted to, no matter how much I thought of smiling crescent moons wearing funny hats and beds made of clouds and deep blue wallpaper with glowing stars. There are times when I think that if I wish for it hard enough, I can time travel to the past and change my mistakes. I tried, but it wouldn't work. I cried and cried and I wanted to scream. Instead of screaming, I put my bathrobe on over my pajamas, put on my slippers and glasses, and went to the Nurse's Station to ask for something to help me sleep. The nurse saw tears staining my face and handed me a box of tissues, then met me at the door of the Med Room to give me a sleeping pill with a paper cup filled with tapwater. The pill was tiny and white, as easy to lose as a grain of sand. I was careful as I placed it on my tongue and washed it down. The nurse reassured me that this night was just a passing moment in time, and that while I couldn't change the past, I could learn from it and I could change my future in positive ways, and live happily. She hugged me and I hugged her back. Even if what she was telling me was standard nurse-to-patient textbook stuff, it still made me feel better and calmed my nerves. When I went back to bed, I curled up under the layers of sheets and blankets, pretended I was laying in the grass by the river, and that the constant hum of the ventilation system was a nearby waterfall. I closed my eyes and drifted into sleep, thankful.

Even though time passes very slowly, I am feeling hopeful. I was granted grounds privileges today, meaning I can enter other parts of the hospital, and even step outside unaccompanied.

Day Five: Sunday, February 4th, 2007

Around noon, I was surprised by a visit from my mom. I led her to the diningroom so we could talk. We're not allowed to bring visitors to our bedrooms, so any conversation we have is eavesdropped upon by the other patients and staff. I don't talk much here, so the other patients must have been surprised to learn that I have a voice.

Earlier, I ventured the hospital grounds on my own. I simply went downstairs to find the change machine and get myself a drink, but I wondered what the others might think of me, an obvious patient with my plastic bracelet, dressed in casual clothes and ballet slippers, confused expression on my face as I explored the hallways. Would they sense I was from the mental health ward, or could I pass for a "normal" patient?

♡ ♡ ♡

Day Six: Monday, February 5ᵗʰ, 2007

My day began with a visit from my doctor. He didn't ask any questions I hadn't already been asked fifteen times before, nor did he tell me anything new. Later in the morning, many phone numbers were given to me, and I embarked upon a game of telephone tag with the payphone, calling up organizations and shelters in Guelph, taking note of yet more phone numbers, operating hours, and addresses. By mid-afternoon, plans had been settled for me to stay in a shelter upon my return to Guelph while I looked for a proper place to live. Another brief visit with the psychiatrist, who tells me I am doing well.

Day Seven: Tuesday, February 6ᵗʰ, 2007

I woke up happy and went through the motions, eating when told to, and even participating during group activity time. We played Trivial Pursuit: 90's Edition, and I moved around the squares on the board with a tiny figurine of Kurt Cobain. I was complimented on my knowledge of 90's happenings. I was in a good mood. Yet I was feeling anxious. A good kind of anxious. I wanted to leave the hospital. So I spoke with my psychiatrist, telling him of how I was feeling, and arrangements that had been made, and my plans for the future. He seemed okay with this, and told me I was free to leave. I packed my things, feeling high with relief and opportunity. Then I was gone.

This is the second printing of *Telegram Ma'am* #9.

Much has changed.

In the intro, I mentioned renting a room with an old lady; that barely lasted a month. I ended up moving in with a guy I'd known for about a week, fucked that up, then rented yet another room with a couple of girls, and that got me through the summer, after which I moved back to my hometown of Lindsay to live on my own for the first time.

Life pretty much got to be too much for me to handle. After a hellish post-hospital, post-break up, post-everything springtime, I needed nothing more than to be myself and try to sort everything out. What it came to was this: I had to severely cut back on drinking, smoking pot, and fucking around, in order to rid myself of unnecessary drama and stupidity, calm myself down, and remember who I was before all this mess started, and who I am now. I'm still trying to figure that out. So far, so good. I mean, my life is far from what I want it to be—I still have too many problems to even name—but I've taken myself out of an unsafe environment, and am at least trying to keep myself alive.

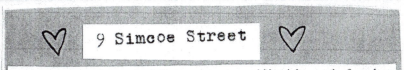

9 Simcoe Street

9 Simcoe Street was a tiny bachelor apartment in an old brick house, the first place I ever lived by myself. I had a futon, a desk, and a shelf, no room for anything else. There were no counters or drawers in the kitchen. I had a tall window by my bed and a little window in the bathroom. This is where I ended up when I moved back to Lindsay, after everything in Guelph fell apart. I chose this place for two seemingly opposing reasons: 1) I thought it would be easier to treat my depression and other mental health issues in my hometown, near my family, and 2) If I killed myself, there'd be less trouble to deal with if I was in the same town as my family. I seriously had visions of my mom having to drive to Guelph to identify my body, and how impossible that would be for her.

I think that when I decided to move back, I really did want to have some kind of recovery, but by the time summer passed and moving day came along, I had spiralled back to wanting to be dead. I needed to take care of the boring things like getting furniture and dishes and stuff, and I chose everything in plain white. No colours, no patterns. I wanted everything to be personality-less, so there'd be less to leave behind. I struggled to paint the walls, knowing that white walls ██ depress me, needing to make this place feel like my home even though I didn't intend to be around for long.

I felt dead while I was living there. I was excited to be near my sister again, and my mom, but I was absolutely not invested in taking care of myself or "getting better." My insomnia was very intense back then. I wouldn't sleep for days and days, but I felt incapable of getting out of bed. I was put on psych meds again, and I overdosed on Lithium. It made me puke constantly, day and night, and when I wasn't puking, I'd pass out and dream that I was puking. I didn't know what was real anymore.

When I read the zines I made while living in that apartment, I'm not sure how I did it. I remember crying because I felt so totally incapable of writing, which I knew was the only thing that could keep me alive. I lived near the Rainbow Bridge, which I would bike over to get to my sister's place. Sometimes I'd just bike along the river, searching for reasons to live.

TELEGRAM MA'AM

Issue #10

October 2007

$2 Canada & US $3 International

♡ INTRO INTRO INTRO ♡

This issue is mostly about all the places I have lived in this year, and my last days in Guelph before coming back to my hometown of Lindsay. I tried to write a love letter to that city, but it sounded very disjointed and strange, so I chose not to include it.

October is my birth month and also one of my favourite times of year. I am looking forward to rainy nights, pressed leaves on the sidewalks, and surprises.

One night, when I was feeling blue, a friend said to me:

You do have a place in the world, right next to me. We're strange, but there are two of us, so you and I will always fit with each other, if no one else.

I'm trying to remember this every single day and night.

Advertised was a furnished room with a separate bathroom, after which there was a phone number with the message, 'TALK LOUD'. I called, and after much difficulty understanding one another, and me repeating myself louder and louder into the receiver, I finally secured an appointment to take a look at the place over the weekend.

I was looking at two places that Saturday, and decided to view this one first. It seemed promising. The place was on the 9th floor of a downtown building. It was a fairly large apartment with retro orange furniture, doilies everywhere, and a balcony with an amazing view of the city. The woman renting out the room, who turned out to be 97 years old, was sweet to me and said she liked my tattoos. The room itself was kind of small, but it had a large closet, a dresser with a mirror, a desk, a nightstand with an attached lamp, and a single bed. I told her I'd let her know my decision very soon.

There was another place to look at, but I had already concocted a wonderful imaginary life for myself in this apartment: drinking tea and knitting, sharing stories, retreating to the solitude of my little bedroom when I needed time alone or wanted to write. I thought choosing this place would keep me out of trouble.

The other room I looked at was in a beautiful Victorian home, and housed a few university students and musicians. In hindsight, I'm sure I would have felt much more at home in that place, but I decided not to take it because it was further from downtown than I would have preferred, and there were too many people around for me. So I went back to the old woman's place to tell her my decision. She was very pleased, saying she was glad to be having company and hoped she could make her place feel like it was my home, too.

It was toward the end of February when I moved in. The first few days were alright, but I was feeling uncomfortable, like an intruder, and like I was being watched all the time. Of course a twenty-one year old and ninety-seven year old living together is not exactly an ideal situation, but I thought I would make the best of it. I thought it would be cute and quaint. She did tell me a lot of stories about her family, growing up in Poland, traveling the world, moving to Canada, and so on, gave me yummy baked things and showed me pictures. Once, she invited me to have wine and cheesecake with her and her friends. Later, her friends accused me of stealing a bottle of wine that had merely been misplaced, and apologized very embarrassed at their assumption when it was found ten minutes later in the liquor cabinet of all places. Soon enough, I discovered that this place was not what I had been expecting at all.

She kept the television intolerably loud for twelve hours everyday; she gave me the bottom shelf of the refrigerator, then let her food spill and spoil mine; she used my so-called separate bathroom, and took it upon herself to move my personal belongings to wherever she saw fit; she checked in on me at night to make sure I was in my room (I didn't have a lock on my door, so she would just walk in); she made me keep my cat trapped in my room even though I had previously been told Amélie would be free to roam the apartment; and, as I started to gain a bit of a social life, she would make panicked long-distance phone calls to my mom in the middle of the night telling her she couldn't find me, and once tried to report me missing when I spent the night at a friend's house. Eventually she made me leave her notes letting her know when I was out, where I was, who I was with, and when I would be back.

It was too much for me. I felt like I no longer had any independence at all, living under the constant watch of this old lady. I just wanted to live my life without having to report it back to someone else all the time. My brief stay at what was supposed to be my new home, and my new life, lasted about a month. I left by the end of March. It didn't take long to gather my things and move them on in to the next place.

The next place was stranger still.

In March, I met a boy at a show at the Vinyl who I thought was quite charming. It was a You Say Party! We Say Die! show, and once the band had finished their set, we went out into the cold night to smoke pot on the rooftop of a nearby punk club. I don't remember what we talked about, but I moved in with him a week later.

It was a weird arrangement. Technically, I was renting a room from him, but I only used it for storage. I didn't have my own bed yet, so I slept with him. We drifted into something like a couple, although we didn't define it as such. We spent our days prancing around town, taking pictures, drinking hot chocolate, and watching movies, and our nights getting drunk and dancing at local bars. Because we were always together, people assumed we were a couple. But we never were.

Not much time passed before we supremely fucked up, and it was time for me to leave again. In May, I packed up and left him behind.

♥ ♥ ♥

On June 1st, I moved into a room in the apartment of a friend I had met through the last boy I was living with. I warned her that I moved a lot, but would try to stay 'til the following spring since she didn't want to worry about finding another roommate, and I was just sick of moving altogether.

The same night, I went to another You Say Party! We Say Die! show, this time with the ex-boy I had originally moved to Guelph for. After that, I never saw him again.

I had a hard time calling this place *home*. By this point, I didn't even expect to actually find a place I would stay for more than a couple months since I was now in the habit of moving so often. I hadn't even been fully unpacking anymore because I always knew I'd be needing those extra boxes again pretty soon.

This is where I was living, though, when I finally decided to buy myself some furniture. I hadn't had much of my own furniture before because I'd been living with people who already had their own. What furniture I did have was used, and I'd gotten rid of it anyway either because I didn't have room to store it between moves, or because it was filled with memories and reminders of things in the past that I no longer wanted to think about.

Shortly before I left the last place, I had purchased a futon for myself, but that was all I had that was *new* and *mine*. So y mom came for a visit and took me for a trip to Ikea, where I decided to buy everything white. Clean slate. I bought myself a white desk, white chair, white nightstand, white bookshelf, and a white rug. Assembling each item wasn't much fun, but I was proud of myself and felt quite accomplished.

Around this time, I decided to cut a lot of people out of my life, and just be alone for a while. I didn't like the way I felt when I was with other people. So I stopped answering calls and emails, deleted my contacts and online accounts, and stopped going out to bars. I slept through the day and stayed up all night holed up in my bedroom reading a book or writing in my journal. I only went out when I had to, for trips to the post office and the grocery store. I would emerge from my bedroom at sunrise, take out my bike or walk along the river, and sit by the water and under the trees reading, writing, and daydreaming for hours.

♡ ♡ ♡

Back at the apartment, I was uncomfortable. I would either avoid the place because it depressed me and made me feel trapped, or I would sink into it and allow myself to become trapped, only leaving my room when I was hungry, and then I would try to do that only when I thought no one else was around; I didn't want to bump into someone and feel pressured to make useless, fake small talk while I prepared myself a sandwich. So all the time, I was focused on avoidance.

One of my roommates and I took to busking. We were both learning guitar and thought this would be a fun way to practice and make some extra cash at the same time. We were both shy, and this seemed like a good, low-pressure way to get used to playing in front of other people. After our first time, I stopped bringing my guitar because I didn't know a lot of songs. Instead, I played tambourine, and she played guitar. It sounds silly, but I've always wanted to play tambourine.

We met a lot of weirdos, of course. There was one man who was drunk before the work-day was over, and tried to play my guitar as a drum against the sidewalk; a man who told me his fears about God, Satan, torture in mental hospitals, and Helter Skelter, among others — he got freaked out by the lyrics to *American Pie*, which my friend was singing beside me; there was another drunk who harassed us and everyone around us until we had to call the cops and they took him away; and there was a group of students who insisted on taking their pants off before hanging out with us for a while.

A lot of men offered us money for sexual favours, money to "come home and play some songs" for them. They were pretty insistent, sometimes even pulling wads of cash out to show that they were serious. They would always say the same thing: "I know a way you girls could make some *real* money." We'd tell them we were making real money and we didn't need theirs.

Of course, there were kinder people, too. For instance, the old lady who played my tambourine and told me about polka dancing; and the man who gave us a $100 bill, saying his wife was divorcing him, and he would rather us have the money than her.

But for some reason, people took it upon themselves to ask us very personal questions about where we worked, where we lived, and what we did with our money. Somehow they seemed to think that just because we were playing music on public streets, our minds and our selves were public property as well.

After a night of busking, we'd get home around three in the morning, pour our money out onto the coffee table and spilt it up, and laugh about all the people we'd met, all the memories we'd made. Mostly we talked about how great it was to make so much tax-free cash, and bragged to everyone else the next day. ♡ ♡ ♡

But soon enough, I had decided to leave. This time, I wasn't just leaving the apartment; I was leaving the city, returning home. It was such a difficult decision to make, but I knew it had to be done. There were a few reasons. For one, I had been feeling extremely lonely all summer, and wanted to be near my family again, thinking that being able to talk to my mom more often would make me feel safe, and hanging out with my sister would distract me from the dark thoughts plaguing my mind and encourage me to *do something*. I'd always wanted to live by myself, and had just managed to find a bachelor apartment in Lindsay, the town I grew up in, that I could actually afford on my own. Although I was in love with Guelph as a city, I no longer wanted to be there. I wanted another chance to start over. One of my most important reasons for leaving, though, was that a year before this, I had moved to Guelph to be with my partner; we weren't together anymore, and now everything in the city reminded me of him. Staying in a city I loved was no longer worth the risk of having another nervous breakdown, or bumping into him on the streets. I had to get away.

Most times I moved, I would flee in such a hurry that I hadn't yet found another place to live, and would stay with my mom until I did. She'd made the two and a half hour trip to Guelph for me so many times, and often on incredibly short notice, as in, "Come pick me up right now, I am freaking out!" I would throw what I could into my Hello Kitty backpack and some garbage bags, fill up her car, and come back later for the rest of it. I would always be in tears, angry or sad, or both.

The spare room in my mom's apartment is not big enough to store an entire lifetime's worth of acquired junk, but that is just what I had to do, time and time again. Furniture, stacks of boxes, and piles of garbage bags filled with clothes left little floor space, sometimes not even a trail to lead me from the door to the bed.

The first time I stayed in my mom's apartment was when the boy and I had split up. I was so heartbroken I could barely speak. I slept most of the time, occasionally emerging from the spare room to watch *Friends* reruns and check my email. It was Christmastime; the place smelled like cinnamon.

Afraid of being spotted in the streets, I refused to leave the apartment, convinced that anyone who saw me would know that my relationship and my new life had failed; that I was worthless, stupid, and couldn't make it on my own.

I stayed there off and on, alternating between my mom's apartment, the apartment the ex-boy and I were still sharing, the local hospital, and a homeless shelter. I'd sleep with near strangers just to have another place to stay for the night. Everywhere I went, I felt guilty; I thought no one wanted me around. I was cold all the time, confused and lost and lonely.

The reason I felt so guilty staying with my mom was that this was the first place that had simply been *her own* since my sister and I had moved out. It was a nice little home for one, decorated with things she had chosen to put on display, used for her own routines, her own life. I felt like an intruder using her dishes and eating her food, spending time on her computer, keeping my bath products in her shower, and letting my laundry pile up in her spare room. She was just finally free of me, and then I returned. I felt like a royal fuck-up.

Continuing my life in Guelph after I'd signed the papers for my new apartment and set a date for the move was difficult. Whenever I left Guelph, I'd be so antsy to get back; now it was just the opposite. I wanted to leave.

On the one hand, I was eager to have my own place waiting for me, and wanted to be there right away. But I was also sad about the whole thing. I loved this city and had been planning on staying much longer. Now my time was ticking out. This was a new feeling to me.

During my last days in Guelph, I made a point of having final visits to some of my favourite places. I spent a lot of time along Speed River, hiking through the brambles and marshy areas, or sometimes staying on the trails, taking lots of pictures, reflecting, and so on. I took my last trip up the many, many steps leading to the Church of Our Lady Immaculate, a last look at the statuette of the Virgin Mary, and the view of the city below. The church sits atop a pretty big hill and is the tallest building in the city. I took a few pictures at the Greyhound station, where I have spent so, so much of my time. And when I filled out my change of address forms at the post office, the staff were sad to see me go, and wished me luck with my new life. I got a little teary that day walking back from the post office, hoping I'd made the right decision.

I told almost no one I was leaving.

Before I moved into my new apartment, I painted. I'd wanted to paint for such a long time but hadn't quite had the opportunity. In our first apartment, the boy and I had discussed what colours we wanted each room to be, but we never got around to doing anything about it. After that, I'd been renting rooms, of course, and never stayed long enough to make painting worthwhile. But now I'd be on my own, free to decorate however I pleased without the obligation of discussing it with someone else first.

Painting is important to me because it makes a place feel much more like a home, which is what I want this place to be. Well, it is what I wanted all those places to be, but I guess that just wasn't meant to happen. I am so sick of white walls!

So I chose a shade of green called Aqualine, and with the help of my mom, had the place finished in less than a day. The kitchen and bathroom already had turquoise countertops and tiles, so even though I'd thought of this colour at least a year and a half previous, it was still the perfect choice for this apartment.

I also had to buy a lot of things before moving in. Just very general items like dishes and cutlery, but the costs sure added up quickly. It was nice, though, a relief, to be able to choose these things on my own, and not just get stuck with what someone else happened to have.

Whenever I'd question my decision about coming back here, I would remind myself that this time I was not running away, I was not escaping; instead, I was moving *toward* something. I'd made a healthy decision to get out of a bad environment, a place that was, essentially, eating me alive, and live instead in a place that may not be exactly ideal, but is certainly better for me, for now.

I have always been planning my escape. My escape from this town, my mind, my life, from just about every place I ever lived. Now, finally, I can stop running and just breathe.

Now when I visit my mom's, it feels a little strange to me. Unfortunately, I automatically associate that cute little apartment of hers with my broken heart. The other day when I went in, that holiday cinnamon scent was back, and my mind was flooded with a rush of images: my boxes taking up so much space; me standing alone on a cold, snowy night; screaming my lungs sore at the ex-boy; opening my Christmas present from him; long car trips where all I could do was cry; wearing just a slip, my hair greasy from not having the energy to shower for days; and so on. This all came back to me the moment I walked in the door.

Of course, it is not the same at all. The apartment is back to its old self, sans my belongings. It's nice to go there and know that I don't have to stay any longer than I want to; I have a home to go to, my own bed to sleep in. I am training myself to think of that place as what it really is – my mom's home – instead of what it was to me – my last resort when I had nowhere else to go.

My 22nd birthday is coming up. I'm a little frightened. I'm not afraid of growing older or being an adult. I know that it is just a number and I will always be a child. I'm not sure if I can pinpoint exactly what it is I am afraid of.

My last few birthdays have been good ones. Special ones, even. This year, I am single, and I am back in this small town... I want to do something to make it wonderful, but I'm not sure if anyone else will care, and I don't want to let it pass by without somehow marking the occasion.

There are important birthdays: 10 because it is the first double-digit; 13 because you are finally a teenager; 16 because you are old enough to drive; 18 because you are a legal adult; 19 because you can drink; 20 because you are finally *not* a teenager. Then there is a big gap. I think 28 should be special because 27 is supposed the worst year, so if you can survive that, you had better celebrate. 30 is special just because it is, and also because of Saturn's Return. Then 40, then 50, then 60, then 65. 22 means nothing.

It's probably a big deal because I typically feel abandoned, unloved, and unwanted, and I don't want to feel that way on my birthday.

Since I moved back, life has been alright. I have good days and bad days, just like always, but I generally feel like I am in a better place, physically, mentally, and spiritually. It's nearing the end of September as I write this, so I've been back in Lindsay for almost a month now. I've been hanging out with old acquaintances and going to shows, spending time with my sister, focusing more on my writing and other art projects... really just trying not to waste my time. I just want to do something with my life. I want to stop fucking up.

TELEGRAM MA'AM

Issue #11

February 2008

$2 Canada and US / $3 International

AN INCOMPLETE ALPHABET

Lately I have felt such a lack of inspiration. It is partly due to the winter, partly due to my depression. Now that we are halfway through the winter, I'm feeling a little better. It's an uphill climb, but I am getting there. I have been thinking over the last couple months all the things I wanted to write about for this issue, but every time I brought my pen to the paper, or turned on my computer, I would become completely frozen and break out in tears. I could not write. Then on a warm day, it struck me to write my own alphabet. Using each letter as a writing prompt has helped me regain my inspiration and finally write again. I'm still having difficulties in my life, and I am not completely happy, not by a longshot, but as long as I can still create, I know there is hope.

BAKING

When we were kids, our nana always baked for my sister and I, and sometimes she would let us help out as well. We had an annual tradition of baking Christmas cookies with icing and sprinkles, and we always loved making pancakes. Nana would also bake her famous apple crumble, Hello Dolly, and cakes for special occasions. A few years ago, she copied all her recipes and gave them to my mom, my sister, and I. Before I moved out on my own, I made yet another copy of all the recipes and bought my own little recipe box to keep them in. Over time I collected more recipes from my family and from zines, and this winter, my sister and I have been trying them out. So far, we have made bran and coconut muffins, banana bread, apple crumble, cherry dream cupcakes, and oatmeal and chocolate chip cookies. We keep some for ourselves and share the rest.

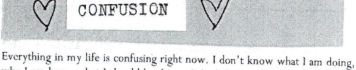

CONFUSION

Everything in my life is confusing right now. I don't know what I am doing, why I am here, what I should be doing, I don't know if I should find a new place to live, meet more people, stay in the same apartment, keep away from people... I don't know if any of my ideas for art projects will ever come to fruition or if they will merely stay in my head. I don't know how to begin, hot to end, how to change, how to be. I am always lost.

DESTRUCTION

In January, I decided to destroy all my paper journals. I'd been keeping them since I was fifteen (my journals from childhood and my early teens had already been thrown out as a teenager), so there was a boxful of eight years of my life to get rid of. I've always felt like my journal are a huge part of who I am. I recorded all sorts of memories, conversations, feelings, moments, fears, *everything*, but my life and my mind were in such a bad state that I felt like all those journals and everything they contained were weighing me down. All I could do was get rid of them. For a long time, I had thought of burning them, but I don't have a firepit on my property, so I figured drowning them would be my next best option. So I filled my kitchen sink with soap and water and put my journals in one at a time. Slowly the pages came unglued and ink ran, staining the water shades of red, purple, pink, and black. I let the ink run until I could no longer read my own words, then turned each page to make sure all of them were soaked. When every page was soaked, I pulled them out individually, drained them, and threw them away. Some thought I would later regret this decision, but those journals and everything they contained were weighing too heavy on me, and I just needed to make them disappear.

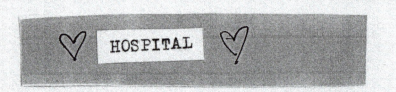

HOSPITAL

This winter, I have had two more admissions to the Mental Health ward of the local hospital. In November, I was admitted for another overdose, and they kept me there for about two weeks. While I was there I spent a lot of time hiding out in my room just writing in my journal, reading a book, or knitting. The psychiatrists changed my meds and sent me home. Then in January I was admitted again when I had a particularly bad panic attack on my first day of group therapy. This time they told me I couldn't hide out anymore and would have to interact with the other patients and spend time in the common areas instead of staying in my bedroom. So I tried, and they released me after a week with yet more med changes. At this point, the hospital feels like a second home to me.

MEDICATION

By now I've lost count of the amount of meds I've been on. I haven't always been medicated. I was twelve the first time I was prescribed antidepressants, but I stopped taking them when I was thirteen and didn't take anything else until I was nineteen. Since then I've been on and off at least five different pills. They worked for a while, but lately, when it comes to antidepressants, nothing I try works at all. It's frustrating because I know there must be something out there that could help me, I just can't seem to find it. In the meantime I'm trying more pills than I can remember, hoping and hoping, yet they never pull through for me. I'm determined, though, to find one that works. I feel insane without them.

OTTAWA

In February, my sister and I went to Ottawa to each get another tattoo. I'd been looking forward to this trip all winter long, and brought designs that I'd had for a long time. In the darkest days of my depression, the anticipation of a road trip and new ink was all that kept me going. My tattoo was inspired by *Little Acorns* by The White Stripes. On my upper left arm, I got a framed black & grey portrait of a squirrel carrying an acorn, and a banner with the lyric, "Be like the squirrel." I know it seems silly, and maybe it is, but at the same time, it means a lot to me, and I'm glad to finally be able to carry this message with me wherever I go. The song basically tells the story of a woman whose life seemed to be falling apart, then one day she watches a squirrel from her window gathering nuts for the winter, and decides that if this squirrel can take care of itself with the harsh winter coming on, so can she.

RESOLUTIONS

I think New Year's resolutions are kind of overrated, but I made a few this year, and they have been going pretty well so far. My biggest resolution was to quit drinking. Drinking used to be fun for me, but it was starting to become a problem not only for me, but for others who were around me when I was drunk. I was tired of having to apologize for my behaviour afterward, and not only that, it was costing me a lot of money that could be better spent, and alcohol doesn't mix well with all the meds I am on anyway. There have been several times in the past when I have tried to quit drinking, but they were half-hearted attempts and didn't take long to fail. This time I am concerned not only with spending too much money and making a fool of myself in front of friends and strangers, but also with my own mental health. I don't particularly think this will last forever, but for now it's what I need, so as of New Year's Day, I am a sober girl.

THERAPY

With my release from the hospital in December, I signed up for a few different Group Therapy sessions held in the outpatient centre of the mental health ward. They were called Enhancing Self, Personal Transformation Skills, Depression & Anxiety, Living with Anger, and a group for young women. The haven't been as helpful to me as I thought they would, and sometimes I feel like I am just putting in time 'til my name comes up on the waitlist for one-ob-one therapy, but I continue to go to each group in the hopes that someone will suddenly say something to transform my way of thinking, or sometimes just to have something to do with my day. If I weren't going to therapy a few times a week, I would probably just stay in bed all day moping, so even just the walk to the hospital is helpful in its own little way. One thing that really bothers me about group therapy is having to listen to the problems of everyone else, and because I don't like to speak in groups, I don't get to talk about my own problems. But two hours spent in each session is another two hours that I am surviving, so I figure even the things I don't like about group therapy are good for me, really.

UPS & DOWNS

I feel like I am an expert on ups and downs these days! My head is always bouncing, unable to just find a comfortable place and stay there. I have been down more often than up, and it's hard to handle, but I am surviving. This fall, I was diagnosed with Bipolar Disorder, and it was around that time that I started noticing just how bad my ups were, how absolutely crazy I was at times. No one else knew, but I knew something was wrong, so I talked to my doctor about it, and he prescribed Lithium for me. Since then my crazy ups have gone away, but my depression hasn't lifted at all; in fact, it has been much worse this winter, possibly just because of the season, but partly due to my brain's chemicals and my past always creeping up on me as well. So I was also given an antidepressant, the fifth one I have tried, and I am hope-hope-hoping it will do the trick.

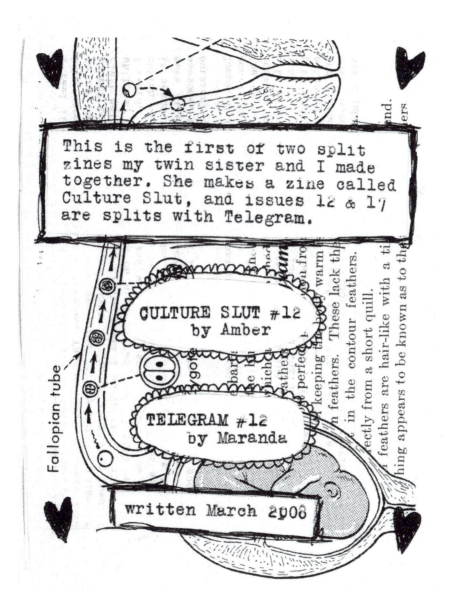

This is the first of two split zines my twin sister and I made together. She makes a zine called Culture Slut, and issues 12 & 17 are splits with Telegram.

CULTURE SLUT #12
by Amber

TELEGRAM #12
by Maranda

written March 2008

Fallopian tube

Culture Slut #12
by Amber

A few weeks ago, Maranda and I were in line together at the bank. We stood next to each other, probably discussing the tattoos that we were going to get the following weekend, because that's why we were withdrawing so much money in the first place. I was wearing a pink and green plaid coat, she was wearing a similar one in black. I have lighter hair, hers in black. We both dye our hair a lot, but I tend to go with lighter colours like blonde and pink, while hers always stays dark, usually black or red. We both rock the Bettie Page bangs. We wear rhinestoned glasses — mine are turquoise, hers are black. Basically, we look the same. I come in Technicolour, and she is the Black-and-White version. We didn't plan it this way, it just happened.

There was a middle-aged woman in front of us in the line. She turned around slowly, looked us up and down, didn't even try to be subtle about it. She kind of rolled her eyes at us, you know that expression. Maranda and I burst into laughter. Why did she look at us like that? Because we dress strange? We're used to being stared at, but she didn't look at us the way people usually do — with curiosity or intrigue — she looked at us the way our peers did when we were still awkward teenagers, wearing dog chains, too much black eyeliner, and oversized clothing. The woman ignored our laughter. A few moments later, we were at the font of the line. The bank teller was excited; she has twins too, in their thirties now.

When we were kids, we thought that we were going to be famous one day. That's what twins do. We only knew the twins that we saw on television. (That is not entirely true. We have cousins who are twins, fraternal, one year younger than us. We have a book of the family tree, going back to the late 1800's and there are several sets of twins along the way.) Obviously, there was Mary-Kate and Ashley Olsen. We were religious *Full House* viewers. And who could forget

Heather and Erica from *Degrassi Junior High*? They were usually shy girls, but were forced to defend themselves against anti-choicers when one of them chose to have an abortion. You tell 'em, Heather and Erica! Phoebe's twin sister Ursula made occasional appearances on *Friends*, there were fraternal twins Brenda and Brandon on *Beverly Hills 90210*, and of course we read all of the *Sweet Valley Twins* books. Later on, we discovered Kim and Kelly Deal's sweet indie rock tunes. I don't know what we thought we were going to be famous for. A sitcom? Doublemint gum commercials? When we were only four days old, we appeared (with Mommie Dearest) on the front page of the *Toronto Sun*, having been the heaviest set of twins ever born at Etobicoke General Hospital. Perhaps we started planning our fame on that very day?

Needless to say, we never became famous. We are something like local celebrities though. I know this, because everywhere I go, friends and strangers tell me that they just saw a girl who looks just like me, only dressed n black. The cashier at the grocery store said that to me yesterday afternoon, while I was paying for my veggies and orange juice. She said, "You have a twin, don't you? I see her in here sometimes." I said, "Yep, she looks just like me, but with black hair?" She said, "That's the one. I have a twin, too, you know. She was always the slimmer one." I said, "That's cool, I always like meeting twins."

People have asked if we ever find ourselves jealous of one another. It is kind of a hard question to respond to, although I've given it a lot of thought. I can't think of any specific instances where I have thought, "I wish I had what Maranda has," but certainly there are times when I'm made aware of the fact that she is more talented than I am, like when it comes to art and writing. She was always good at drawing, even as children her sketches were always more realistic than mine. She is also a much more eloquent writer than I am, although I would imagine it's because we have different interests as far as reading material goes. I am much more likely to be reading feminist themed non-fiction and zines, whereas she likes to immerse herself in really great fiction. Sometimes I think that I'm a terrible writer, but then I just remind myself that I have different interests and a different style than she does.

We've also been asked how we might react if the other were to die. This is not a hypothetical situation, as my sister has been dealing with depression and mental illness. She has attempted suicide on more than one occasion, so I've been forced to think about how I might deal with her death. I was completely unaware of the first attempt until a short while after the fact. I was living in Ottawa at the time, and she was in Guelph, so we mostly communicated through the internet. It wasn't until about a week or so after the attempt that she updated her online journal, telling everyone what had happened. She had been in the hospital for a week, and therefore had no contact with me. I don't remember how I reacted, besides crying to my roommate. I wondered, the next time she attempted, would she succeed? Sometimes I feel disconnected from her, because there are times when I simply cannot relate to the things she's saying, and that's a new feeling to me. I've always felt overprotective of her, like I am the big sister or something. She was always more shy than I was, always trailed behind me a little when we went places, and I always had to take charge. When she fell off her bike as a child, or was pushed around by people at school, I always thought that it was hurting me more than her, and I wanted to keep her away from it, not only for her own safety, but for my own. Now I've had to come to terms with the fact that there are some things I'll never be able to protect her from, like depression, and asshole boyfriends, and that stupid credit card debt. If she were to die, I still don't know what I would do. I know that I would be a wreck and I would curl up in bed (or maybe on my mom's couch) and cry for days and days. I know that it seems to crass to admit, but I almost feel prepared for her death, in a strange way. And I certainly don't mean that I am looking forward to it in any manner, but sometimes she seems so determined to die young, that it is hard for me to ignore. I hope she makes progress with her mental illness, but I still feel (unhappily) prepared for her death, because I've been forced to contemplate it on so many occasions.

♡ ♡ ♡

It's been said that twins who were separated at birth turn out to be exactly the same. They usually don't know that they have a twin, so they aren't actively trying to be different, to stand out, to prove that they are their own person. So the separated twins wind up living similar lives, studying the same things in school, giving their pets the same names, and trimming their hair the same way. Maranda and I dressed the same as children, because that's what twins are supposed to do, I guess. I once threw a temper tantrum at age five because she didn't want to wear the same sweater as me. We had our colours; I always wore pink, she always wore purple. We love a lot of the same music, we're both into zines, we have matching tattoos, and we both proudly proclaim ourselves feminists. But in some ways, we turned out so, so differently.

WHAT NOT TO DO

Sometimes people say really stupid things to Maranda and I based on the fact that we are twins. So we thought we'd write this little list of what NOT to say or do to twins, because hey, you don't want to offend us, do you?

1. **"Twins are totally hot. You guys should do porn."** A surprising amount of loser teenagers and frat-boy types have this mentality. I don't know where the twins-as-fetish (or 'twincest' as some people lovingly refer) thing came from, and I don't want to know. It just plain gives me the creeps. Before making a comment like this to twin girls, please think logically. We are sisters. We've been best friends since we were babies. We share the same parents. There is nothing hip or hot about incest, and we don't appreciate the suggestion. Even if you're joking. It's gross.

2. **Try to refrain from staring at us for too long.** We know that people sometimes find twins intriguing and interesting, or just plain weird, and we're cool with that. But when we're walking past you on the street, we are not there for display purposes. Please try to keep your eyes to yourself. When you stare at us for too long, we notice, and it makes us a little uncomfortable.

♡ ♡ ♡

3. **Don't ask us if we have different interests.** Of course we have different interests, we're DIFFERENT PEOPLE. Yeah, we've got some things in common, the same way many siblings and friends do, but we are not exactly the same. It is quite naïve to assume that we agree 100% of the time.

4. **Please don't treat us as if we are interchangeable.** Okay, so this doesn't happen to us quite as often as it did when we were younger, but I imagine many other twins face situations like this, so I'm going to address it. Please don't treat us like we are the same person. For example, when we were younger, a friend might phone and ask me if I wanted to hang out. If I was busy, they would immediately say, "Well, is Maranda around?" It just felt like they were thinking, "If Amber isn't available, I'll just get Maranda instead." And that was kinda weird and unfair.

5. **Don't set us up on double-dates.** I know that the whole idea seems very cute, but frankly, it's also kind of awkward. People always tell us how great it would be if Maranda was dating my boyfriend's brother. It makes for some uncomfortable situations. Just because we look similar doesn't mean we wanna date look-a-like siblings too.

6. **Keep gift-giving interesting.** For our entire lives, we were given the same gifts at birthdays and holidays. We were given the same outfits in coordinating colours, the same Barbie dolls, the same accessories... There were even times when we were told to open our gifts at the same time so that one wouldn't spoil the surprise for the other. I've said it before, I'll say it again: WE ARE NOT THE SAME PERSON.

7. **Don't be all, "Ooh, catfight!"** That's stupid.

♡ ♡ ♡

TELEGRAM #12
by Maranda

I feel like I'm reporting from behind a thick, velvet curtain, or in a corner hiding within the shadows. *This is what it feels like to be the sick half of a pair of twins.* I try not to think of myself on those terms, but sometimes it just cannot be helped. I can't help but notice that it always seems I am spiralling downwards while my sister is standing on her own two feet. I take one step forward, two steps back, and watch her soar ahead of me. Since childhood, Amber has always been the more popular one, or at least it seems that way to me. When we go out together, she is the one more likely to be approached. It's like she was born with these awesome, friendly vibes that I can never have. I feel like such an outsider compared to her.

Compared to her. I know other people are comparing the two of us, conveniently forgetting that we are two individual people. We look the same, so we must be the same, they think. We do have a lot in common. We like a lot of the same music, we're both into things like zines, feminism, live shows, and taking random pictures. We hang out a lot, and have a lot of weird inside jokes that nobody else would understand. But we're different, too. Amber is more outgoing than I am, more able to make conversation with strangers and friends alike, and because of this, she meets more people and makes more friends. She gets things done, and I procrastinate. She has a job, and I don't. She has a boyfriend, and I don't.

It does sometimes feel like Amber is the functional one, and I am the broken one. As we find out more and more about the mental illnesses in our family, we have to ask ourselves, 'How come only one of us got the depression gene?' And it's easy to be envious of her life, which seems so much happier than mine, but I know better because I know she has her problems, too, and neither one of us is better or worse than the other.

Amber is usually the one I go to when I need some cheering up. We often make plans to work on projects together, but when we do get together, we're more likely to just watch DVD's and talk about nothing in particular. I remember one winter day when we decided it would be a good idea to buy tambourines, so we went into the local music shop and left not only with two tambourines, but two acoustic guitars as well. Somehow when we were in that store, we suddenly wanted to learn guitar and start a cute little two-piece. More than one year later, I can barely play one song, and she can't play any. This zine is certainly one project we talked about for a very long time before actually writing anything.

Although we talked about it for quite a long time, we didn't fully decide to write this zine until the two of us were living in the same town again. In 2006, Amber moved to Ottawa and I moved to Guelph, cities which are about 5 ½ hours apart, the greatest distance there has ever been between the two of us (excluding trips across the border and overseas). During this time, we would write letters to one another, send zines and colouring books in the mail, chat online, and just generally try to keep in touch and be there when we were needed. In the winter of 2007, Amber moved back to our hometown of Lindsay, and in the summer of the same year, I followed suit. Now, at last, we could work on all those projects together! We intended to write this zine right when we were reunited, but other things got in the way. Now that we are each at our 12th issue of our perzines, it seemed appropriate that this one would be the split.

Growing up, it was always great having a twin sister because I always had someone to come along with me if I wanted to go anywhere, always had someone to play with, someone to talk to, etc. I think that may have hindered me as an adult, though. I am so used to having someone with me all the time that I feel uncomfortable when I have to go anywhere alone. When we are together, I tend to let her do most of the speaking. I'm uncomfortable with little things that some people might never even think about, like being the first to enter a room (I try my best to make sure someone else enters before me), talking to retail staff, etc. On the other hand, if I am somewhere where nobody knows I am a twin, like when we were living in separate cities, for example, I am more relaxed because I know that no one is comparing me to her. It's easy to be myself when I know that no one think I am quieter, uglier, whateverer than her.

Sometimes it feels like Amber is my protector. She has always been braver than me, has always been more of a leader. It makes me feel guilty, but I'm trying to become a little better about that. At the same time I am also learning to accept that that's just the way things are. Although we are alike in many ways, we clash in many ways, too.

There are questions that people always ask us. Sometimes they're interesting, sometimes I just get sick of it. But for the purposes of this zine, I'm definitely interested in talking about them. One question we get asked a lot is if it is weird being a twin or having another version of each other in the world. I don't think of Amber as another version of myself. Despite the fact that we look alike, we are different people. It's also never occurred to me that it would be strange simply because Amber has always been in my life. To outsiders, the idea of having a twin might seem weird, but to someone who has always had a twin, well, no, it's not at all. It's just life. Growing up, having a twin was like having a built-in best friend, someone to be with you wherever you go.

We also get asked about dressing alike. When we were kids, we always dressed the same, but Amber would wear pink, and I would wear a matching outfit in purple. As we grew up, we started dressing differently from one another, but there were still a few incidents in our teenage years when we would accidentally wear the same skirt or something, and sometimes there would be a fight about it, other times one of us would simply change into something else. These days, as mentioned before, Amber is the Technicolour one and I am the Black & White one, and she is still attracted to pink while I still go for purple. Amber wears more t-shirts and jeans while I like to wear dresses, skirts, and patterned tights.

Do you feel it when the other one is upset or injured? In the past, there have definitely been occasions where I felt upset for no reason just to find out that something had been upsetting Amber that day. And if I see her get hurt, like stubbing her toe or something, I always burst out with, "Ouch!" even thought I can't actually feel it. Sometimes our lives will have strange parallels, like a few years ago she was breaking up with her boyfriend just as I was getting together with mine, then a couple years later, they were getting back together just as mine and I were breaking up. It was pretty weird for both of us. What's funny about this question, though, is that everyone always wants to know if we feel it when the other one is hurt, but no one ever asks if we feel it when the other one is happy.

Until I worked on this zine, I didn't quite realize just how much I use this means of expression in a confessional form. Although it's on my mind fairly often, I guess I haven't had a lot of opportunities to talk about how I really feel about the ups and downs of having a twin. In a way, I felt like each time Amber and I sent a piece of the zine to one another to take a look at, we were sending a letter with little secrets inside. She told me things I never knew, and maybe I did the same.

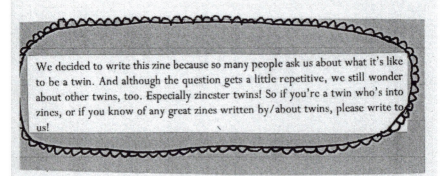

We decided to write this zine because so many people ask us about what it's like to be a twin. And although the question gets a little repetitive, we still wonder about other twins, too. Especially zinester twins! So if you're a twin who's into zines, or if you know of any great zines written by/about twins, please write to us!

TELEGRAM MA'AM

June 2008 $2 Canada and U.S. $3 International

Name.—The centipede owes its name to the fact that it possesses many legs (*centum*, hundred; *pes*, foot).

Habit. cool, moist places under bark of rotten st s, in some secluded co of ar ar the situa ti his little an us nu ot

as w vi

flat te for the ce openings or to bject ery lose to the ground. Co ering or exoskeleton protects the body her echanical injury. Seg numer us segments of he body allow t and turn in every direction The number varies with species and the age of the individual.

From Comstock's "Spider Book," courtesy Doubleday, Page & Co.
Fig. 86. A centipede

#13

I thought that once the snow melted and the sun started shining again, everything would be a little simpler. I thought it would be easier to get out of bed, to work on projects, to smile. At the same time, I didn't really believe I would survive winter at all. It's only May, and I am already dreading next November, when the snow will return. I want to spend all my time working on zines and other art projects, hanging out with my friends, riding my bike, and finally learning how to play my guitar, but getting out of bed is so hard, let alone forcing myself to actually do something once I am up. Sometimes I'd rather just wrap myself up in my blanket, let the music play, and drift in and out of sleep forever.

I've been frustrated lately at the thought that nobody actually knows who I am, and I wonder who they do know me as. Do you ever wonder how you appear to others? Do you care? For a long time, people seemed to think that I was shy and sweet, and for a while that may have been true, maybe it still is, but I am much, much more than that, and I think there are people who find that disappointing. I can't be sweet all the time. Unfortunately, I seem to be either sweet or obnoxious, and I can't find a happy balance between the two. Twenty years of my life were spent keeping to myself, I finally got tired of it, and now my nonsense comes out in ridiculous bursts, alienating everyone who thought they knew me.

Then again, they aren't who I thought they were either. If I don't think anyone can ever truly know who I am, then how can I expect to truly know who anyone else is? And if we don't know one another, then how can we fall in love?

I'm a little lost these days. But that's nothing new.

I have a tendency to think that the life I am living right now is just practice for my next, *real* life. *Next time this happens, I'll know how to say no, Next time this happens, I'll tell him how I feel before it's too late. Next time this happens, I won't act all shy and coy. Next time this happens, I'll start dancing earlier. Next time this happens, next time, next time...* And on and on. It's not that I have any regrets. I don't. I know I've fucked up a lot, and I know things could have turned out differently, but I'm fairly satisfied with the decisions I have made up to this point; I have learned a lot, and I am grateful for my experiences. I'll use that experience to write ten thousand novels of my life disguised as fiction. Regret is a waste of energy. If you can't change it, don't dwell on it. It's just that my life doesn't always feel like its happening. It feels more like what *might* happen *if*. it's like a Choose Your Own Adventure book, which is an analogy I use all too often, but it's true. I'm still convinced that if I try hard enough, I can go back to page 9 and choose page 10 instead of page 11. Twenty-two years, and I have yet to accept that this is my life and I'm not going to get another chance.

These days, I'm finding it quite difficult to write. One, usually incomplete, sentence comes to me at a time, and sometimes I'll write it down on scrap paper, the back of a drugstore receipt, in the hopes of using it later for some big, important art project, but it just gets buried in all the other scraps on my desk, and I forget where I was going with the idea anyway. Other times I don't write it down because I come up with all my best ideas when I am trying to sleep, and instead of getting up to write them down, or keeping a notebook by my bed, I tell myself I'll write them down tomorrow, but I rarely remember them.

For most of my life, I have had a strange habit of counting syllables. I count them in fours and eights, which is weird because I don't like even numbers, and I imagine each syllable on a different finger. I also think of some letters and sounds as having a cold temperature, and other letters and sounds having a warm temperature. When it comes to numbers, evens are sharp and odds are soft. It's not something I think about doing anymore, it's just something I do. So sometimes, when I'm trying to fall asleep, and I don't want to get up to write down my great idea, I will make a note of the syllables in my idea, and remember which fingers are hot and which fingers are cold. If I remember the formula the next day, it will usually lead me back to the initial idea. Then I can write it down and let it get buried in my scraps with the others.

I stopped taking my meds. I think that was back in February? I was on several when I quit. There was Lithium, plus an anti-psychotic, and yet another antidepressant. I've been on so many now that I have trouble remembering all the names. Wait, I think I can actually write a list of all of them: Lithium, Zyprexa, Remeron, Trazodone, Wellbutrin, Lorazepam, Effexor, Celexa, and Luvox. I *think* that covers it. Anyway, they're all gone now. Some of them were good at putting me to sleep, which is great since I've had pretty horrible insomnia since the age of twelve, but they weren't really doing what they were supposed to be doing, and I was exhausted with trying new pills all the time, so I just thought, fuck it, and stopped taking them altogether. Although I feel like they are a form of poison, if they worked, I'd continue taking them. But at this point, I've just had enough. It's not just the meds that are a problem, but the fact that nobody really seems to know just what the proper diagnosis is. So far, I have heard depression (obviously), severe depression, anxiety, social phobia, agoraphobia, and bipolar. I think they should just combine them all, add a few more to that ridiculous list, and call it Being Maranda. Because I don't think they're going to find me in a textbook.

The thing about taking all those pills is that it makes me feel like I am *supposed* to be sick, like I am *supposed* to be unstable, and so I find myself unable to get better because I don't think I'm expected to. It made me feel like I would spend the rest of my life taking pills and having occasional freak-outs, and manic episodes, and depressive spells, and visits to the doctor. And I thought that I would let myself fuck up all the time thinking it would be okay to just say, "Sorry, I'm sick, you'll have to forgive me." Basically, by doing something that's supposed to make me 'better', I would refuse to get better. Not taking meds, in a maybe kind of backwards way, is like taking control of my illness.

And honestly, I also stopped taking them because they were giving me a bad reaction to alcohol, which is sometimes the only thing that makes me happy (*sometimes*, not always and not only), and it seriously wasn't worth it, and I was mighty fed up with side effects like weight gain, shakiness, memory loss, etc. The side effects of life are bad enough without the side effects of meds, so it's just better for me this way.

I still visit my doctor regularly so he can see that I'm not on the brink of suicide, but at least I no longer leave with a new prescription every time.

In the winter, I started going to group therapy for outpatients at the hospital. I would wake up early and trudge through the snow to get there. The city was on strike, so the snow wasn't being plowed, and I would have to walk out on the road, or sometimes my mom would give me a ride on her way to work, dropping me off an hour early, so I would read until the first session began. I was involved in several different groups. I felt uncomfortable in most of the groups. Aside from the young adults group, I was the youngest person in each session, and everybody seemed to notice. I kept to myself for the most part, even when I thought I had something of value to offer, because I didn't want to give anyone the opportunity to mock me or shoot me down. I'm sure they wouldn't intentionally do that, but although we were there for similar reasons, we had different experiences, and I wasn't sure they'd be too accepting of mine, so I didn't talk too much about it. I did learn a lot, though, and it's not always easy to keep what I learned with me at all times, but I do try. It was so uncomfortable, though, because we'd be sitting around these big tables in a room with no natural light, and I did not want to be with these people at all. I was going mostly because it was a safe place for me during the day, I thought it might help me sort my head out briefly, and I didn't feel I was ready to be out of the hospital yet, but the local mental health ward doesn't like to keep anyone too long, so you get kicked out before you're ready to handle to real world on your own again. They're really more of a transition centre than a treatment centre. I didn't like the other people in my groups. They'd make comments that were anti-woman, anti-queer, and they'd make all sorts of generalizations about certain 'types' of people, and they would just generally say a lot of things that I didn't agree with. And that's fine, I know we can't all agree on everything, but it takes a lot to offend me, so to be feeling offended on a regular basis was a bit terrifying. I try to surround myself with people who have similar sorts of ideas as me, similar interests and opinions and politics, bright, intelligent people who have open minds and want to change the world, people who are into art and sharing and learning, and because I close myself off to the typical small town mentality with which I am currently living, it's a big slap in the face to suddenly be in a roomful of it, and not feel articulate enough or confident enough to tell them everything that is wrong with what they are saying. Whenever I try to fight it, I get so frustrated that I end up yelling, crying, leaving the room, or all of the above. And that's just not a good argument, so I usually just keep quiet, and that's not good either, but it's less disruptive.

I'm learning to use words like 'should' and 'shouldn't' and 'right' and 'wrong' less often these days. Words like that put pressure on me to try to behave a certain way, to have certain reactions to the statements of others, and basically to live by somebody else's rules, and that just can't be healthy for me. I'm only going to live this life once, and there's no reason to spend it appeasing others. I feel like I have been such a disappointment, although I can't pinpoint exactly why. But instead of dwelling on this, I'm just going to let it go, and be who I am, and not care what anyone else thinks. It's much easier this way, once you get the hang of it. I've let go of the guilt of all my fuck-ups, and I am moving on.

Therapy ended last week. The young adults group. And I think I'm alright with that. I think I'm doing better than I was when I began those sessions, and I think they have helped me. But it's still kind of weird to know that I will no longer be making that weekly walk through downtown and up to the hospital. I'm curious about what's going to happen to everyone else in that group. Although most of them are not people I would choose to spend time with outside of the hospital, I have still become attached to them in a small way. When you get used to seeing someone all the time, it's weird when it ends. I know things about their lives that nobody else knows, sometimes I understand them, sometimes I don't, and I just want things to work out for everyone. They've already been labelled as cutters and sluts and crazy, and so have I, and maybe that's how they identify themselves as well, but I really hope they don't let those labels haunt them forever. I hope they grow and change and recover.

I guess this is where I need to say that I don't think 'slut' and 'crazy' are insults. I kind of go between thinking sluttery is empowering and thinking it doesn't exist at all. If somebody knew nothing about my personality, my personal life, my past experiences, my childhood, my relationships, my interests, my politics, my beliefs, and only knew the amount of people I've fucked, the circumstances under which I fucked them, and just how and when and where I fucked them, they'd think I was a slut. Sometimes I think I'm a slut. But I am not ashamed. I feel no guilt. I have reasons for everything I've done. I think calling somebody a slut completely disregards the fact that they are a human being just like the rest of us. Instead of seeing someone who likes reading books and writing stories and eating sandwiches and riding their bike and whatever else they like to do, you see someone who fucks around. Nothing is wrong with being a girl who fucks around, but nobody can be identified with that habit alone.

The trouble with mental illness is it's too easy to identify yourself as someone with a particular condition or disorder, and let that identification become who you are. Language has a lot to do with it. People tend to say, 'She is bipolar', or, 'She is schizophrenic', or, 'She is depressed', instead of, 'She has bipolar', 'She has schizophrenia', 'She has depression'. It's not just the language, though. It's stigma in society, and even stigma in the mental health community; the way Hollywood portrays mental health issues; a million things, I'm sure. Being treated for bipolar disorder very much focuses on the fact that you are ill and you need to get better but you might not and you're gonna have to take these pills and there's not much else we can do to help you, good luck. Finding help is a joke. The doctor doesn't know what to do with you. The professionals think that if you're not OD'ing and cutting on a daily basis, you're okay. Waitlists for therapy and other treatments stretch years long. You have to find ways to help yourself. You have to talk to your family, even when they don't understand you or find certain things about you difficult to accept. You have to eat healthy foods and get out of the house and wash your hair even when you want to stay in bed all day and sleep, even when you'd rather forget the rest of the world, even when you want to disappear. You have to build what they call a "support system" or "support community." How do you do that when you're alone? How do you do that when it's easier to spin out of control and destroy yourself?

I want to be okay, I really do. I have this wonderful imaginary future where I spend my days writing zines and novels and riding my bike and writing letters for my friends and travelling and visiting everyone and feeling content then one day meeting some exceptional person and falling in love and working on creative projects together and everything is a.o.k. But as it is, they are just thoughts because I find it far too difficult to force myself (and I shouldn't have to *use* force anyway) to write everything I want to, and get out of the house, and I can't afford to visit all my friends, and sometimes, in my more cynical moods, I can't see myself falling in love again because I feel comfortable with so few people and I connect with so few people and I think I'm a weird person to be around. In my better moods, I know all of it is possible if I work towards it and I don't need to worry about that whole love thing because there's plenty of time and love only finds you when you're not looking for it.

♡ ♡ ♡

Sometimes I have these days that make me go, "Yes! This is why I am alive!" Like, the other day, I was biking by these kids who looked maybe between eleven and thirteen, and they said, "I love your pink hair!" so I waved ad thanked them. The next day, I walked by their house again, and they told me they loved my hair again. Then on my way back from running errands downtown, one of the girls ran across the street and gave me a hug. She didn't say anything at all, but I hugged her back and said, "You are so adorable." I continued walking, and when I heard more footsteps behind me, I turned around and saw two more girls running to catch up with me, so I stopped, and when they caught up, they hugged me, too. It was the cutest thing ever! We introduced ourselves, and one of the girls told me she's a twin, too, and we talked about how much we love meeting other twins. They said they had homework to do, and went back home. I continued down the street, beaming. No we wave and say hi every time we pass one another.

♡ ♡ ♡

Every morning, as the birds begin to chirp, whether or not I have gone to bed, I am still awake. The sounds of birds chirping first thing in the morning is one of my favourite things. Sometimes I wish I had recordings of them to listen to when I am blue, but that would surely make the authentic bird songs seem less special. In the nicer seasons, I like to take out my bike, my camera, and a book just as the sun is rising, take a ride around town, and lose myself in stories. This morning, I rode my bike through downtown, taking pictures of the empty main street and my hair flying in the wind. I meandered through residential streets, daydreaming. When I was tired of riding my bike, I headed down to the river and sat down at a picnic table to read my book. I am re-reading *The Secret Life of the Lonely Doll: The Search for Dare Wright* by Jean Nathan. Dare Wright wrote my favourite children's book, *The Lonely Doll*. A few others biked by, glancing at me as they passed. I smiled but they turned away. Hearing thunder in the sky, I returned home. Being outside, alone, so early in the morning, makes me feel a little hopeful. Before I left, I was laying in bed crying, wondering what to do with myself, beating myself up, tossing and turning. After the solitude of a 5 AM bike ride, I am still heavy in the eyes, but feeling inspired and refreshed.

People are constantly asking me about my tattoos. They want to know where they came from, if they are real, what they mean, why I got them, where and when I had them done, who the artists were, whether or not they hurt, and on and on. I will answer their questions nicely, but I very rarely go into details of what they mean I why I chose them because the background stories of my tattoos are extremely personal to me, would take *forever* to explain, and mean absolutely nothing to anyone else, so I think it's a waste of time and effort to tell anyone too much about them. Depending on who is asking me, I get annoyed. Strangers seem to think that because they are visible, it's their business. I don't take well to strangers asking me personal questions about my decisions. Strangers also seem to think it's okay to touch my tattoos. Huge invasion of privacy and personal space! It's like they think the tattoos are separate from my body, and they are only touching the ink, not my skin. It's completely creepy and uncomfortable when a stranger grabs my arm with one hand, and caresses my tattoo with the other. I don't understand why anyone would think that behaviour is okay.

It was when my mom, sister, and I first moved to this town that I got my first real bike. It was a pink bike with training wheels, and my twin sister got the same one, of course. We weren't allowed to go too far because we were very young, but I remembering biking in circles around the housing complex all day long, and down the hill to the park. We always took good care of our bikes because bored neighbourhood kids liked to throw bikes into the river for fun, and we didn't want to fall victim to them. We have a cute picture of the two of us on our front lawn perched atop our matching bikes wearing matching pink jackets and matching blue sweaters with red hearts that our nana knit for us, the same sweaters we wore for Grade One picture day. We eventually took off the training wheels and grew too big for those bikes, but we had to continue riding them around a little longer because we couldn't afford new ones yet. When we were able to get new bikes, I got a purple mountain bike, my favourite colour, with white handlebars, and it was wonderful. We were allowed to bike further now, around the little streets in our neighbourhood, but not downtown, and not across the river. Sometimes we would go downtown with our friends anyway, and we felt like such rebels. I was always afraid of getting caught. When we grew out of those, I switched to a green mountain bike, but I didn't use it for long before retiring it forever because it was around that time that my anxiety about being in public was creeping up on me, and I was entering my goth phase, so a bicycle was much too sporty for me. It was years before I would ride a bike again. I didn't want any modern contraption, so my nana gave me her vintage 1960's bicycle, a pretty little blue thing, and I named her Lulu after a Louise Brooks film. I didn't bike too far with her either because I was still nervous about being outside, nervous about being hit by a car, nervous about my bike being stolen, nervous about a lot of things. When I moved to Guelph, I took her with me, and I did go bike-riding a lot in the summertime, once I moved to an apartment building, my bike spent a lot of time locked in the closet. One day, she was lost in a misunderstanding, my ex throwing her into the dumpster while I was out of town. My nana had another similar bike, though, and she gave that one to me as well, and I named him Eddie after Eddie Vedder of Pearl Jam. I like naming inanimate objects. I wasn't as nervous as I used to be, and I took Eddie out pretty much everyday.

When I moved back to Lindsay in the fall, my mom gave me the perfect wicker basket for him, and my poppa made little leather straps with buckles to fasten it to the handlebars. The Spring, I was especially active with my bike, but it broke turning a corner. The chain guard came loose, and the pedal spun up and dented it. I walked it home and borrowed one of my sister's bikes for a couple days before finding the absolute perfect bicycle. When I woke up today, it was 36 degrees. My windows were open, and I brought out my little purple glow-in-the-dark fan for the first time of the year. As I walked under the sweltering sun, I spotted a gorgeous bike parked in a driveway in the distance, and hoped and hoped it was for sale. I went over to check out the bike, and sure enough, there was a For Sale sign hanging on the handlebars and an envelope instructing me to leave $20 in the mailbox for the bike. What a steal! So I wrote *THANK YOU!* on the envelope, put some cash inside, left it in the mailbox, and hopped on. It's a wonderful vintage one-speed bike, which I named Jolene after the Dolly Parton song, in a gorgeous shade of sky blue with rainbow stripes under the seat, a rearview mirror and bell, and it doesn't squeak obnoxiously like all my other bikes. I'm in love!

♡ ♡ ♡

When extra bedrooms are needed, a second floor could be added, shown by this plan. The small Bedroom on the first floor would be shortened to allow for the staircase and this room used as a study.

I've been in a fit of madness lately, confused about what day and time it is because I haven't been sleeping, riding my bike all over town for hours at a time, writing more in a couple of days than I have written all year, writing zines and journals and letters and notes and emails. Although I have been desperate for human contact, I have been isolated in my apartment, scared to death of reaching out to anyone because I worry that no one likes me anyway so I don't want to bother them. When I do hang out with other people, my anxiety gets the better of me, and I have to leave early. I think that everybody is watching me, and that certain people are putting thoughts into my head. I try to have a good time, but I am uncomfortable and can't enjoy myself, so I come home, and then I feel all alone again. So I write.

I am in the midst of a manic episode.

This is certainly not the worst episode I have ever experienced. In fact, it is probably the best. I have been productive and artistic, I have been creating things and sharing them. I have been drinking less, and I haven't done anything too destructive. I've been drinking lots of water and eating my fruits and raw vegetables.

This is the reason I stopped taking Lithium. Medicated, I am much too lethargic to get anything done. I stay in bed all day, I spend too much time on the internet, and when I do go out, I drink too much and make a fool of myself. Then I pass out, and do it all over again. Mood stabilizers take away these highs, and I need these highs to survive.

I will take pride in my madness.

In simple terms, bipolar is something like experiencing the same emotions as everyone else, but 1000 times more intensely. It has affected my entire life. Every little thing I do, every little thing I say, every little thing I think, is sprinkled with my own special brand of insanity. I have too many neuroses to count.

As time passes, I am learning about what it is that triggers episodes of mania ad episodes of depression. I am learning how to better spot these episodes, and understand the difference between reality, and what is going on in my mind.

Aside from bipolar, I also experience depression, suicidal ideation, self-injury, social phobia, anxiety, paranoia, delusions, OCD, and auditory hallucinations.

I am not an easy person to form a friendship with.

Things that have triggered manic episodes for me are break-ups (not just of serious relationships, but ay relationships and friendships at all), and delusions (I tend to imagine that if someone is being nice to me, it is part of an elaborate scheme to fuck me over, that I am being cheated on, that I am being compared to other girls in bed, that people are talking about me behind my back, that everyone is avoiding me, that I am too ugly to be seen with other people, that I am being used, that any nice thing somebody says to me is a lie to make me happy, that I will never be good enough at anything for anyone, etc...).

Things that have triggered depressive episodes for me are those listed above as well as disappointments (not finding what I am looking for, not being understood or agreed with, not being able to do the things I want to do or go the places I want to go), cancelled plans (this seems fairly petty, but when someone cancels their plans with me, I tend to take a total nosedive and refuse to get out of bed), and thinking about things that have upset me in the past.

I am typically depressed at all times, but there are episodes when it gets much darker. I have extremely brief moments of happiness. Riding my bike makes me happy, but I sink again when I return home, and drinking makes me happy, but I sink again the morning after. New books make me happy, but spending my money makes me feel guilty.

Basically, I am always unsatisfied with life. Even if I did not suffer disappointment, even if no one ever cancelled plans, even if relationships were easy, and even if I understood that my delusions were not real, my head would still be playing tricks on me, my brain chemicals would still be wonky, and I would still be all messed up.

I've done some pretty awful things while experiencing a manic episode. Up until recently, these episodes were completely undiagnosed. I did not know what was wrong with me, nor did anyone else. I thought that this behaviour was me, and that I was simply an awful person. I spent a lot of time thinking I was a toxic person, and everyone should keep away from me lest I fuck up their lives for good. I have destroyed relationships and burned bridges. There are people who will never speak to me again, and they will never know of my diagnosis, never know that that wasn't really me. They will forever think I am horrible. They will tell stories to their friends about their crazy ex, that crazy girl they knew, and they will warn people to keep away from me.

I am not proud of the things I have done, but I do not want to feel ashamed either. I am not bragging or showing off. I just want to share.

Here are some of the things I have done during the worst of my episodes and delusions (some good, some bad; some with explanations, some without):

- destroyed eight years worth of journals

Writing is pretty much the only thing that keeps me alive. I have been keeping journals from the age of five through to today, with a gap around the age of thirteen and fourteen when I was paranoid about having them read, so I threw them out and quit writing for a while, and a few months earlier this year when I was too depressed to write. I had an addiction to buying notebooks, and would fill one up within about four months or so, then have a boxful of blank notebooks to choose from for the next one. Over time, I began to realize that one reason I kept journals was that I thought if I did not write something down, I would either forget it, or it had not happened at all. I would write down every conversation I had, every place I went, everything I bought or was given, every thought and every idea, and analyze it all to death. I wrote several times a day, and would chastise myself for leaving out details of a particular encounter that I did not remember until after I had written about it. My journals, throughout the years, went from mundane to cute to explicit to embarrassing, and always neurotic and depressing. In the winter of 2006, my then-partner told me he had been reading my journal. This was while I was in the hospital, and I had to spend a few more days there with the knowledge that he was at home reading my most personal thoughts, until he finally gave it back to me. This was also the only time I had ever let my journal out of my sight; I didn't have it with me because I had OD'ed and been rushed to the ER a few days previous, and hadn't brought anything with me, not even my shoes. He would make references to my journal entries in conversations. I continued writing anyway. But this winter, extremely suicidal and unable to sleep, I decided I should destroy my journals. I had been thinking about it for a while, but I was afraid I would grow to regret it, that I would want to read my journals later, that I would need them for something. But at the same time, I wanted to forget everything and start all over again. If nothing happened until I wrote it down, then by destroying my journals, it would be like nothing had happened at all. I could leave everything behind, forget it. My past constantly plagued me, and I felt like this was my only chance for an escape. Without a place to set them on fire, I drowned them in my kitchen sink. The ink washed away, and everything was gone. I stayed awake for days making sure everything was destroyed. I knew it was a crazy thing to do. Later, discussing journaling, I had a particularly bad panic attach realizing what I had done, and I found myself in the hospital again. But I still don't regret it. Today, I will still write occasional entries in my journal, but they are not the same, and I destroy them afterward.

- destroyed and vandalized personal property
- bought unnecessary, expensive things
- spent money I did not have
- acquired $7,000 credit card debt (so far)
- physically attacked people
- nearly set fire to my apartment for revenge
- sent ridiculous emails at ridiculous hours
- gone for days without sleep

- acquired spur-of-the-moment tattoos
- had (sometimes unsafe) sex with strangers
- quit various jobs, sometimes quite dramatically
- moved (sometimes with little to no notice)
- attempted suicide on several occasions
- cut and burned myself
- drank way too much way too often
- involved myself in ridiculous and sometimes dangerous relationships
- traveled to places I was not familiar with to meet people I barely knew
- moved in with someone I barely knew
- ridden my bike for hours in the early morning with no sleep
- stayed up all night writing non-stop
- ended up in many fights and arguments brought on by misunderstandings an bad communication
- lost many, many opportunities
- alienated everyone

And that's just what I can remember.

Auditory hallucinations are voices, basically. They usually make themselves heard when I am lying in bed, before I have fallen asleep, but they can come to me at any time. The voices do not speak directly to me. It's more like listening in on snippets of somebody else's conversations, always strangers, although sometimes I hear their names. I usually only pick up a sentence or two at a time, sometimes not even that much. They rarely make much sense because they are not complete thoughts. And they are easy to forget. I could hear ten different people in one night, and not remember a single one of them the next day. These voices have been with me my entire life. I was put on medication briefly to make them go away, but that was pretty silly as they were never a problem. I think the voices were stronger when I was a kid. It always sounded like there was a news broadcast playing nearby. The news voices are mostly women, and the conversational voices are mostly men. Voices are not the same as thoughts; they sound real, and they cannot be controlled. A few nights ago, I listened to the voices and wrote down what they were saying.

"That's a cherry sour campaign."
"Are you? Because I am."
"Eggplant was a wisp."
"I am going to combine that tint."
"The point in relative fashion is not…"
"Something will come along with your spilled ink."
"I can't live past midnight."
"Quit suffering."

The manic episode I was experiencing when I began to write this zine is wearing off, I think. It must have lasted more than a week, but it's a difficult thing to keep track of. Towards the end, I was beginning to feel like a child again. Well, I always feel childish. I'm a nostalgic person, and I am obsessed with the past. People tell me I am naïve. I would rather be naïve than cynical.

Anyway, I went to the exotic pet store the other day, and got so lost in all the animals, wishing I could be a multi-coloured fish. The way they move, and all the oranges, yellows, and purples, are so mesmerizing. I think I wouldn't mind living in the water, not having to think about anything at all. But being trapped in a tank might not be very much fun. I don't suppose animals like fish feel the love the people who keep them have for them, but I suppose if they did, then being in a tank would feel awfully safe. I felt kind of delirious in there, and could have stayed for hours. It was nice, though. It made me feel some connection to the girl I used to be, who I know is still inside me somewhere.

There are times when it seems I will not allow myself to get better. Recovery terrifies me because I know there will be a relapse. There always is. I am never able to fully enjoy my happiness because I know it will end. I know is sounds pessimistic, but that's the way it always has been, and I can't imagine a time when that would stop. Because I know it can't last, happiness, to me, seems dangerous.

Six months ago, I was added to the waitlist to see a therapist at Community Counselling at the hospital. Last week, I went into the office to speak to the receptionist to get an idea of how much longer I should expect to wait. Approaching the desk, I was disheartened to see the sour face of the receptionist from the inpatient mental health ward, who had apparently been moved downstairs. She had always been rude to me for no reason at all, and I was so disappointed to see that I would have to deal with her all over again. Sure enough, she argued with me, and accused me of lying until I was frustrated to tears, and left without an answer to the only question I had asked. But the next day, she called with an appointment for me. When I was added to the waitlist, they neglected to inform me that it is only a 10-session program, so now I have been added to yet another waitlist, this time for a longer-term program. These waitlists will be the death of me.

I filled out a bunch of forms, covering technical things like my health card number and my address, then scales between 1 and 5 marking my self-esteem, anger, levels of happiness with relationships, etc. After that, I met my therapist, a middle-aged woman with a dreamy voice who calls me *darling* and *hon*, has long black hair and angel trinkets. The first thing she said to me was, "Do you think those shoes are going to take you home?" I was wearing my ruby shoes, and was so lost in my head that I missed the *Wizard of Oz* reference. Most of this session felt kind of like an interview, with her asking me simple questions and telling me about herself and her practice. She reassured me that she had plenty of experience treating people, especially women, who have been diagnosed with bipolar.

There were, unfortunately, things she said that I did not agree with. She told me that although all of us are unique, our experiences are not. I know she was getting at the idea that people with bipolar often have similar experiences and behaviours because of their condition, and I am not alone, but it came out sounding more like all of our experiences are the same, and she knows everything about them. It made me feel like there was no point in telling her about myself if she's heard it all before, and I also wanted to tell her that that couldn't possibly be true because even if we have the same or similar experiences, we interpret them differently, react to them differently, and internalize them differently, so although they may appear the same outwardly, they are not the same at all. She also told me I must have a lot of confidence to dress the way I do. But truthfully, my confidence levels are very low, and it takes less guts for me to dress different from everyone else than it does to dress the same and try to fit in. If I did that, I'd be afraid of being caught as a fraud. I didn't tell her that I usually dress in black, and had only recently started dressing like rainbows because black was too depressing.

The session didn't last long. She did not invite me into her office until fifteen minutes of the set time of the appointment ha passed, and then spent some time making phone calls that should have been made before I entered her office. But at the end of the session, she told me she thinks I will be an easy person to work with because I seem very open and honest, yet still mysterious. I told her I have no choice but to be honest because I feel like I have been lying my entire life, and I can't keep anything inside anymore. She said I seem like a creative, articulate girl whose family loves her. She also told me I am a lonely person who obviously lacks meaningful relationships, I abuse alcohol, and I allow others to use me. I told her I use them, too. And she said I have a lot issues regarding sex that I need to talk about. All of this was interesting to me because I like finding out what others think of me, how they interpret the things I say, the way I conduct myself.

I've been seeing therapists off and on for most of my life. The only therapist I recall ever helping me in any sort of tangible way was three years ago, when I was nineteen. We only had twelve sessions together, but in that time she helped me understand that the bad, paranoid thoughts I had/have about myself and others often have no evidence to prove they are true, she helped me become less of a recluse, and she prescribed me Effexor, which, although I am no longer fond of medication, made me a stable and happy person for a year and a half, and for that I will always be grateful.

I still want a therapist who makes me feel like she cares. I'm still afraid of not getting my views across when I am in therapy, never being able to make the therapist see just what life is like for me, and just the way my head works.

Well, this is not only something I feel with therapists, but with pretty much everyone. I am terribly inarticulate when speaking, and tend to think of the right thing to say after the moment has passed. I need to write to express myself. I have always been better at writing than speaking, probably because I have time to think of what I want to say, I can scribble out my words or backspace them if I need to, and my ramblings aren't interrupted or distracted by somebody else. Also, I'm never sure how I feel in the moment. I need time to think about what has happened and figure out how I feel about it. When I'm having troubles with someone, I write them a letter. I can recall times when I wrote letters to someone while they sat in the next room and waited for me, then I sat nervous and shaking while they read the letter.

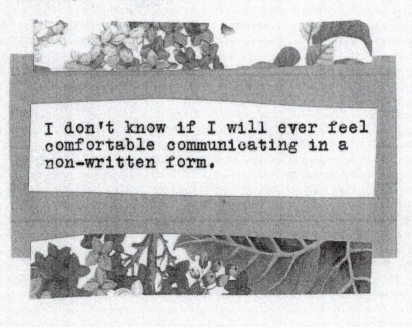

I don't know if I will ever feel comfortable communicating in a non-written form.

TELEGRAM MA'AM

Issue #15

October 2008

$2 Canada and U.S.

$3 International

or trade for your zine

Today is the first day of October, and now I feel like it is officially Fall. October is a beautiful month, and it is always at his time of year that I fall in love with the world. The leaves are changing colour and falling to the ground and rain paints their colours on the sidewalks. The air smells wonderful, I can wear boots and sweaters again, my birthday is coming up, and so is Halloween. I want to dance along the sidewalks and take lots of pictures.

I had a panic attack during Intro to Psych. I left class for a few minutes, got some air, and came back. Another day, I began to have yet another panic attack, and instead of just getting a few breaths of fresh air, I left class, hopped on my bike, and got the fuck out of that place. Sore throat and eyes a little blurred, I made my way back home, not entirely sure what I would do when I got there. I kept thinking, *I was born on the wrong fucking planet*. All these thoughts danced around my head, lists of everything that was wrong, lists of everything that will go wrong, lists of ways I have completely fucked up everything by leaving school. I've just added another few thousand dollars to my debt, for absolutely nothing. It was just another expensive lesson, I have learned over and over and over again that I cannot live a "normal" life, I cannot even interact with other people without wanting to kill them or kill myself. I thought about swallowing my sleeping pills, but I don't have enough to do any real damage, and I'm not interested in going back to the hospital. I thought about cutting myself, but I've got enough scars right now. I haven't made any decisions about what to do, except to write, because it'll keep me alive a little longer.

I applied for the Early Childhood Education program at the local community college in the summer after two nights in a row with no sleep, feeling strangely alive and hopeful. My therapist encouraged me to do this; she thought I was ready. Therapists in general always give me this false sense of hope that only lasts a few hours after each appointment until I crash again. So anyway, high on therapy and lack of sleep, I applied and was accepted, and spent the next few weeks filling out a ridiculous amount of forms. I didn't think I'd ever be going back to school, and just the idea of it was very weird for me. Just getting a package in the mail from the college was kind of overwhelming, but I was excited about the whole thing, and somehow got through the whole enrolment process and started attended classes in September.

The first week was all orientation stuff, and one thing that really stood out to me was one of the staff telling first-year students that a lot of us weren't going to make it 'til Christmas, let alone complete the entire program. I kind of figured I'd be one of the ones who didn't make it, but I pushed that thought away and pretended everything was okay.

Unfortunately, school was not the miracle I hoped it would be. I really thought there was a possibility of magically changing my personality and my entire life simply by going to community college and studying something I wasn't even sure my heart was in, in a town I have spent most of my life in and hated passionately, surrounded by people who I don't get, and who I know will never get me. I had pretty well deluded myself into thinking I would somehow make friends and have a social life and be a top student and stop hating myself.

I do this all the time. I think that one stupid little thing will change everything and I will suddenly be happy and none of this will matter anymore. But of course, what always happens is that I am reminded of my inability to cope in the real world, and I retreat back to my bed, the hospital, or somewhere else where I can be hidden from the world.

My panic attacks faded a little over the spring and summer, but they have become more frequent lately, and I don't know how to handle them. Over the last few months, I noticed that whenever I go out, I always have to leave early, in need of solitude, or if I am not able to come home, I go out on a walk, then return to wherever it is I am required to be, and hope to be able to go home soon. But when I go home, I don't know how I will make it through the night.

Ever since we were little girls, everyone told my sister and I that we were so smart, so artistic, so mature, blah blah blah. I know a lot of people get told these things at some point, but I feel like I was somehow expected to grow up to be some amazing person, a famous writer or something, and I kind of assumed that something wonderful would happen on its own, so I made no effort to actually do anything with my intelligence or my creativity. In the meantime, the world abused me and suffocated me, and now I have turned into an absolute mess who cannot go to the grocery store without getting angry at someone. I still want to be a writer, and I have a million ideas for stories that I *need* to write, but I just want them to be written already, I don't want to actually take the time and effort to write them down on my own. I wish I could hook something up from my head to the computer that would translate all my ideas and images to proper words, and I would have a book in front of me, and publishers would immediately have bidding wars over my great novels. I wish all the people who fucked me over in the past would go to their local bookstore and just happen to find a book with my name on it and be completely blown away that I grew up to be Someone, and they did not.

Anyway, studying Psychology did nothing but strengthen my bitterness at the world and the mental health system. Everything they tried to teach us was so simplified and untrue, and it just reminded of how horrible people who try to treat mental health issues are when they have not experienced those kinds of problems themselves, or when they are ignorant to the fact that not everybody's experiences are the same, medication is not the right form of treatment for everyone, and that people with mental health conditions are not Other People, Somewhere Else in the World, they are your students and your colleagues and your so-called friends, they are everywhere around you, and you are pissing them off.

I don't feel like I can fight back against everything. Or anything, really. I know it's completely counter-productive to keep to myself, but it's all I can handle right now. If I could surround myself with people who are like me, and understand my anger and my issues and my craziness, I'm almost positive I would be okay, but there aren't enough of these people in my world, and they are all far away. I rely on communication through the internet and snail mail to get me by. I don't care how conceited this sounds, but I feel like I have to dumb myself down to hang out with the people around here. This means I don't have any *real* conversations, thus have no *real* friends, and it only contributes to my hatred of... everything. I know I'm being negative but I can't help it. I am fed up with having no local friends and not being able to move to a place where I would be closer to the friends I do have.

The truth is, I figured this would happen. I wanted to brag to everybody about going back to school so they would be proud of me, but I also wanted to keep it to myself, not wanting anybody to know because I thought I would fuck it up. So that day I ran away from school, it just felt inevitable. I knew I wouldn't make it. I had told my therapist I was scared of going back to school because I would have to pretend to be a well-adjusted person, and I would have to follow a schedule and answer to other people. I told her I felt like I would be living a lie, and the last time I felt that way, I ended up in the emergency room having my stomach pumped as that was the only way I knew how to say something was wrong. But she told me this was the right time, that I could be someone else and not go insane, that all this mess would be in the past. And I believed her, naïve girl that I am, that I *could* be someone else, that I *could* be successful!. And of course I did have another breakdown, though thankfully did not take it far enough to be hospitalized. And I know this was my choice, but I still want to scream at her that she pushed me too hard.

Yeah, maybe I'm a little bitter about that, but I am at least confident that school is not the right place for me right now. I felt like such a hypocrite there since I don't truly believe in formal education. I was not meant to be there, I never was. So now I'm figuring out what to do next.

♡ ♡ ♡

I like reading about towns and cities. I like reading about coffeeshops and sidewalks and bedrooms and memories. I like writing about them too and I want to share my stories.

In Lindsay, Kent Street is downtown. If you're not on Kent Street, you're not really downtown. When I was kid, I wasn't allowed to go downtown. But sometimes my friends and I would ride our bikes there anyway. She lived downtown, so she knew her way around, and I would follow her, hoping nobody I knew drove by. Once we went to a little trinket store and I bought a glass frog that fit on my fingertip and a glass wiener dog smaller than my thumb. They sat together on my shelf for years, these little secrets collecting dust.

I liked to play on the Iron Bridge, though I was often too scared to walk across it all the way. It was this big bridge where the train used to run, high up above the river, big gaps between each wooden beam and no barriers, so I was afraid my feet would slip through, that I would fall down to the river and drown. My sister and I would sneak over to the bridge, or sometimes our babysitter would bring us there. We would collect rusty nails and such from the train tracks and bring them home, feeling like they were so special but not really knowing what to do with them, and our mom would tell us to bring them back outside, that we'll get hurt.

Eventually, they tore up the train tracks and rebuilt the bridge, made it a safe place to walk and bike and jog, but you can climb the barriers and dangle your feet over the edge and it's not so scary anymore.

There's another bridge further down the old-train-tracks-now-gravel-trail. I don't know if it has a name, I guess I just call it the Other Iron Bridge or The Bridge Past the Iron Bridge or something. It's smaller and less scary, just a small bridge with a little road underneath where kids used to throw rocks at the cars below. Maybe they still do.

You used to be able to follow those tracks out to the highway and beyond and there were so many trees and weeds and so much farmland and you'd really feel like you were out in the middle of nowhere and it was a dangerous feeling at night but so amazing when the sun was shining.

But if you go there now, it's all gone. It is a field of mud with houses in various stages of development, new roads, new street signs. One day, my memories will fade away with the train tracks, and I'll wonder if it ever happened at all.

The tracks were near these yellow brick townhouses, where my sister and mom and I used to live, the first place we lived when we came to this town. Nayoro Place, a name that has something to do with our sister town in Japan, but we always called it The Complex. There is one road that runs through it, in the shape of a messy circle, with a set of mailboxes at the entrance, a park on a hill at the back, and a little road off to the side leading down to the river. Low-income housing, where all the poor people all lumped together. I had a friend who lived next door, and we would knock secret messages on our walls from one bedroom to the other.

I bike by there sometimes, or I walk, and I get a really weird feeling from that place. Like a combination of nostalgia and fear and curiosity and rage.

I used to work in a drugstore, and I still get a weird feeling when I go in there as well. It's easy to shoplift because they don't have scanners or cameras and nobody is paying attention. I used to steal chocolate bars and pads and magazines, and now I steal headache pills and paper. I hated working there, so now I just feel bad when I go in, remembering how mean the customers were. After working there, I've been sure to be the nicest customer ever wherever I go. I've had customers yell at me till I was crying because there was no prize on their lottery tickets, old men hit me with rolled up newspaper to get my attention, and of course the classic complaining-to-me-about-the-price, like I have anything to do with it. I used to have small breakdowns during my shift, and I would have to serve people with tears streaming down my face, unable to speak. Once they almost fired me, but I cried so much in my boss's office that I guess he probably just felt bad for me, and I ended up staying there for a year and a couple months, which is the longest time I have worked at one place.

But yeah, I wonder if the other employees hate it as much as I did, I wonder if they consider walking out during every shift, if the customers make them cry… There's this one girl who started on the same day as me, and she's still there, and it must have been six years ago.

Near that drugstore was where I used to get my photocopies, after I'd overstayed my welcome at the 7-Eleven. It was so convenient, right in the middle of the town, the cheapest place, too, and the staff are always nice to me. It was never busy in there, probably because the supplies are overpriced. Then they moved farther up Kent Street, and it's such a long walk now, uphill, but I do it anyway because I like it there and the few times I went to the other office-supply-and-photocopy-shop, they were just mean, they've got a reputation for being rude, so I just don't go there anymore, and I tell everyone else to stay away as well. And now I wonder if the lovely ladies at the copy shop are going to read this as they copy it. I swear, I like you, I just don't like your seventeen dollar notepads that cost ten dollars across the street.

Another drugstore a couple blocks down, I used to hang out on the rooftop. You could go around the corner and down an alleyway behind the office of the daily newspaper where there was a fire escape and at the top of the fire escape was a garbage can that gave you a boost to get onto the rooftop. There was another level on the front of the building where you could climb up higher and look over downtown, dare yourself to jump, hide from the pedestrians below, or you could stay on the bigger roof and look into the windows of empty apartments and you could open them up, but you couldn't climb in because of the bars.

I used to dream those apartments would be mine someday, this cute little place to call my own, and I would decorate it with thrift store furniture and be free.

Sometimes the neighbours would see us and yell at us and call the cops. When the cops showed up, they wouldn't come onto the rooftop, they'd just stand at the top of the fire escape and tell us to come down, warn us that the roof was old and weak and could collapse and kill us at any moment. And we'd come down but we'd always go back up. I'd skip school to hang out on that rooftop, and I'd spend my nights there too.

It's weird, the different associations, different stories, that go along with the same places. Well, not weird, but neat. Like the Old Mill, down by the river near our historic Academy Theatre. These crumbling brick walls surrounded in grass and water, with bars on the windows and a view of the liftlocks, rocks to climb over that let you inside where you can climb on the beams and crawl through these tiny hidden waterfalls. People take their wedding photos there. If you go by at any time in the warmer seasons, especially in June, you are almost guaranteed to see a bride and a groom and a photographer and people in fancy dresses and rented suits. I guess it makes a nice background, I guess it looks quaint and serene and maybe even beautiful. But that place to me is where bored teenagers go to drink and to fuck.

We used to have this really neat coffeeshop that I went to a lot when I was much younger, even though I didn't drink coffee. It was all brick walls and hardwood floors and mismatched furniture. There was one wall at the back designated for everyone to write on, and I remember writing Smashing Pumpkins lyrics when I was thirteen and being sad when the wall was painted over.

There have been several coffeeshops there, but they never last long, they always go out of business. My sister used to work in one of them, but I hardly ever went in because I was too shy.

After living here for more than a year, this tiny apartment of mine is finally feeling like a home. The trick was not only to have an electric heater installed and keep the place clean and organized, but also to grow more comfortable with myself over time, and try to enjoy things as they are instead of always wanting to change or wanting to run away.

Of course, I still fantasize about running away. I fantasize about a lot of things. But I know that my problem is myself, and I can't run away from myself. Like they say, wherever you go, there you are.

I take things one day at a time, one half hour at a time. I read a few chapters of a book. I watch an episode or two of *Daria*. I make a bowl of soup. I read some zines. I organize my desk. I take a nap. I read another few chapters of a book. I knit. And I'm still alive, so I must be doing something right.

It seems my most effective form of escape is simply to stay where I am.

I can't stay inside all the time. I have appointments to attend. I have groceries to purchase. I have laundry to do. The best days are when I have no obligations at all. I like staying home. (And I like that I finally feel comfortable calling this place my home.)

There are some things I must ignore in order to feel at peace. Like, the fact that I am very deeply in debt. Or that I need new glasses. Or that my legal name change is going to cost money and there is going to be an unbelievable amount of paperwork to take care of. I will deal with these things in the new year, or when winter is over.

I must make plans for this winter to keep myself busy. I imagine I'll be doing pretty much the same things I have been doing these days, reading and writing, knitting... Maybe I will write an epic novel. I must also continue to eat lots of fruits and vegetables and not settle for junk food.

There is not a lot I want to do with my future, which must be one reason why I have so much trouble getting by. Because it feels like these days are not leading up to anything. There will be no change, there will be nothing special. Just me in my apartment, avoiding everyone, surrounded by unfinished projects.

I don't want to grow up.

There is no way I can escape, physically, anymore, because of money and fear and my health. I won't go anywhere because I know where I'll end up: right here. My life is fairly stable right now, more than it has been in years, and I cannot risk giving that up. Although I want to move back to Guelph, I know that I wouldn't be able to afford to live on my own there, not right now, and I need to live alone to save my sanity. I would end up with noisy roommates who think I'm weird, and I would be far away from my family. Although I would like to escape, I cannot deal with the reality of actually running away. If I had a friend to run away with, it would be different, but I don't, so it isn't.

Sometimes I have to tell myself to quit daydreaming. My mind makes up conversations that I am never going to have. It gets a little out of hand, and I get angry. Sometimes I move my mouth and make wild gestures when I am daydreaming. Sometimes I pace my apartment because I can't concentrate on anything, but I can't do nothing. I have to remind myself that my daydreams are not real. Sometimes I forget what conversations I've had and what conversations I have imagined. I can't not daydream, but I have to learn to keep my daydreams under control. (As much as I despise saying that.)

Last winter I hated my home so much. Now, when I look around, I try to make note of all the things I do like about it: the green walls, the vintage cupboard handles, the postcards and art on the walls, my little cacti and other plants, my green shelf, all my books, the fancy-looking radiator, the fact that the heat now works, the fact that I am alone. It could be so much worse than this.

Every now and then, I do find myself thinking about the future. The things I would like to accomplish, rather than the angry imaginary conversations I have not quite learned how to control yet. I think about what I would like to do if there comes a time when money and my mental health issues are not holding me back quite the way they are right now.

I would like to live in a little wartime house with a vegetable garden and a big oak tree. On the outside, it would have colourful shutters and overgrown plants and a cute mailbox and maybe a little fence with a gate because I will be cranky and will not want others to cut across my lawn or not clean up after their dogs. There would be a little shed to keep my bike, and a garage in case I ever decide to get my license. Maybe I would have some garden gnomes. Inside, each room would be painted a different colour. Green living room, yellow kitchen, purple bedroom, red bathroom, pink laundry room, orange craft room. My furniture would be soft and comfortable. I would have a real bed instead of a futon, and a loud loud loud stereo. I would have a hairless cat. Everything would be mine.

I don't know where this house would be. Ideally, I would like for it to be in Guelph, yet I keep imagining it in Lindsay. I just instinctively imagine the house I lived in when I was 12. I certainly do not want to live in that house again, nor do I wish to stay in this town.

When I dream about the things I want to do, I imagine them happening somewhere else, almost never in this town. It is unfortunate, but instead of trying to make this town a better place for myself, I find myself waiting to leave, waiting to find another place. I talk a lot about the things I'd like to do, but I never act upon them. I wait. It's like it's never the right place or the right time. Not big things. I'm not going to change the world. But I want to make public art, and I want to have dance parties, and I want to leave my zines in random places to be found by others, and I want to rollerskate, and I just want to run around and have fun and not worry, but I've never felt comfortable enough to do that here.

Writing about this reminded me of a little house in Guelph that I used to call my dream home. I took pictures of it. It is on a corner of two streets whose names are not coming to mind, but I could walk you there right now if I had the opportunity. I could also look at the pictures right now and tell you what the street signs say, but it kind of breaks my heart to look at those pictures. It is a little beige house with a green iron fence. I used to imagine buying it one day when I was older. I hadn't thought about it in a long time, and being reminded of it now also really breaks my heart.

There was never a time in my life when I did not feel homesick. I always have this dreadful feeling in the pit of my stomach. I remember being in Grade Two, feeling so sad when I was at school. I remember my mom picking me up at school and taking me home for macaroni and cheese or mushroom soup for lunch, and then being sad when I had to go back to school for the afternoon. I used to fake sick a lot so I could stay home. But I also felt homesick when I was at home. This feeling never left me. It followed me throughout school and throughout my teenage years. I still feel my heart aching and my stomach twisting, even today, and I can't figure out where I'm supposed to be. It aches the most when I think of Guelph.

The streets are too familiar here. There is no mystery. If I decide to go for a walk, I know that I am not going to see anything new. At least when I am in other cities, I can turn onto a street I have never seen before. The only streets that are new to me in Lindsay are the housing developments popping up all over town, destroying the old train tracks and trails and fields. I cannot get lost in this town. No matter where I go, there's some house an old friend used to live in, there's a Tim Hortons, there's some guy blasting music obnoxiously from his car, there's a school with a scent I still remember, there's the chance of bumping into people I don't want to see, there are the same cracks in the same sidewalks, the same anxiety that makes me turn around and go home, disappointed but not surprised with the lack of wonder, the lack of excitement, the lack of anything at all.

I feel so restless, unsure of what to do with my energy, like I would have to leave town to dispel this feeling, and I do not have that option.

I think perhaps I was meant to be alone and it is finally becoming easier to accept, and to accept happily. I just like to have days where I feel productive. If I spend time with people, I feel like there was something better I could have done with that time. I could have read a book, I could have written a zine. I could have had something to show for my day (or night). In the past, I preferred being alone, but I would go out if I was invited, thinking maybe this will be the night that changes my life. It never is, so I stay inside now, and I like it that way just fine.

It's funny how things change. Just as I was wrapping up this zine, feeling alright with my home and my mind and the winter ahead, everything got flipped upside down. I'm gonna be moving again. Shock horror. There are mice in my apartment, and I've been unable to get rid of them. There's no way I can sleep here. I've been staying with my mom, and we're moving into a new place together in February. I'm not very comfortable staying in her apartment, for various reasons, but I think it will be better once we've moved again. Then again, I always think it will be better once I've moved again...

I've now committed myself to spending at least another year in this town. Here I am, trying to get out as soon as possible, and I just dig myself in deeper. But I guess, really, staying here a while longer would be the more responsible thing to do. I just don't want to feel like I all my plans are slipping further away from me.

I'm not feeling so great about winter now that a lot of my ideas and projects have been set aside. It's like I'm wasting time, waiting for the snow to melt, just like every other winter. But at least I still have things to look forward to...

Telegram Ma'am

Issue #17

February 2009

$2 Canada and U.S.

$3 International

or trade for your zine

TELEGRAM #17
by Maranda

When I was a kid, I wanted an older brother. I used to imagine that Amber and I would share a room, and he'd be in the next room, with messy hair and loud music, and we wouldn't act like we knew each other in public because he'd probably think he was too cool for us, being older and a guy and all, but at home, we'd be friends. I thought it would be cool to have someone around who was older than us, who could teach us and warn us and give us a heads up on what the future was gonna be like, and I also thought that having an older brother would be a good way of finding out what's going on inside a guy's head, what his life is like, beyond the way he'd act out his life to the kids at school. I wished so hard, but I knew it could never happen.

One night in November, my mom and my sister showed up at my place to talk to me. I knew something was up because I'd never had them both over at the same time before. When my mom said she had something to tell me, I made all these ridiculous guesses at what sort of family secrets she was hiding, even jokingly suggesting that I did have an older brother. Instead, she told me that Amber and I have an older half-sister. Apparently our dad had a daughter with another woman a few years before he met my mom.

I wasn't surprised when she told me. It kind of felt like I had known it all along. It didn't feel like I was being told some big family secret, some dramatic thing, it didn't feel like I had just found out there was some other part of me out there somewhere, a part of me who probably doesn't even know that I exist. It was just like, "Oh, by the way…" and I laughed about it.

In fact, it wasn't even really kept a secret on purpose, at least not for this long. My mom had actually forgotten about it until an aunt reminded her, asking if she had ever told us, and of course she hadn't, she hadn't even thought about it.

My mom and my sister didn't stay for long, maybe ten minutes, standing around in my kitchen, making stupid jokes about the whole thing. When they left, I wrote a little bit about it in my journal, and I got back to writing the letter I was working on before they showed up.

My mind was racing, though. Had my half-sister been in contact with my dad? Did she know anything about him? Did she know anything about us? What was she like? Where did she live? Would she want to hear to from us? Should we try to find her?

I've never been close with my dad. I barely feel like he is a part of our family. Even before he and my mom split up back when I was four, even when he was still living with us, I didn't really know who he was. He was just this mysterious guy who sometimes was around, sometimes wasn't. But I have small memories that remind me that there was a point in my life when I loved him.

He drove a cement truck, and he would leave really early in the morning, before the sun had risen. I would wake up really early, too, and go into his bedroom to see if he was awake yet. I didn't know it was out of the ordinary for him to have a separate room from my mom. I would play with him and follow him around the house, and I would wave to him as he drove away in his cement truck.

His mom, my grandmother, died when we were very young. I didn't know her very well, or see her very much. I had a dream about her when I was two or three and I thought it was real throughout my childhood because it was the only memory I had of her. In my dream, she was in a wheelchair on our front lawn, injecting a giant syringe into her arm, and I wanted to play with the needle, too.

As the four of us – my mom, sister, dad, and I – drove to her funeral, Amber and I got really excited that Dad was in the car with us, because that never, *ever* happened. It was so unusual for all four of us to be together. My mom still jokes about it now, how excited we were.

For all the horrible things he's done, we mostly just joke about it now. Once, before they had separated, my dad, an alcoholic, promised my mom he would quit drinking. He went on for weeks saying he hadn't had a drink, but she went out to the shed one day and found that it was stacked to the ceiling with empties, the shed was full. So while he was at work, she returned all the empties, kept the money for herself, and nobody ever spoke of it.

We make jokes, but I can't imagine what it must have been like living with him.

We lived in a haunted house. It was this beautiful yellow brick house, and Amber and I would see ghosts wandering the hallways at night. We would say to our mom, "Mom, who's that man?" and she would say, "What man?" and we'd say, "The man in the hallway."

Mom saw the ghosts, too. She could see smoky figures in the hallway just like we did, and she knew it wasn't just her imagination, or just some tricks her eyes were playing on her. There were a few haunted houses in that town, and we just happened to end up living in one of them.

She told me she could feel the presence that was haunting our home leave the day we moved out. She was sitting on the couch, packed boxes all around her, waiting for the movers to show up, when suddenly there was the most vile, sickening scent. It was overwhelmingly strong, the scent of death, and then it just swept out of the house and disappeared.

I had the same nightmares as my sister, about flying down the staircase, and about my mom's evil twin. Even though it scared me, I loved that floating feeling. Those nightmares followed me for nearly a decade, a different staircase every time we moved, always flying, not knowing how to land.

In some of my nightmares about my mom, her body was made of blue velvet, and she had little round eyes made of the silver candies my nana used for the eyes of her rocking horse Christmas cookies. But in most of my nightmares, she looked like herself. My sister and I would be hanging out in the living room watching TV with our mom, and then we would hear a key in the lock on our front door, and it would be our mom, again. We couldn't tell which mom was real, the one in the living room or the one at the door. We didn't know which one to run away from. Sometimes I would race up the stairs and down the hall into her bedroom. I would hide under her bed, knowing she would find me, and when she found me, I didn't know if she was going to tickle me or hurt me. I had these nightmares from as early an age I can remember, until around the age of eighteen. We always called the evil one Scary Mom, like that was her name.

As we were growing up, we would stay at our dad's place on alternate weekends. He didn't know what to do with us, so we mostly just ended up going to the bar with him, drinking dozens of Shirley Temples until we thought our bladders were going to burst. I didn't know that was out of the ordinary either, that kids weren't supposed to hang out in bars. We were supposed to keep it a secret, but my mom knew, and she would ask us if he knew the bartenders names, if he acted like he was friends with them, and he did, which meant he was a regular. He wasn't allowed to be drinking when he was with us, it was in the separation agreement, but of course he did anyway. Amber and I used to stock his fridge with bottles of beer. There was one shelf for the beer, one shelf for the Diet Pepsi his girlfriend drank, and one shelf for condiments. We ate blueberry waffles and drank a lot of chocolate milk.

Amber and I always brought books with us when we went to his place, but whenever we tried to hang out in our room and read or listen to music, Dad would complain that we should be outside. So we'd go outside and end up complaining that we were bored, and then Dad would complain that we were complaining. Sometimes he would rent video game systems for us to keep us busy.

When we got back home on Sunday evening, our mom would make us take baths right away, to get the smoke smell off of us. She'd take our clothes and do a load of laundry, and we'd scrub ourselves with soap and shampoo. I'd always be sad when I came home, even if I didn't have fun at Dad's house.

A lot of the time, he just wouldn't show up. Amber and I would have our bags packed, and the time would tick by, us standing there in the living room expecting a knock at the door any minute now, checking out the windows every time we heard a vehicle. We might get a call saying he wasn't going to show up, or we might not. I don't understand how someone could disappoint two little girls like that.

We stopped visiting him when we were twelve, and we don't talk to him very much now. He sends us cards for our birthday and for Christmas if he remembers, and sometimes he includes a cheque, a scratch ticket, or a gift certificate. He used to call us on Christmas morning, always when he knew we were at our grandparents' so he could appear to be making an effort without actually having to talk to us. I send him letters sometimes, and he always tells me to keep in touch, but never writes back.

I've pretty much stopped caring about my half-sister. I don't want to try to find her. I'm curious about who she is, sure, but it doesn't matter anymore. I can't imagine she would want to hear from us.

My sister moved to another city, and I am getting used to not having her around. I miss her. Since she left, I've been dreaming about her most nights. My dreams were sad and a little scary, but they've been getting better. I kept dreaming that things were going wrong and she had to come back. I dreamed she came back after only a week in the city, I dreamed she decided to go to university, I dreamed she was working at 7-Eleven and everyone was worried about her, I dreamt she went missing... I even dreamt her boyfriend had a twin brother and I liked him but I couldn't tell them apart.

February 15th, 2009
Hello Amber!

Life here in Lindsay is nothing terribly spectacular, but I've been doing alright, and I'm in one of those moods where I feel like everything will probably be okay. I haven't been feeling as lonely as I thought I was gonna feel with you being gone. I think it's pretty neat that we're able to live such different lives and still have this weird connection, you know?

I'm glad that things are going well for you in Montreal. I haven't really felt like you're far away or anything, it's pretty weird. They asked me at the post office the other day if I miss you, and I said, "Yeah, but even though I've lost a local friend, I've gained an awesome penpal."

Amber and I were always planning a small town revolution, and even though she's no longer in this town, I don't feel like the dream is dead. I was disappointed at first when she told me she was leaving, especially so soon, but I am also determined to start liking this town a little more, and to make whatever time I have here fucking magnificent (or at least something more than just bearable). Because what else can I do?

Since Amber left, I've been dreaming up new ideas and projects and adventures. I'll bike by myself and I'll write letters and stories and zines and distribute fliers and learn my rollerskates. And I'll visit her in Montreal.

We've still been talking a lot. We send each other snail mail and emails all the time, recipes and inside jokes and serious discussions and daily happenings.

It's like were both starting new lives, we've both opportunities for new adventures. We both moved around the same time, and moving to another place, no matter how often I do it, always feels like some sort of fresh start... So Amber will be like my long-distance partner in crime.

TELEGRAM MA'AM

issue #18

October 2009

INTRO INTRO INTRO

Your Pretty Face Is Going Straight To Hell is one of my favourite zines, so I'm really excited to be making this split with Tukru., and so pleased to have it ready just in time for Hallo-ween.

When I started writing this zine back in the spring, I had in-tended to write about long-distance friendship, pen pals, meeting people via the internet and zines and so on, but it actually turned out to be more like a love letter to my bike, with notes on adventures with local

friends, anxiety, and small town life.
  Around the time I began this zine,
I noticed a lot of people asking me
how I have the guts to do such silly
things, like ride my ridiculous bike
around Lindsay, when I am so shy and
have depression and anxiety, so I guess
that's why I ended up writing so much
about it. Things can be difficult in a
small town because you can never just
be invisible and anonymous. It seems
like everybody knows who you are. You
can't get away with anything, there
are no secrets. Like the other day, my
mom said to me, "I heard you bought a
cookie jar this afternoon." A workmate
of hers who I had never met had spotted
me at Salvation Army and reported the
sighting to my mom, complete with a
description of the cookie jar.
  Anyway, I've spent a lot of time
riding my bike, learning the basics of
bike repair, and perhaps thinking a
little too much about what it means to
be a weird girl in a small town, and
and applying what my bike has taught
me to all other aspects of my life.

I feel like I've been pedalling my
way to finally not giving a fuck
about what anyone else thinks. If I'm
having fun and not hurting anyone,
what's the problem?
xxxxxxxxxxxxxxxxxxxxxxxxxxxxxxxxxxxx
X TELEGRAM MA'AM #18 WAS MADE WITH
THE HELP OF: peppermint tea, Joan Jett
on full blast, night-time mini-skirt
bike rides, and Suzy Lee, my Underwood
portable typewriter.
SPECIAL THANKS TO: Vincent for causing
a ruckus with me, Amber for being the
best sister ever, Dave for being unspeakably awesome, aMy and Clara Bee
for giving me a place to stay when
I'm in the city, Erin for sending me
such colourful letters, and Tukru,
of course, for making this zine with
me. I LOVE YOU.

JOLENE AND ANXIETY

I try to go outside every single day. I don't always make it, but I try. There are times when it helps to have a destination in mind, and other times when I just bike along random streets till I feel like I have biked on every street in town, and then I come home. Other times, I just hang out in my backyard. Fresh air is essential.

When Spring finally came along, I was nervous about riding my bike again, even though I practically lived on it last year. I get like that. If I haven't done something in a long time, I get nervous about it. So I started small. I picked up my bike, a vintage Firestone Monterey who I named Jolene when I found her last year (the tale of Jolene and my past bicycles and also tales of other objects I have given human names can be found in my other zines), from my nana and poppa's house, where I had been storing her, and I biked home. It was probably only a five-minute bike ride. It was exhilarating, but I wasn't feeling up to doing much biking beyond that, so I tucked her away in the backyard.

I started to take my bike out at night. I'd bike along the quiet, bumpy streets under the stars and get used to the feel of her handlebars, wrapped in orange, turquoise, and rainbow handmade streamers, remember the parts of her that make little squeaks, reacquainting myself with the pedal brakes and rearview mirror and little bell.

It was good to do this alone. I was too anxious to get to know Jolene again on sunny streets filled with other people. The downtown roads are too dangerous to bike on because drivers aren't looking out for cyclists, yet pedestrians get pissed off when you use the sidewalk. It's a bit of a conundrum.

So I would ride my bike at night, but I would stay in on Thursdays, Fridays, and Saturdays to avoid the drunks littering the streets, fighting and catcalling and cheering. They make me feel uncomfortable anyway (like last Winter when I was walking through downtown at night and a few drunk teenagers/20-somethings argued amongst themselves over whether or not I was a boy or a girl, then told me to go home and slit my wrists), but especially so when I'm with Jolene. My bike is kind of a target for sad people who get off on making fun of strangers because my goal is to make my bike look like a circus tent or parade float. She's a sky blue bike with a lot of accessories like the set of goldenrod and violet streamers I knit for her after the other ones were ruined, a bell that sounds like a doorbell, plus tons of colourful ribbons on her wicker basket, and she is old and kind of fancy.

After a little while, I was confident enough to take Jolene out during the day. I don't want to let my anxiety and the townspeople's fear of people who aren't like them to get the best of me, and now I tell myself that me and my bike belong here just as much as they do. I still stuck to the smaller streets when I started taking Jolene out during the day, but eventually I had the guts to take on the downtown streets, too, and now, once again, it is second nature. I get nervous, but I do it anyway.

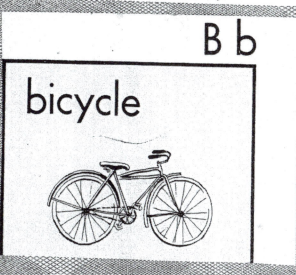

bicycle

B b

There is also a trail I follow that leads to the conservation area, with all sorts of little trails branching off from it, and if you keep following the main trail, it will take you to nearby towns and maybe eventually across the province. Last year I followed it for an hour and ended up in Fenelon Falls, which is about a fifteen-minute drive away, I think. Sometimes I go there for frozen yogurt at the health food store, or for thrifting adventures at what is the best Salvation Army in the area. I haven't biked that far this year, though, not yet. But I've been biking to the conservation area. Part of the trail is paved, and it attracts other cyclists and joggers. I like going there in mornings and afternoons, but not in the evening because that's when everybody else is out after work and after dinner, and it's just not the same. So I go when I think I'll be the most alone.

The other day, I biked to the conservation area and I hung out by the beach for maybe an hour or so writing in a notebook about my memories of that beach, which isn't much of a beach anymore, just a bit of sand and a swamp on the edge of the lake.

I went to summer camp here when I was a kid. I was shy and didn't get along with the other kids. I wore an oversized t-shirt over my bathing suit and refused to go in the water. I clung to my mom's legs and cried some mornings when she tried to drop me off, making her late for work on countless occasions. And I made a lot of bracelets. This went on every summer for a few years.

I know that hundreds and thousands of people have been there, but I still sometimes like to pretend that it is a secret place only I know about. And I feel a little annoyed when other people show up, usually with dogs, like they are intruding in my space, which they aren't. This place is for everyone, and just like I belong here as much as they do, they belong here as much as I do.

Eventually I start to feel restless or hungry (I almost always forget to bring snacks), and I head home.

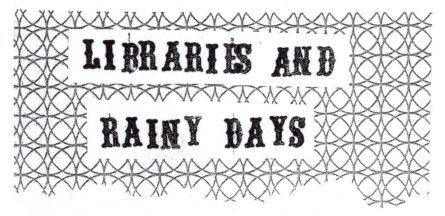

LIBRARIES AND RAINY DAYS

Sometimes I take my bike to the library. I am always telling myself that I need to spend more time there. I used to go to the library almost everyday when I was a teenager, and then I just sort of ignored it for a long time. I don't go looking for anything specific, I just wander the aisles and see what tickles my fancy. At bookstores, I spend most of my time in fiction, but at libraries I spend most of my time in non-fiction. Sometimes I hide little fliers with small town manifestos and riot grrrl manifestos between the books or tucked away in their pages. Sometimes I sit down and write in my journal, or I start one of the books I've picked up off the shelf, but once again, I start to feel restless, and I go home.

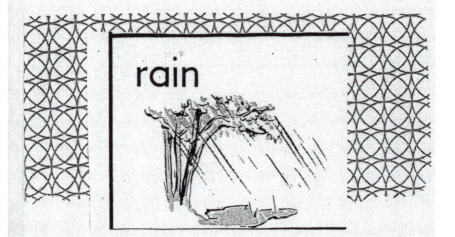

rain

A little while ago, when I left the library, it was pouring rain. It was a grey day, but I thought the rain was over with, so I was wearing shorts and a t-shirt. My bike was soaked, and I was soaked before I even had a chance to unlock it. I thought that if I sat on my bike seat, it was gonna look like I peed my pants, but the rest of my pants were wet anyway, so I threw caution to the wind and took that risk. The traffic was a little chaotic because the rain was ridiculous and some of the streets were blocked off by construction. I biked carefully but with a giant smile and went through all the puddles, covering my legs in mud. The raindrops clung to my glasses making it difficult to see properly. I laughed out loud by myself. I just thought it was so silly that everybody panics when it rains, meanwhile I was having so much fun. My bike basket was filled with books and I had my purse on top of them to keep them as dry as I could. As I got closer to my house, the raindrops hitting my arms started to feel more like little knives, it was so cold. When I got inside, I stripped naked in the kitchen and made myself a cup of tea.

LONELINESS

There are times when I feel so happy and free on my bike but then when I get home, it just turns to sadness, that I have all this energy and no one to share it with. I take off my shoes, drink a glass of water, and think, *Now what?*

As much fun as I have on my own, riding my bike can also be really lonely sometimes. It depends on my mood. Sometimes it depends on the day. I have little reason to pay attention to exactly what day it is; I don't work regularly, I mostly keep to myself. I know when it's a weekend because the post office is closed, but that's about it. If I'm out on my bike, I know if it's a Friday or Saturday night, like I mentioned before, and I feel anxious. Sometimes I just stay in so I won't have to see anyone (or so no one will see me). My anxiety makes me think thoughts that are absurd. It makes me wish I were invisible, which might be strange for someone so consumed with loneliness, but I guess that's just one of my many contradictions.

If you gave me a map of this town and asked me to put a red mark on every place here that makes my heart hurt at least a little bit, Lindsay would be swimming in a sea of blood. That's what keeps me inside. If I had a way to bike around those places, keep them out of my view, I would. But as it is, I'm surrounded. And I don't know how to handle this feeling, beyond writing about it.

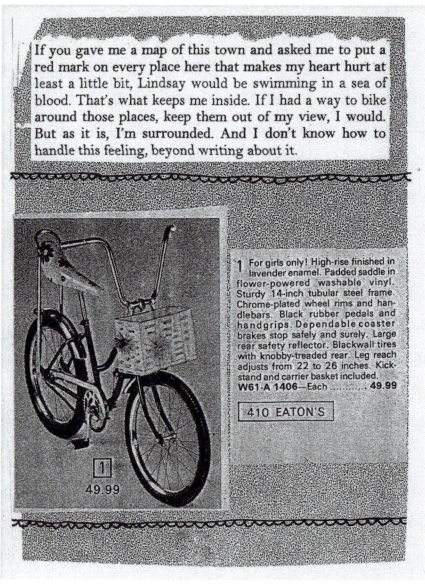

1 For girls only! High-rise finished in lavender enamel. Padded saddle in flower-powered washable vinyl. Sturdy 14-inch tubular steel frame. Chrome-plated wheel rims and handlebars. Black rubber pedals and handgrips. Dependable coaster brakes stop safely and surely. Large rear safety reflector. Blackwall tires with knobby-treaded rear. Leg reach adjusts from 22 to 26 inches. Kickstand and carrier basket included.
W61-A 1406—Each 49.99

410 EATON'S

1
49.99

YOU DON'T BELONG HERE

I've been told so many times that I don't belong in this town. The general consensus seems to be that I am too weird, too smart, too different. (Meanwhile, *millions* of people are told they are weird and smart and different, so what does that even mean?)

It seems it is mostly people who are older than me say it as a compliment, and people who are younger than me say it as an insult. For those who mean it as a compliment, maybe they think they're just being silly or that I will be flattered, but maybe they haven't actually thought about what it means to tell somebody that they don't belong somewhere.

Lindsay has been my home for most of my life. I moved here when I was five, and I have been here ever since, except for the year and a bit that I lived in Guelph. All small towns have misfits who desperately want to leave for whatever reason, and although I want to leave as well, I don't think it's fair to assume that I don't belong here or that I would be happier in a city. I've been told so many times by so many people that I should be living in Toronto or Montreal. But I know that I would never be able to live in a city that big. It's overwhelming and expensive. I like visiting my friends in cities, and I've been going to Toronto pretty frequently lately, but I know that it's not somewhere I want to live. And I resent being told that I somehow belong there, and not here.

city

On the other hand, I'm sure that those who mean it as an insult would be quite happy to see me leave, although I can't understand why. Every time I get made fun of, I feel like the entire world is hopeless. I think of their parents being bullies, and their future children being bullies, and it just never ends. I'm really tired of feeling like I need to hide or run away. Maybe I don't belong here, but I would rather find that out for myself than have somebody else tell me so.

BIKE ACCIDENT

Jolene's front tire blew. It was my fault. I rode through a construction site downtown, where the road around the new sidewalk had not yet been paved, so the corner of the sidewalk was elevated from the road, a bump that I knew was too big for Jolene, but I didn't want to get off my bike, I just wanted to get out of there. I have little patience. Less than a block later, all the air had been let out of my tire. So I got off my bike and walked her home.

Although a broken bicycle is always disappointing, I was a little bit delighted at learning how to fix it myself. That's something I've been meaning to do for years: learn how to fix bikes. It only makes sense that if you're gonna ride a bike, you better know how to fix it. But it's on that long list of things I say I want to do and almost never get around to doing.

But here was my chance. I looked up how to patch a tire, and I went out to purchase my very first bike repair kit. Sadly, when I got home, I found that I couldn't even unscrew the bolt to take off the wheel, therefore I could not patch my flat tire. I was frustrated almost to tears. It really bothers me to not be able to take care of things on my own. I don't like having to rely on others. But I tried and tried and tried to unscrew that bolt, and it wouldn't budge the littlest bit, so I knew that I would have to bring it into a shop.

Thankfully, there's a bike shop downtown that offers repair service, so I brought Jolene in, and hung out at the library while the guy fixed my bike. When I went back an hour later, she was all ready to go, although I was told I ought to change the tires sometime soon because they're pretty worn out. After only a couple of days being without my bike, those pedals sure felt wonderful under my feet.

I didn't get to fix my bike on my own this time, but next time, I will be prepared. It's kind of a dream of mine to have a home with a little shed where I can store and repair bikes, and lend them out to those who need them.

road

SHARPIE BICYCLE NIGHT

A little while ago, a friend and I declared it Sharpie-Bicycle Night and attacked downtown Lindsay with, yes, our Sharpies and our bicycles. I had been riding my bike barefoot that day, much to the chagrin of my mom, who warned me that bare feet are dangerous. I laughed at her, then went out to the driveway where I tripped on the curb, sprained my toe in some weird way and ripped it open. It hurt so much I could barely walk on my left foot. So I cleaned up the blood, put on a Hello Kitty band-aid, took care in putting on my shoes, and went out. It was a painful bike ride. Any time I got off my bike, I had to limp awkwardly. Once the sun set, we took out our Sharpies. He wrote silly things and I wrote feminist slogans. I was happy to finally have someone to commit tiny acts of revolt with. And I smile whenever I pass the brick walls, lampposts, and signs bearing our handiwork. I don't mind feeling childish about it. I like graffiti.

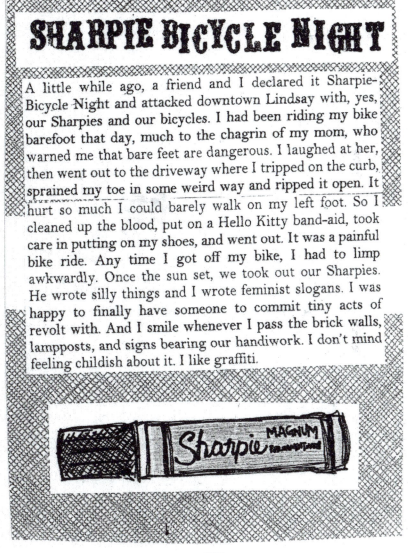

SMALL TOWN NEGATIVE ENERGY

There are a lot of bad vibes in this town and I try not to let it get me down. Everybody seems so full of negative energy, it's like a poison.

Another friend and I let ourselves into one of the local high schools recently and wandered around the hallways. It gave me the creeps. All I could think about was my own high school hell ten years ago and how nothing had changed. Just being near lockers and school colours and echoing stairwells filled me with rage. And the high school kids were still making fun of me for looking weird. It's like, really, that's still amusing to you? Making fun of people? Why? Wouldn't it be easier to just leave me alone? They probably thought I was a fellow student. I look really young. I'm 23, but a lot people still ask me what grade I'm in when we meet.

And I still get yelled at from car windows when people drive by. I don't get it. I want to sit down with everyone in this town and ask them:

Does it make you feel good to put others down? Are you afraid of people who are not like you? Do you think you're so wonderful we should all be like you? What do you hope to accomplish by making fun of strangers on the street? What makes you think I don't belong here just as much as you do? Do you really think you're that clever? Are there not more positive things you could do with your energy? What made you choose me as your target? Will you ever grow out of this behaviour or will you pass it on to your kids? Are you capable of empathy? Remorse? Love? What are you afraid of?

FAMILIARITY

One thing I like about Lindsay is the comfort of knowing where everything is.

Sure, adventures and new places are great, but there is something to be said for familiarity. Everything is within walking distance, and I always know exactly where something is, or exactly where to find something. That can sometimes be reassuring.

Having a few places I enjoy being in Lindsay makes me feel better, even though I'll also have days where all I can think about is getting the fuck out of here. But there is some good in this town, I'll admit it.

THE LILAC FESTIVAL

Our town has a public lilac garden that has been here for maybe ten years, I think. I had never gone until this year. It was one of those things I always meant to do, but never got around to it, or never had anyone to go with.

Lilacs are my favourite flowers. When I was a kid, I would pick bunches of them for my mom. Lilacs were also my nana and poppa's wedding flower. When the lilacs bloom, I know that Spring is truly here, and although it makes me sad that they only bloom for a few weeks, I think that's probably why I appreciate them so much, and part of what makes them so special.

So I finally went to the Lilac Festival this year, with a friend. I hadn't realized there were so many varieties of lilacs. There must have been at least twenty different kinds, probably more, in all sorts of shades of purple, pink, and white. We went on a rainy day, which turned out to be a rainy week. I think it rained everyday of the Lilac Festival. That's okay with me because I like the rain, but I'm sure many people probably didn't bother going because of the weather, and it makes me sad for the organizers and also for everyone who missed out.

Anyway, at the time that we arrived, we were the only visitors. We wandered from bush to bush. Some of them had plaques indicating who they were planted in memory of, or donated by. I joked about having one planted in tribute to my awesomeness. And I took a lot of pictures because I was so desperate to keep them with me. We stayed by ourselves for the most part, but now and then one of the festival volunteers would come around and strike up a little conversation. I would have preferred to be left alone, but I also thought it was very sweet how enthusiastic they were about the plants, telling me about their favourite breeds.

There was also a small table under a tent where they were selling lilac-themed mugs, and bread and cuticle cream that had been made with lilacs, and of course, a few baby lilac bushes to plant at your own home.

After a little while, a bus full of tourists showed up, and we decided that was as good a reason as any to make our way out of there.

ZINE GATHERINGS

Zine events give me a good reason to get out of this town for a little while, hang out with my zinester friends and pen pals, and meet other people in the zine community.

Unfortunately, I also get pretty nervous at zine events, not only because of my anxiety, but simply because of the nature of the thing. Zines are something I work on by myself, and I hardly talk to anyone who reads my zine in person because they are scattered all over the world. It's like brain-to-paper communication, rather than face-to-face. Walking from table to table, checking out everybody else's zines and other projects is really uncomfortable for me. My anxiety goes on overdrive, and I start feeling like they will be offended if I don't buy something from their table, and sometimes it's just not something I'm interested in, or I don't have enough money, or whatever, and I also worry that they might feel just as uncomfortable as I do, and I don't know whether or not I should acknowledge the silliness of it all, or pretend that everything is okay.

And then of course I feel awkward when I'm behind my own table, too. I never know if I should be making eye contact and greeting everyone or if I should let them be to look at my zines, and I hate being asked questions like, *What's a zine?* or *What's your zine about?* I also don't like asking people for money for my zines, but obviously I can't afford to just give them away.

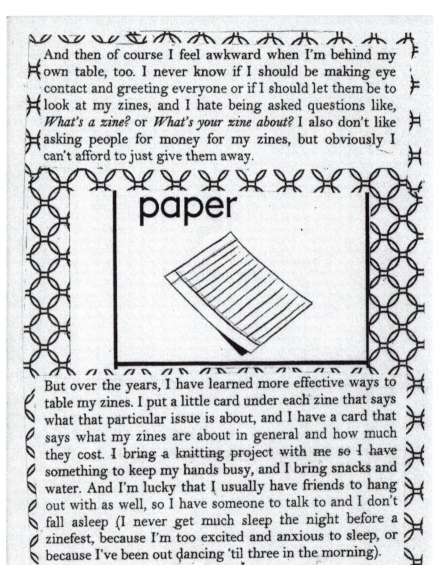

paper

But over the years, I have learned more effective ways to table my zines. I put a little card under each zine that says what that particular issue is about, and I have a card that says what my zines are about in general and how much they cost. I bring a knitting project with me so I have something to keep my hands busy, and I bring snacks and water. And I'm lucky that I usually have friends to hang out with as well, so I have someone to talk to and I don't fall asleep (I never get much sleep the night before a zinefest, because I'm too excited and anxious to sleep, or because I've been out dancing 'til three in the morning).

SUMMER PICNICS

Summer hardly feels like summer this year. It hasn't been as hot as usual. I keep getting excited about Spring, then realizing that in fact it is gone, and we are already halfway through the summer. I'm already a little afraid of fallen leaves gathering frost, and that's months away. What I need to do is take advantage of the season. Ride my bike everyday. Wear lots of sunscreen. Go on picnics and other adventures.

I did go on a picnic a little while ago, with a friend of mine. We brought blankets, egg salad sandwiches, pickles, fruits, chips, and pomegranate pop. We went off a trail at the edge of town and wandered until we found a nice little spot on the lake where we were under the shade of a hundred trees, listening to the toads croak on the water. We played Dictionary Pictionary while eating, and then we went to explore the area and climb trees that grew out over the water.

PANIC ATTACKS

I've been having some pretty intense panic attacks lately, and have been trying to figure out exactly what it is that's been triggering them, and how to get through them. Panic attacks are not something I can avoid, so I'm learning how to accept them and deal with them and know that each one is not the end of the world.

THE HOSPITAL

While having a panic attack during my shift in a food bank warehouse that I very briefly volunteered in, I walked out and biked straight to the hospital, not knowing where else to go and not wanting to go home. I was really fed up with this happening all the time, and not being able to hold down even a casual volunteer position without freaking out. I hadn't seen my therapist in a while because I had skipped my last appointment and never made another one. But I figured I ought to go back since, once again, I could not cope, so I made an appointment with her.

After the hospital, I had pretty much stopped crying but I didn't want to go home yet, so I rode my bike down to the river and sat down under a tree. I read a book and wrote in my journal until I had calmed down and then I went home.

ANOTHER ACCIDENT

And in the midst of processing my recent panic attacks, and trying to find ways to get through them without doing too much damage to myself – I got hit by a car while riding my bike.

I wasn't surprised at all. I've been waiting for this to happen since I took up bicycling, especially within the last year or so. I'm always careful when I'm on my bike, especially in certain areas of town, and my sister was hit by a car while she was riding her bike last year, so I am always very aware of the dangers. I'm also aware of the history of hostility between drivers and cyclists, and I'm not really interested in being a part of that, but I keep it in mind.

I was riding my bike through the fast food district, which I think is pretty much the most dangerous area in town to be riding a bike, so I am always extremely cautious. The block I was on is basically a series of drive-thrus, and drivers don't typically look both ways before pulling out onto the road, so I'm always watching them. I bike slowly and I make eye contact with drivers when I can so I know they see me, and they know I see them.

So I was biking along, approaching a car waiting to pull out, and the driver was only looking left to check her lane, not right to make sure there were no bicyclists or pedestrians. I stopped, barely in time, and yelled at her before she pulled out, but she didn't hear me, and ran into my bike, just the front of the tire that was in front of her car. I was really screaming now, and it still took her a moment to notice what was going on and stop her car. She backed up and I laid my bike down in front of her car to make sure she couldn't drive away, and went to her window where I proceeded to yell at her about how fucking stupid she was to not look both ways. Although I've been expecting this to happen for such a long time, I also felt like I was in shock. I hadn't been hurt, but I was really worried about my bike, and I was taking out my rage at every single careless driver on her. I yelled for quite awhile before she called the cops. Thankfully she admitted right away that it was her fault, so that was one less argument to worry about.

When the cop showed up, I gave him my side of the story and my information, then rode my bike around to make sure it was alright. I was crying and laughing at the same time, and just wanted the whole thing to be over with so I could leave. Once that was all taken care of, I continued along on my trek to the record store and promised not to let the incident ruin my day.

FEARS

One of my biggest fears is of having my bike stolen. Jolene is my best friend. I've never loved any other bike the way I've loved her. My bedroom window overlooks the driveway, and Jolene stays just around the corner at the end, unlocked because there is nothing there to lock her to. I leave my window open and I am aware of all the noise that goes on around me. Mostly just drunk kids walking by at night, and random people walking their dogs. I feel like I'm paranoid, but I keep a good eye and ear on what's going on, and if it sounds like somebody is abnormally close to the house, or overly rowdy, I look out to see what's up. Once I thought I heard somebody in the driveway, but it turned out to be animals rummaging in the recycling bin. During the day, I check to make sure she's still there, and I get a little panicky just before I turn the corner at the end of the driveway and see her shining chrome leaning against the wall. Since I don't have a shed or any sort of shelter for her, I keep her under a shower curtain clipped on with clothespins, and I think even that's enough to make sure she's safe because who wants to bother dealing with the hassle and noise of freeing her from the curtain anyway?

I don't like leaving her out of sight even for just a few moments while I send some letters at the post office or pick up some groceries. I've never had a bike stolen from me, but I don't want to assume that it will never happen. I remember how when we were kids, people would steal bikes and throw them into the river for fun. I remember being taught about bike safety at school and being warned about thieves. It makes me feel like I shouldn't get too attached, and I always have a bit of cash saved up in case I need to get my hands on another bike. But it's too late, I love Jolene, and I want her to be mine forever.

I resent feeling this way. I feel like it's taken for granted that bikes get stolen and that's just the way it is. I can't imagine taking somebody else's bike, I think the guilt of taking it and the paranoia of getting caught would make me feel all tangled up inside. And I really can't imagine how I would feel if one day I went out to get Jolene, and she was gone. I know I would cry. I know I would be checking out every bike I come across for the rest of my life, making sure it isn't her.

ASSERTIVE

COMMUNICATION

Riding my bike around town has taught me how to be a little more assertive, and take up space. My mantra lately has been, *I belong here just as much as anybody else.* I am usually a very friendly person, I like to be polite and courteous, I like to help out when I can, and I like to keep out of the way. Those are all positive traits, I suppose, until they start affecting your own quality of life or level of comfort in a situation. Sometimes I feel like such a doormat, and I'm trying to get out of that habit. Although it's something I did in the past, and still do sometimes, I don't think it's always necessary to thank somebody for letting me by when I had the right of way anyway, nor do I think I should edge as close the curb as possible when I'm biking on the side of the road and a vehicle is coming by. I read somewhere that, when seeing a cyclist on the road, a driver is much more likely to give the cyclist as much room between their vehicle and the bike as the cyclist is giving themselves between their bike and the side of the road, and I'm hoping this is true.

Because I obviously can't talk to drivers when I'm on my bike, I have to learn to communicate in different ways, like using hand gestures and eye contact, and sometimes even smiles. How I communicate with drivers depends on my mood. If I'm already in a bad mood and you piss me off, I'll be sure to let you know, via my angry *What the fuck are you doing?* face, or sometimes I just end up muttering obscenities to myself. If I'm a good mood, and not letting others' negative energy get me down, I'm more likely to smile and forgive you when you nearly run me over. I'm not exactly consistent in my communication with others, but I do what I can.

DEAD LEAVES

The better part of 2009 has been spent learning and re-learning all the streets in this town, knowing where all the cracks and potholes are, the bumps, and the smooth new pavement, getting a feel for the flow of traffic, pedestrian, vehicular, and otherwise. Whenever I'm in a car on a bumpy road and the driver comments on it, I say, "Try riding a bike on this road!" Let me tell you, it can be difficult. I just happen to live in an area with some of the worst roads in town. It can be dangerous, especially when your bike is already questionably jangly, like mine, but it can also be a lot of fun if you're in the mood for adventure.

In the summer, I liked walking all over town barefoot, even that time I walked too far and got blisters and had to steal a pair of shoes to get me home. I liked feeling safe and protected with the comforting scent of sunscreen, and I liked hanging out in the backyard with a book to read and my journal to write in. Those days are fading away.

The leaves are turning colour and falling now. Soon they'll hide all those imperfections on the roads and sidewalks that I have gotten to know so well, and I will have to be extra careful. That's okay. I am fascinated by the change of seasons, and I really do love Fall. I like the sound of the crunching leaves under my feet, I like wearing cardigans and maryjanes with my colourful tights, I like the cool breeze coming through my window and the anticipation of what's to come.

I will keep on riding Jolene until it's time to put her in storage for the season. I'll get through the winter knowing she is waiting patiently for me. We'll have more adventures next year.

OUTRO OUTRO OUTRO

Sometimes I feel a lack of communication within the zine community. It's far easier these days to get your hands on somebody's zine without actually corresponding with them at all, especially with sites like Etsy and PayPal. I want to encourage anybody who's reading this zine to get in touch if you feel like it. Tell me your stories, say hello! There's nothing better than finding a bunch of letters in my mailbox. Don't be shy!

MARANDA ELIZABETH
P.O. BOX 1689
GUELPH, ONTARIO
N1H 6J9 CANADA
©

schoolformapsATgmailDOTcom

schoolformaps.etsy.com

TELEGRAM MA'AM 19.5

the revamped winter survival issue

2010 / 2011

chai spice tea

Sometimes making it through the winter isn't as easy as just keeping your hands busy or going for a walk. Sometimes you don't even bother getting out of bed. These things, connecting with others and making things aren't always enough and aren't always possible.

My plans for Winter 2009/2010 are pretty much to write a lot of letters, write a lot of fiction, watch old movies, drink tea, catch up on all my unread books, eat fruit & drink water & take my vitamin C, and go on evening walks for fresh air and exercise. It sounds so simple. We'll see how it goes when it's really snowing...

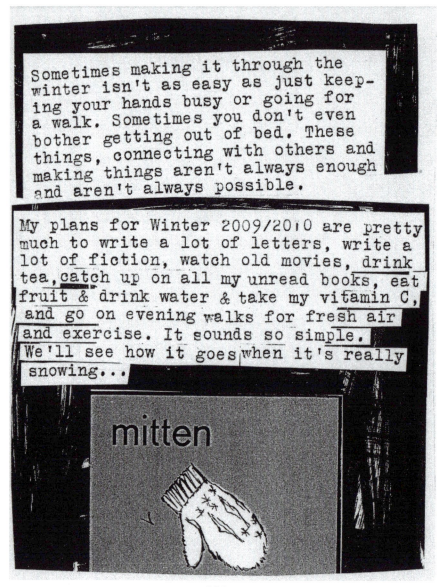

mitten

INTRO INTRO INTRO INTRO INTRO INTRO

2010/2011

One of my favourite things to do in October is just wander. I like taking pictures of trees and graffiti, the crunching leaves beneath my feet, the gorgeous pink and orange sunsets, and the spooky feeling I get while walking late at night around Halloween. I also like checking out the decorations and haunted houses, and pondering costumes that I'll never wear because I don't like parties, and almost never actually go out on Halloween.

Well, this year I did dress up. I recently joined the local roller derby team, Royal City Rollergirls, and dressed up as a dead, or at least severely injured, derby girl. Black & purple eyes, stitches, fake blood. You don't really know how fun it is to dress up like you're dead and rollerskate to Rob Zombie songs until you get the chance to do it.

— stitches

— fake blood

— lots of safety equip.

— red rollerskates!

Halloween is my favourite holiday, but I usually spend it alone. This year, I treated myself to a soy pumpkin spice latte, a new daily planner for 2011, and I wandered all over town in the dark, peeking into windows where orange and black streamers were hanging from the ceiling, watching the flashing lights and scary faces in a garage turned into a haunted house, and listening to cute kids yell, 'Trick-or-treat!' at every doorstep. I ate enough Rockets that week that my stomach began to think they were a legitimate food group all on their own.

I get sad when November hits, though. I look forward to it in a way, because it's a challenge, and I'm starting to like a good challenge, but I do get pretty low as well, and it's not always easy to keep myself motivated to get through the season. That old feeling of I-must-get-into-hibernation-mode got me pretty early this year, but I am trying to resist. I don't really want to hibernate. I want to practice rollerskating, I want to make local friends, I want to volunteer somewhere, I want to write write write, and teach myself better time management skills. But I am easily discouraged, and being alone in my apartment feels so safe.

So I'm being careful and trying to find a balance, and hopefully this zine will help keep you motivated and alive as well. Are you ready to take on this season? Let's do it together! We'll think of it as an adventure.

maranda ♡♡

WINTER WINTER WINTER

Me and Winter, we sure have a history. I want to like Winter, and I really do try. It's hard, but I'm getting closer. Last year, I made a winter survival zine, filled with lists and ideas and projects to help make your (and my) winter wonderful. I know a lot of us truly hate this season. But one day I just said to myself, fuck this, I live in Canada, I need to learn to love Winter. And there are some pretty great things about the season. I can't deny that the first snow is beautiful, even if I'm only watching it from my window. You know how sometimes you're walking down the street, and a wind sweeps by and all these leaves are plucked from their branches and come raining over you, and you feel like you're in a movie, or something? I really love that feeling, even though it means the branches will soon be bare, and then they will be frosted.

When I made the winter survival zine, I made it really quickly. Just a bunch of tips and tricks banged out on my typewriter and little illustrations from a children's alphabet book thrown in. Something to carry around in your pocket and share with your friends. This time, I want to include more stories, make the zine a little more interactive, and talk about how the winter survival strategies worked out for me last year, and how I'm gonna tinker around with them this year to make them even better.

I write a lot of lists. I honest to goodness could not live without them. I have daily to-do lists, an everyday-to-do list, and a things-to-do-before-I-die list, among others. They are essential. And around this time of year, I find myself writing winter lists. My biggest concern right now is self-care. I don't feel like I've been taking care of myself as well as I need to be. Maybe that's true for you, too. I seem to be over-extending myself, then getting upset when I realize I'm falling behind on everything. So I'm taking little steps to catch up, and if I don't finish something "on time," so what. I'll do it later.

Do you remember the worst winter of your life? How about the best winter? Did you have a lot of control over those winters, or were outside factors thrashing you around to and fro? What would you like this winter to be like, and how can you make that happen?

Daily
- drink water
- stretch
- write
- read
- eat fruit
- take meds
- take vitamins
- moisturize
- smile

Before I Die
- learn simple bike repair skills
- own my own home
- see Marilyn Manson live
- learn how to dance the Charleston
- ride in a hot air balloon

Winter has always been scary and anxiety-inducing for me. Every time it rolls around, I can never see an end. I still remember when I was a kid, they would set up winter sports and obstacle courses in the schoolyard, encouraging us to compete. I would refuse to participate, just standing there against the brick wall waiting for it all to be over. As I grew older, I had a fear of ice. I don't know why, but I was so afraid of falling that I would practically tiptoe everywhere I went. And after I dropped out of school, I stopped going outside in the winter at all. Although I had no name for it at the time, I developed agoraphobia, and eventually refused to leave the house. I couldn't even walk from the back door to the driveway to get a ride somewhere, and I couldn't go out on the front porch to check the mail. It was really bad. I went to therapy and met the first therapist I ever actually liked. She taught me how to walk outside again. She would walk beside me on the sidewalk, and sometimes I could only take a few steps before I became overwhelmed with anxiety and had to go back. Each appointment, we would walk further, but it was always a relief to return to the cozy confines of her office, housed in an old brick building with creaky hardwood floors. Once we could walk through downtown and back to her office together, we switched it up and she began walking fifteen feet behind me so I could get used to walking alone. It was scary. I couldn't always do it. I liked walking on rainy days best because I could hide under my umbrella. Once I had an intense panic attack and had to stop on a bench on a concrete platform and try to teach myself how to breathe again. That's what I think of every time I see that bench.

The best winter I've had so far was last year, and that's because I went into it with positive intent, almost over-prepared. And although I crashed at the end and ended up being hospitalized again, I still had some pretty good times, and I learned what I need to do differently this year to keep myself safe.

First things first. I've moved! And while having a home that I really love definitely helps in the winter, I am also very aware that the last time I lived in this town just happened to be the worst winter of my life. Circumstances have changed, *a lot*, and I know that it can never be that bad again, but I am concerned about having certain memories triggered, etc. So I need to be careful. I'm living in a town that I love and an apartment that I love, and I am feeling much more in control.

Twenty-Seven Ways to Survive Winter

1. Make your own scarf. If you don't know how to knit already, now's a good time to learn. Choose a colour that'll keep you feeling happy and cozy & warm on cold days. You'll have something nobody else has, you'll get lots of compliments, and you might even get a few folks asking for their own handmade scarf as well.

I'm not actually making my own scarf this year. I've been dealing with chronic pain in my hand, arm, shoulder, back, and neck, and I just can't knit like I used to. But I did find a gorgeous purple pashmina for $10, and it is my new favourite thing. Fashion is more important to me in Winter; I think if you're gonna be out there braving cold and snow and ice and wind and general discomfort, you might as well wear something both practical and cute. It's pretty crucial to have a coat, scarf, mittens, and boots that you really love.

2. Scented candles are your best friend when it's snowing and you wanna stay in. Apparently scents are the strongest memory trigger, even moreso than music, so choose a scent that'll agree with you, not one that'll make you think of things you don't wanna think about. I stick to scents like vanilla, cinnamon, and apples. And I get a lot of candles at the dollarstore. I don't care if those are the poisonous ones, they're the only ones I can afford.

3. Eat bananas. They're good for your mental health and they're delicious. When they start to turn brown, put them in your freezer. You can use them in a bunch of yummy recipes (like banana bread or shakes), or you can mash them up and eat them as a pretty perfect vegan alternative to ice cream.

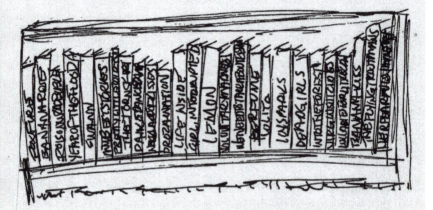

4. Reorganize your books. Because it's fun and inspiring and if you find any books you don't want anymore, you can pass them onto your friends, sell them, or trade them for other books. Making sure they find good homes brightens up somebody else's winter as well, and you might feel better yourself with less clutter.

5. Don't use the internet today. Seriously. Staring at the screen for long periods of time can strain your eyes and drain your energy. Do something else today.

I'd just like to say that in trying to minimize pain, I have to spend as little time on the computer as possible. Although the issues I've been having are currently undiagnosed, there is a possibility that it is at least partly due to Carpal Tunnel Syndrome. Using a computer is extremely painful for me. It starts in my hand, and before I know it, my arm and my neck and my back are all aching and tingling and it can get pretty excruciating. So although I often feel like I spend a little too much time online, the fact that it has also become physically painful encourages me to get off the internet. I always feel a little healthier for having done so.

6. Write letters. Snail mail is the best ever. I'll admit, I'm not as great at keeping all caught up on my mail as I used to be. Sometimes I am experiencing too much pain to write, sometimes life just gets in the way. Sometimes both. But snail mail will always be my true love. In fact, having a P.O. Box instead of a regular mailbox at my front door is another winter survival strategy of mine. This'll force me to get out no matter how cold it is; if I wanna check my mail, I've gotta get dressed and trudge through the snow. I'm actually looking forward to it.

7. (Related to 6.) Send me your own winter survival tips.

8. Take lots of pictures. Preferably outside.

9. Last year, I made a game of trying all different kinds of tea. It was an effective method of surviving the season since you pretty can't ever run out of flavours. It's also how I realized I like the scent of fruit teas, but not the taste. I like peppermint tea best, and chai tea as well. I have recently become a little obsessed with soy chai lattes, and I try one at every café I happen to find myself in.

10. Get tattooed. It seems like I get most of my tattoos in the winter, not on purpose, that's just the way it works out. If you've got the funds, it's nice to have something like that to look forward to. Also, I genuinely enjoy the way the needle feels as it fills my skin with ink. When asked, I liken it to be scratched by kittens for a prolonged period of time. I also kind of want to learn how to give myself a tattoo.

11. Solo dance party! Turn up the music and dance all by yourself!

12. Learn something new. Knitting, crocheting, embroidery, cross-stitch... Old lady crafts rule. Alternatively, take up a crafty skill you used to be really into but haven't done in a long time. This winter, I'm considering sewing some banners with scrappy fabric and hanging up little inspirational messages in my apartment. It's been a long time since I've sewn anything. Either I lose interest, or my sewing machine breaks down.

13. Library adventures! In my hometown, the library has monthly sales in their basement where you can buy as many books as you want for a small donation. The books are donated to the library, and the basement is filled with hundreds and hundreds of them. I always looked forward to these Tuesdays, and would often come home with, like, ten books for ten dollars. It was amazing. Now I've got this huge collection of books I haven't even read yet. And I miss those days. Here in Guelph, I still spend a lot of time at the library. I find a quiet little corner to sit in and I start writing. It's a good place to people-watch, to get out of your house, to get inspired.

14. Have your pet's photo taken with Santa! I don't actually celebrate Christmas anymore, but the opportunity was too adorable to pass up. A few years ago, I took my cat, Amélie, to have her photo taken with Santa, and it was the cutest ever. We lined up with a bunch of dogs and bunnies and such, many of whom were all dressed up. It cost $10, which went to an animal shelter, and now I've got the photo framed on my wall.

15. Set small goals. For example: Send at least two items of mail a week, read one book a week, go outside everyday, etc…

16. Write a list of things you like about Winter.

Here's my list:

- warm drinks
- the sound of crunching snow beneath my feet
- wearing thick socks
- wearing lots of layers
- seeing other people wearing silly hats
- seeing dogs in sweaters and boots
- coming up with new winter survival plans
- cooking and eating soup
- scratching hearts into frost on windows
- knowing that the snow will eventually melt

17. Build a blanket fort. Last year, some friends and I built a fort on my friend's bed and hid under all the blankets watching bad movies and sharing a bottle of wine. If I get around to building a fort this winter, I know I'll be tempted to leave it up all year 'round.

18. Cut & paste! Make a zine, make a collage, glue receipts into your journal, decorate shoeboxes and use them for storage, make your own envelopes...

19. Eat soup. Better yet, make your own soup from scratch. I really enjoy making squash soup and carrot soup. I don't even follow the recipes anymore, I just sort of get the basics and make it up as I go along. I make a big pot so that it lasts a few days, and every time I heat up another bowl, I add another vegetable or whatever so that it's different every time.

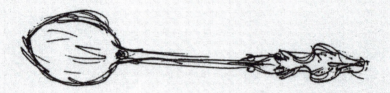

20. In the first edition of this zine, the 20th winter survival tip was Travel. But now that I'm no longer living in my claustrophobic, anxiety-inducing hometown, visiting other cities is not really my top priority right now, plus I can't really afford to anymore anyway. Bus tickets are getting expensive. Besides, I live in a pretty wonderful town and I love my home, and I think it's about time my longer-distance friends come visit me now. I used to really love taking the Greyhound and exploring new streets and stuff, but I guess that has changed a little. So if you're living somewhere where you need an escape, get a bus ticket and disappear for the weekend, but if you love where you are and you've got a friend who needs an escape, invite them over to your place instead.

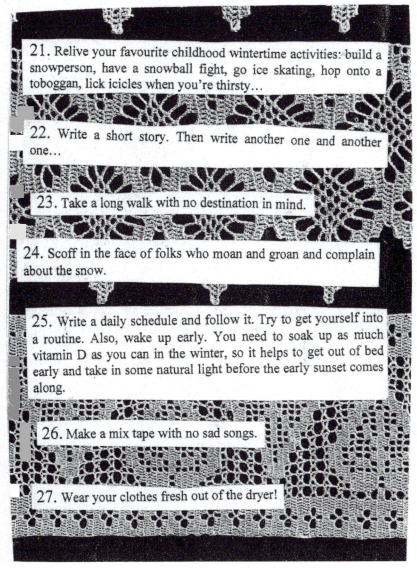

21. Relive your favourite childhood wintertime activities: build a snowperson, have a snowball fight, go ice skating, hop onto a toboggan, lick icicles when you're thirsty...

22. Write a short story. Then write another one and another one...

23. Take a long walk with no destination in mind.

24. Scoff in the face of folks who moan and groan and complain about the snow.

25. Write a daily schedule and follow it. Try to get yourself into a routine. Also, wake up early. You need to soak up as much vitamin D as you can in the winter, so it helps to get out of bed early and take in some natural light before the early sunset comes along.

26. Make a mix tape with no sad songs.

27. Wear your clothes fresh out of the dryer!

A Special Note About Naps

Let it be known that I am avid nap enthusiast. I was gonna use 'Take a nap' as one of my winter survival tips, but the truth is, naps can be tricky things; they are both good and bad and I gotta be careful about them.

Sometimes if I'm in a crummy mood, I take a nap and wake up feeling better. Other times, I end up feeling worse. I feel especially depressed if the sun sets while I'm napping and I wake up to darkness. I don't have a solution, I just wanted to mention it. Naps are cool but use them wisely!

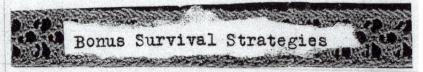

Bonus Survival Strategies

Lately, one of my favourite things to do is fill up my backpack with books and notebooks and pens, take a walk to a nearby café, and just hang out and write for awhile. I always order a soy chai latte or peppermint tea. And I usually take a picture of my drink as well, or sketch it in my journal, simply because I like the look of it. It's fun to taste the same drink in different places, and I like seeing the different mugs they use. One place gave me my drink in a beer mug! I choose a small table, preferably near a window, and I just write away.

When I don't have the money for a yummy drink, I go to the library instead. It gets me away from all the distractions in my home and ensures that I get some writing done, and that I get some exercise walking to and from the library as well.

It's also a good idea to carry a travel mug with you so you can drink yummy things while you're out wandering – it's also cheaper if you make those drinks at home, plus it creates less litter.

I never used to drink coffee. Cafés always intimidated me. I wouldn't go in because I didn't know what to drink, and I didn't want to stand around all uncomfortable trying to make a decision, not really knowing what anything is and not wanting to ask. The first time I had coffee was when I was fourteen. I was at a psychiatrist's office filling out one of those questionnaires that asks if you have ever considered setting fire to buildings, hurting yourself or other people, etc., and telling an old man what I could see in those ink blot tests. Filling in the little circles with a freshly sharpened pencil, and drinking a mug of coffee with extra sugar. I didn't drink another coffee for nearly ten years after that, and the scent always reminded me of that day. Now I drink two big mugs every morning, otherwise I don't truly wake up. Sometimes I add vanilla extract or cinnamon. It has been the most effective antidepressant for me.

I think having some kind of daily routine is important, but I don't get too stressed if I'm not really following it. It's more like something to work toward, not something totally set in stone the moment you write it down. The meds I take make me sleep a little longer than I'd like to, so I wake up late and feel like part of my day has been wasted. Then my brain gets buzzy and overstimulated at night, so it's hard to go to bed at a decent time. I always feel like I haven't accomplished enough to let myself sleep just yet. And while I think it's pretty important to get out and get some fresh air and sunshine most days, I think it's just as important to give yourself permission to stay in and have a pajama day and do whatever you want. Be kind to yourself.

One reason it's so important for me to make some kind of routine for myself is that I am on disability, so it is totally up to me to structure my days. I'm not always able to do everything I've planned, but at least most of my time is purely my own. I'm not obligated to show up at a job or a class at a set time everyday, but I do like to try to get out of bed early anyway; if I sleep too much, my depression only gets worse, I simply become lethargic. Of course, there are times when I am required to be somewhere at a certain time. Like, doctor's appointments, food bank appointments, roller derby practice, etc. But most days are my own, and the responsibility to find reasons to get out of bed lies solely on me.

I like to wake up with coffee and a good book, and I do stretches as well since my body is always aching. Coffee gets me into a good mood, and then I'm ready to take on another day. I also take B12 vitamins and Ginseng to help my energy levels, and I take Ginkgo Biloba to help improve my memory and concentration, both of which have been remarkably damaged due to all the meds I've taken over the years. Sometimes I take Valerian to help me sleep. It's a tricky process, but I'm managing alright.

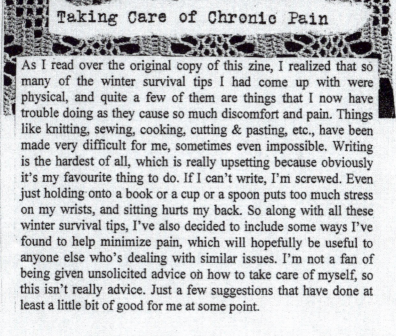

Taking Care of Chronic Pain

As I read over the original copy of this zine, I realized that so many of the winter survival tips I had come up with were physical, and quite a few of them are things that I now have trouble doing as they cause so much discomfort and pain. Things like knitting, sewing, cooking, cutting & pasting, etc., have been made very difficult for me, sometimes even impossible. Writing is the hardest of all, which is really upsetting because obviously it's my favourite thing to do. If I can't write, I'm screwed. Even just holding onto a book or a cup or a spoon puts too much stress on my wrists, and sitting hurts my back. So along with all these winter survival tips, I've also decided to include some ways I've found to help minimize pain, which will hopefully be useful to anyone else who's dealing with similar issues. I'm not a fan of being given unsolicited advice on how to take care of myself, so this isn't really advice. Just a few suggestions that have done at least a little bit of good for me at some point.

- Using a backpack instead of a purse. Since most of my pain is contained to the right side of my body, carrying a purse only exacerbates discomfort. A backpack isn't perfect as I still end up hurting myself when I'm putting it on or taking it off, and even just pulling the drawstring and snapping it closed, but at least the weight of the things I am carrying with me is evenly distributed.
- Doing stretches first thing upon getting out of bed and throughout the day as well. I got one of those exercise balls which motivates me because it's so much fun to play with. There are about a million different exercises and stretches you can do with it. Get creative.
- Using a typewriter instead of a pen to write letters. It's not perfect, but it helps. I love my typewriter, but I'd like to get my hands on one that is quieter and doesn't require so much pressure on the keys.
- Bubble baths. I was really happy when I moved into this apartment and found out I had a pink bathtub! Bubble baths are not quite perfect either (nothing is) since my bathtub is not really big enough for me to stretch out, but immersing myself in hot water and letting my body lay limp for awhile is good for my strained muscles and nerves.
- Going out for long walks. Thankfully, I don't seem to have any problems with my legs, so going out for a walk allows me to relax my arms and shoulders without straining any other part of my body.
- Don't sit for more than half an hour at a time. I tend to sit for long periods of time, so I have to be very conscious of that and stand up and do stretches whenever I can.

- Ibuprofen and Tylenol 3. Once again, not perfect, but sometimes helpful. I don't like to rely on pills, but when that's the cheapest method of treatment available, that's what I'm gonna do. I have been trying to take them less than usual, though, as I seem to have built up a tolerance over time.
- Giving myself permission to do nothing. It's allowed. But not too often, or I fall into a horrendous slump that is very difficult to dig my way out of.

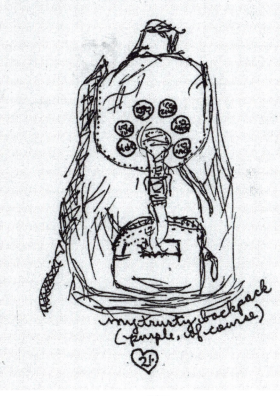

my trusty backpack
(purple, of course)

BOOK RECOMMENDATIONS

These are a few books that motivate, inspire, and/or comfort me. I won't bother writing reviews; I think you will seek out whichever ones interest you the most, and I'm sure you'll find some other wonderful books along the way. Happy reading & happy winter!

Juicy Pens Thirsty Paper (and anything else) by SARK
Writing Down the Bones (and anything else) by Natalie Goldberg
The Artist's Way by Julia Cameron
Hello, Cruel World: 101 Alternatives to Suicide for Teens, Freaks, & Other Outlaws by Kate Bornstein
Journal of a Solitude by May Sarton
Walden and Other Writings by Henry David Thoreau
Live Through This: On Creativity and Self-Destruction edited by Sabrina Chapadjiev

TELEGRAM MA'AM

issue 2

SPRING 2010

$2 Canada and U.S.

$3 International

Spring! My attic bedroom is overheated,
yet downstairs gets too cold. I wake up
early every morning, even weekends, open
my handmade curtains, make a lotta coffee
and begin my day. I read for a little
while and I listen to the birdsongs.
Spring treats me well, sometimes. Good
things have been happening. And I've got
a lotta good things to look forward to
as well, like summer travels to Montreal,
Quebec, and Halifax, Nova Scotia. Thank
goodness for that. Aside from that, I've
also got plans to get more tattoos, move
outta town again, and **write write write.**
Plans freak me out because they seem to
fall through more than I'd like, but this
time, I've got a good feeling.

So, this is my Spring.

Please write to me!

Lately I've been going to a lot of yard sales and junk shops and whatnot. I'd stopped for a while because I didn't have the money or the space, and I thought everything was pretty useless, just clutter, unless I really needed it. But it can be fun. And so what if now and then, stuff makes me happy.

A few weeks ago, we left town to go to this big community yard sale. I met up with my friend, Ashley, who I hadn't seen in years, even though we have literally known one another since the day I was born. She wasn't expecting to see me and we shared a long, tight hug. Her hair seemed to come down to her elbows and had a little bit of pink in it. She was carrying a green&black-striped purse I knit for her years ago and had completely forgotten about.

The morning turned out to be cold; I wished for mittens to go along with my cardigan. I bought a set of giant yellow mugs, dreaming of hot coffeewith cinnamon

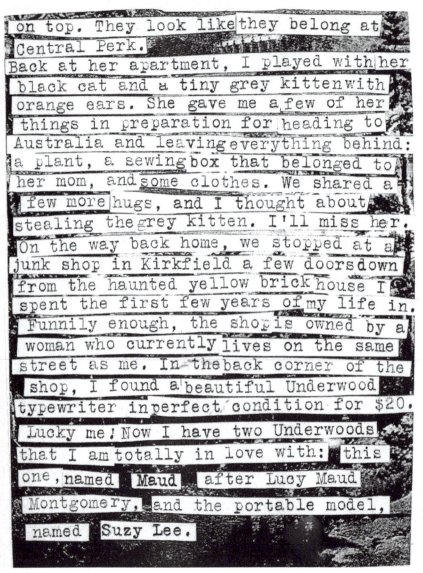

on top. They look like they belong at Central Perk.

Back at her apartment, I played with her black cat and a tiny grey kitten with orange ears. She gave me a few of her things in preparation for heading to Australia and leaving everything behind: a plant, a sewing box that belonged to her mom, and some clothes. We shared a few more hugs, and I thought about stealing the grey kitten. I'll miss her. On the way back home, we stopped at a junk shop in Kirkfield a few doors down from the haunted yellow brick house I spent the first few years of my life in. Funnily enough, the shop is owned by a woman who currently lives on the same street as me. In the back corner of the shop, I found a beautiful Underwood typewriter in perfect condition for $20. Lucky me! Now I have two Underwoods that I am totally in love with: this one, named Maud after Lucy Maud Montgomery, and the portable model, named Suzy Lee.

Things That Help Improve My Mental
Health & Self-Esteem (Even if Only
Temporarily)

- riding my bike

- going vegan

- drinking coffee

- writing fiction

- good books

- quit shaving

- hanging out at the library

- spending less time online

-good mail days

- medication,
  sometimes

- drinking lots of water

- spending time outside (even if it's
just in the backyard)

May 29, 2010

~~Some days just feel~~ magical, like
there's something in the air. After
~~a morning spent yard~~ saling (I got
an olive suitcase for $2 and a beau-
~~tiful wooden desk with~~ drawers and
old handles... I will soonly sand it
~~down and paint it a very light~~
purple, set my typewriters on top),
I attended a writer's workshop held
in the library by a semi-local
writer. The focus was on writing
memoirs. I had no idea what to expect; I'd never been to a writer's
workshop, and I barely know a thing
about the local writing community.
I was the youngest person there.
Everyone else seemed to be late-50's
and beyond. I was afraid the workshop
would be tailored for beginners, &
~~in some ways it was~~, but I also found
it both fascinating and useful. We
~~not only discussed writing~~ & story-
telling, but we were given prompts
~~to write short pieces with~~, as well
as the opportunity to share our
~~writing with one another~~. I decided
I just plain wasn't gonna be shy, &
volunteered several times to read my

pieces. I'm not usually great at coming up with something on the spot, but I was quite proud of what I had written, and I kind of wanted to show it off. I don't think we're encouraged to think of our own writing as GOOD and WORTHWHILE, but mine is, and yours is, and we shouldn't be afraid to say it. If you're a good writer, own it. If you're not a good writer, keep writing. Anyway. Each time I read a piece, I got many compliments, and I didn't blush at all, I didn't try to pass it off as just something silly I had come up with, I didn't try to say

that I could do better, or someone
else could do better. I held my head
high and said thank you.

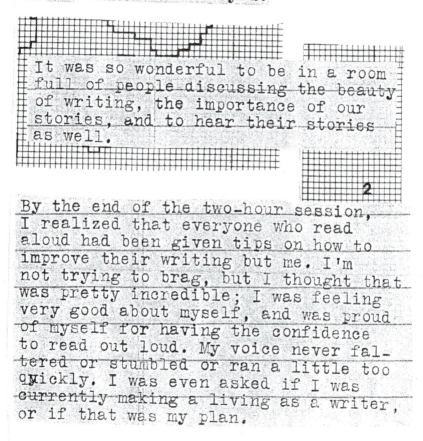

It was so wonderful to be in a room
full of people discussing the beauty
of writing, the importance of our
stories, and to hear their stories
as well.

By the end of the two-hour session,
I realized that everyone who read
aloud had been given tips on how to
improve their writing but me. I'm
not trying to brag, but I thought that
was pretty incredible; I was feeling
very good about myself, and was proud
of myself for having the confidence
to read out loud. My voice never fal-
tered or stumbled or ran a little too
quickly. I was even asked if I was
currently making a living as a writer,
or if that was my plan.

At the end of the workshop, the woman hosting it pulled me aside and after everyone else had left, she too asked me if I was writing as a career, and I said not yet, but that I plan to. She gave me many encouraging words, assuring me that this is something I can do for a living, that I have a talent with words she doesn't see too often, and that she doesn't flatter just anyone. I took those words to heart; I need to hold them close. It felt like such a relief to hear those words from someone who doesn't know me at all, but knows what she's talking about.

Leaving the library, I felt giddy and powerful and maybe even capable of making this happen for real.

Hearing about habits of writers kind of fascinates me. I am always inspired by their discipline and their tricks, and I try to learn from them. When it comes to writing, especially fiction, I am not quite as disciplined as I'd like to be, so I've been trying to change some of my habits and gain better focus. Although there are times when I can write & write & write non-stop, it's definitely not like that all the time. Sometimes I have to force myself to sit down & write (or edit, revise, etc.), sometimes my inspiration comes to me while I'm out and I scribble a mess in my notebook, but when I come home and have a chance to write it all down properly, I'm no longer in the same frame of mind. It has been said that if you are meant to be a writer, you will be writing constantly, you will not be able to stop yourself. Well, I don't think that's quite true. Because sometimes I am incapable or nervous or worn out or uninspired. All those stories are always right there on the tip of my tongue (or my pen or my fingers), but sometimes they just can't be written yet, I'm not

ready or they're not ready or something
is in the way. That doesn't mean it's
not meant to be, it's just not meant to
be right now. I used to think I had to
have published at least one novel by
the age of 25, and several by the age
of 30. I hadn't realized how young 25
is 'til I turned 24, It hadn't occurred
to me that I might live beyond 30. And
I'm not sure how many of the writers I
love were publishing novels
in their 20's
anyway.

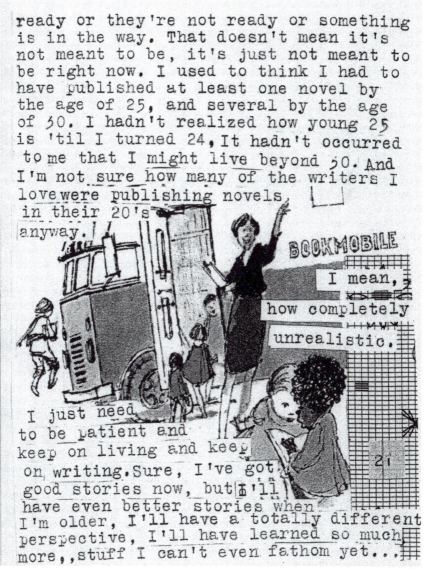

BOOKMOBILE

I mean,
how completely
unrealistic.

I just need
to be patient and
keep on living and keep
on writing. Sure, I've got
good stories now, but I'll
have even better stories when
I'm older, I'll have a totally different
perspective, I'll have learned so much
more, stuff I can't even fathom yet...

21

OUTRO OUTRO OUTRO OUTRO OUTRO OUTRO

This issue is quite different from
more recent issues of Telegram Ma'am.
I thought it would be nice to take a
break from my usual style of writing
and make a zine in a short period of
time. I also wanted to write about
something other than mental health
since that is the focus of so many of
my zines. Although I worried whether
or not anyone would like this zine,
the fact is, it doesn't matter. I
needed to make it, so I made it.
And yes, I am printing issue 21 before
issue 20. I've been working on issue
20 for a long time and will be comp-
leting it as zinester-in-residence at
the Roberts Street Social Centre in
Halifax in July. Hooray!

Thanks for reading!
Send me a letter,
let's be friends!

TELEGRAM MA'AM

issue 20 / summer 2010

Torre Bevans

INTRO INTRO INTRO INTRO INTRO INTRO

I've been nervous about writing this zine. I don't often talk about being on disability, but it's been coming up more and more often lately. People ask me a lot of stupid questions, and although many of them will never read this, I need to write it anyway. I've gone back and forth between feeling guilty and useless for being on disability, to accepting that this is what I need right now and it doesn't matter what anyone else thinks. Taking care of my mental health is a full-time job. I'd like to get to a point where that's not the case, but that's how it is right now.

So I kind of wrote this zine on a dare. I applied for a zine residency at the Roberts Street Social Centre in Halifax, Nova Scotia, back in the winter. I figured if I was accepted, I'd have to make the zine, and if I wasn't, then I had some time to think about it, and/or back out. And I also wanted to get the fuck out of my town and visit somewhere new. I wasn't really expecting to be accepted, but here I am. And here's my zine.

P.S.:   Maranda ♡♡
Please write me! I love letters!

WHAT DO YOU DO?

Ah, the most unimaginative question in the whole wide world. For years, this question has grated on my nerves. Well, I do about a million things. But we all know what this question really means: Where does your money come from? Folks are awfully persistent about finding out. No matter what answer I give them about *what I do*, they want to know *how I pay my rent*. Usually when someone asks what I do, I tell them I write, because, yeah, that's what I do. I spend most of my time writing. From there, they'll either ask what I write then ask how writing pays the rent, or they'll just skip to the rent question right away. Sometimes I outright ask, "Are you asking me what I do or are you asking me where my money comes from?" Nobody answers right away; it's like they've been caught.

One weird thing that happens when people find out I don't have a job in the conventional sense, is they ask me what I do all day, like not having a job means I must be sitting around bored or something. It's like they get so caught up in thinking day jobs are so meaningful and important, they forget that it doesn't work that way for everyone else, that the job you have is not always indicative of having a good life or being a good person or "contributing to society." I kinda feel sorry for them; for me and a lot of my friends, jobs suck energy and take us away from the things we would rather be doing; but for folks who think I must have too much free time on my hands, I wonder if they've just grown so used to their own routines that they don't think about what they would want to do if they had the opportunity to do something else. The thing is, I have so much to do that even without having to show up for work and follow somebody else's schedule, I still run out of time.

Other intrusive questions I get are, "How much money do you make?" and, ugh, "What's your disability?" How about none of your fucking business. I am always so grateful on the rare occasions when I tell somebody what I do, and don't have deal with a bombardment of boring and tedious questions.

APPLYING FOR DISABILITY

Applying for disability was a really fucking arduous process that involved lots and lots of crying and screaming and filling out complicated paperwork. I think I was ashamed for a long time but didn't know how to name those feelings. It's not like I was ashamed of being on disability, moreso that I was annoyed with the judgment that came along with it so I became uncomfortable with letting anybody know.

Filling out application forms for ODSP (Ontario Disability Support Program) involved not only writing down basic information about myself, but getting my doctor to fill out forms and such as well.

When filling out the forms to apply for disability, you are asked, or rather, your doctor is asked, when you are expected to recover from your disability. Is it short-term or long-term? They are more likely to accept you if it is short-term. They are also more likely to accept you if you are older. If you're twenty, they might have to support you for sixty years, but f you're sixty, they might have to support you for only twenty.

How can you predict when you're going to recover from depression? Is it possible to recover at all?

While waiting to find out whether or not I was accepted, I applied for OW (Ontario Works / welfare). That was another complicated process, and my caseworker was a horror to deal with. I was given $400/month, which was the cost of my rent, and all other living expenses went onto my credit card. I got into debt pretty quickly, eventually going through the process of declaring bankruptcy, which in the end, I didn't complete. Anyway. The first time I heard back from ODSP, they told me I had been denied because I had filled out some of the forms incorrectly. I'd accidentally filled out forms my doctor was supposed to deal with. So I got those cleared up, sent them back, and a few months later was finally accepted.

Although they provide more money than welfare, it's still not really enough to live on. Money is separated into two categories: Shelter and Basic Needs. The amount given to cover rent is so low that you have to either live with roommates because even bachelor apartments are too expensive for someone on disability, or use your Basic Needs allowance along with your Shelter allowance to pay rent, and go without proper nutrition and other essentials. There's certainly not much money left over for things like books, music, craft supplies, postage, going out with friends, photocopies, transit, whatever else you're into beyond basic survival (and I'd argue that these things are, in fact, necessary for survival). It's especially difficult when the seasons change and you find yourself in need of a new coat, or new shoes, that kind of thing. There's a careful budget to stick to each month with little to no room for unexpected extras. The Ontario government says a single person needs $1800/month to live, yet won't provide anything near that for those who need it. There is a Special Diet Allowance for those who need extra money for food, but it's generally not available to folks who are on disability for mental health reasons, which is about 50% of ODSP recipients.

The stress of living under a constant threat of coming up for review and having a bunch of strangers decide whether or not I still deserve/require disability payments really fucks with my mental health. There are days when I become so panicked with fear of being cut off that I break down in tears and wonder if I will know how to fight.

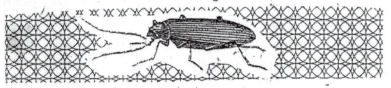

I wonder if anyone else gets as annoyed as I do. I don't get to have this conversation as often or as in-depth as I'd like to because I don't know a lot of people who are on disability. It tends to be something we're quiet about, with good reason.

The knowledge that you're on disability brings innumerable preconceptions and blatant ignorance. They want you to prove that you deserve it, yet they think you're weak for needing it. They think if they can't see your disability, if they can't understand it, you must be lying, it must not be that bad. Obviously you're scamming the government because you're just lazy. If you're not slitting your wrists everyday, you must be alright, you must be well enough to catch up with the rest of them.

How fucked up do you have to be before you deserve it?

Another thing folks say that annoys me: "I'm glad to hear you're doing okay."

Even when I am 'doing okay', hearing it put that way automatically makes me feel worse. Like, if I'm okay I should just shut up, and if I'm no longer okay, I'm going to be a big disappointment. Oh, Maranda's unhappy again, what else is new...

I've been on disability for three and a half years now. A lot has changed in that time, as it usually does. When I applied for disability, I had just gotten out of the hospital(s) after my first suicide attempt, my relationship had fallen apart, and I had lost my home and was looking for a new one. I felt fragile, broken, and useless. Naively, I thought I would use this time to do something really wonderful, like write a great novel, not realizing things would get much, much worse before getting better, not realizing I wouldn't have the energy, the confidence, the mental health, to do much anyway.

WINTER SURVIVAL (AND ANOTHER HOSPITAL ADVENTURE)

Last Fall, I decided I wanted to get out of the mental health system for good. My therapist was leaving her practice, I had been off meds for a while, and I felt happier than I had been in years. It seemed like biking up to the hospital to talk to my therapist was doing more harm than good; it forced me to talk about stuff I didn't want to talk about, and it ruined the good mood I'd been in before showing up for my appointment. I just wanted to focus on good things: bike rides, sunshine, coffee, books, friendship, whathaveyou. As the leaves were falling, I was gearing myself up to have the Best Winter Ever. I wanted at least to survive the winter without a serious depressive episode.

My therapist was supportive of my plan. She told me about the two other therapists I could be referred to just in case, but I wasn't into it. I had had a bad experience with one of them during one of my inpatient stays, and I just didn't want to start all over again with someone new. I felt like I would have to rehash all this stuff from the past that I didn't feel like talking about anymore, and I just didn't want to go through the effort of getting to know one another. Besides, I was afraid the other therapist would turn out to be one more person I didn't like, and wouldn't feel confident sharing much with her anyway.

After my last appointment, my therapist asked if she could hug me. We hugged, and she said she felt like crying. I did too. I'm not very good with goodbyes.

But now I was out and on my own!

We had a late Winter. For the first time in my life, I grew impatient and wished for it to snow. When it did, I thought it was beautiful. I had written lists and lists of ways to survive the winter, and I was prepared. I went for walks in the evening, I ate soup, I wrote a million letters. When the New Year came, I decided to give veganism a try and started writing a list of all the books I was reading, so I can tally it up at the end of 2010.

It turned out to be the mildest winter I've ever experienced. No major snowstorms, no icy sidewalk wipe-outs, no nervous breakdowns. It was pretty swell. And it was my Best Winter Ever. I kind of felt like I had maybe even over-prepared. But I was still glad I had thought it all through so thoroughly and done everything within my ability to take care of myself.

Something happened around the end of March. There was no specific trigger, nothing I could put my finger on. I became more and more uncomfortable in the house I was living in; issues with physical pain I had been experiencing seemed to be getting worse; I felt stuck. Most afternoons, I would go to the library with a book and all my letter-writing supplies in tow, choose a cubicle, and hang out for a couple hours. It became a safe haven. I reacquainted myself with the librarians

I used to see a lot more often, I noticed a pattern of busy times and slow times & quiet times and noisy times, and I overheard conversations here and there; some amusing, some not so much. Unfortunately, my pain was getting so bad that I was having trouble writing at all, and I was feeling more and more, well, *stuck*. I would sometimes consider going straight to the hospital from the library, but I didn't want to admit that maybe I wasn't doing as well as I'd thought. I didn't want to end up *there* again, but I didn't know what else to do. As always, I got annoyed when people said, "You seem to be doing so well these days!" I didn't feel well.

Finally, on one of these days, I walked home from the library, and feeling oppressed in my own home, feeling that old sense of hopelessness and despair that was so familiar, I packed a tote bag with toothpaste and a toothbrush, a few pairs of underwear, a t-shirt, a pair of tights, and two books. (I always have a list of what to bring. When I lived by myself, I kept a post-it on my bathroom mirror with a list of everything I would need in case I had to go to the hospital.) I put a list of past and current medications in my wallet. And then I waited.

But I knew I had made my decision. I wouldn't be able to sleep here tonight. So I put on my coat and boots, grabbed my bag, and went to the hospital.

SOME STORIES ABOUT MY THERAPIST

My therapist was kind of an inspiration to me, cheesy as that may sound. She was someone I could identify with. Of course I had my qualms with her, too; who wouldn't. But overall, I liked her. She was a feminist (like me!) and a writer (like me!). She reminded me of someone, but I could never figure out whom. She always encouraged me to write (even going so far as to look up information on how to find editors and agents and how to submit a manuscript during one of our sessions), and was supportive of my decision not to take medication; as she always liked to remind me, she was anti-medical model. It always bothered her that her office was located in a hospital.

One way she differed from other therapists I had seen over the years was that she often talked to me about her own personal life. She told me about going to school in Toronto, visiting Paris, spending time with her husband.

There was one story she told me that I always remembered. While eating at a restaurant in Paris, this woman stepped out onto the patio where they were seated; she was tall and alarmingly beautiful, and she wore heels that made her even taller. When she took off her coat, she was wearing a white linen halter pantsuit sort of thing. My therapist was floored. Yet nobody else was looking. They didn't so much as glance at her.

"In Paris," my therapist said, "people are discrete. They respect one another's privacy. In Lindsay, they are constantly staring, constantly gossiping."

She was adamant that I belonged in a city like Paris. That I would flourish, given the chance.

Sometimes I miss her a little bit. When I was still attending therapy, it had occurred to me more than once that even where I thought she lacked somehow as an appropriate therapist for me, she did seem like someone I would want to be friends with under different circumstances. She could be my eccentric older friend, or a cool aunt.

I've seen her twice since our last session together. The first time, I bumped into her downtown. It had snowed. I was on my way to the post office and she was on her way to the liquor store. She crossed the street to come say Hi. She asked me how I was, and I was actually doing well that day, so I told her so. I had been working on a writing project and I told her about it, and she told me about her plans for the evening: picking up a bottle of wine to bring to a friend's housewarming party. When we got to the liquor store, we parted ways.

The next time I saw her was the day I went to pick up my bike from my grandparents' house, shortly after being discharged from the hospital. I recognized her from a distance. She has a distinctive style: long black hair, black clothes, black trenchcoat, black boots. I was riding my bike downhill and she was walking towards me on the other side of the street. Her daughter was a few feet ahead of her, riding a bike with training wheels and sparkly streamers. As we got closer, I called out Hi, and she stopped and asked me how I was. "Good," I replied, even though I wasn't. "How are you?" She always says, "So nice to see you," and when she does, she emphasizes the *see* and draws out the *you*: "So nice to *see* yooouuu." We stood for a moment then parted ways, again.

HOSPITAL ADVENTURES CONTINUED

I didn't feel as anxious in the ER as I usually do. Maybe I'm becoming used to it. Of course I was worried about getting involved in the mental health system again, but I felt like I had enough knowledge, or at least more knowledge than in the past, of both sides of the spectrum: medical model and anti-medical model. Something was wrong and I needed to find some kind of middleground between the two. I waited on an uncomfortable chair for a few minutes, spoke to a nurse who asked me the usual questions then took my pulse and my blood pressure, spoke to someone else who affixed my hospital bracelet, then waited some more. As I waited, I began reading Henry David Thoreau's *Walden and Other Writings*, which I would finish along with three other books during my time at the hospital.

After hanging out in the waiting room for an hour and a half, I was brought in to speak with a nurse and psychiatrist. I'd never met either of them before, as far as I could remember. This was the first time I had been brought into a cozy room with proper couches and chairs, instead of a white and blue room with a hospital bed and an IV drip.

I answered the same questions the first nurse had asked me, and more. I was a bit scared of what was going to happen. I knew I would probably be admitted to inpatient, which was why I had packed my bag, but I've never had a positive experience with a psychiatrist, and I was afraid of what he might say and what he might do.

I thought of a quote from *Beyond the Crazy House* by Pat Capponi:

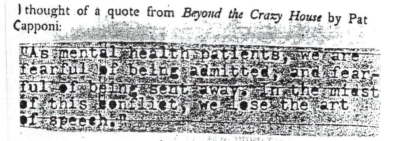

"As mental health patients, we are fearful of being admitted, and fearful of being sent away. In the midst of this conflict, we lose the art of speech."

The psychiatrist spoke more than the nurse. I tried to remain calm and I tried to explain myself articulately, explain how I felt and why I needed help. But every time I tried to speak, he would interrupt me, then ask the same question again. It was exasperating. I told him all the drugs I had tried in the past. He wanted to put me on Lithium again but I kept protesting. "That drug deadened me," I kept telling him. "I won't take it, it will paralyze me." Finally he listened. He took notes all along.

The nurse and the psychiatrist kept leaving and coming back, leaving and coming back. While they were gone, I would alternately read my book or write in my journal. I'd decided that this time I was going to write down every little thing that took place at the hospital, and I was going to keep track of everybody's names so that if somebody fucked up, I could report them by name instead of vague description.

A little after midnight, a security guard brought me up to the Mental Health Inpatient Unit. It wasn't the same security guard as usual. The nurse on duty remembered me from past admissions. She took me into the Interview Room, asked me more questions and I filled out some forms. I was given my first dose of new meds and went to bed around one o' clock in the morning, tiptoeing so as not to wake up my roommate.

ARE YOU CRAZY ENOUGH? CAN YOU OVERCOME YOUR CRAZINESS?

My therapist was anti-medical model, and I was thankful for that at the time since I had chosen to go unmedicated. But some of the language she used in what was probably an effort to get me to see my potential and work toward doing something with myself instead of hiding within my own mental health conditions and shutting out the world was kind of fucked up. I remember her saying to me several times, "You're not as crazy as you think you are," or "You're not as crazy as other people I see," or even, "Other people with your diagnosis go to work, they are doctors and lawyers and writers." I think that last one may have been the worst of all; I'm really tired of dealing with the false notion that all you have to do is get a job and you'll be okay. I don't like that, "If I can do it, so can you" mentality, As well, she would sometimes give me examples of "crazier" things other people did, or crazier things they thought and said — and those supposedly crazier thoughts and behaviours were troubles I had too. I just didn't know how to talk about them so they went mostly unnoticed. Sometimes my crazy thoughts are embarrassing to talk about, and I don't know how to bring it up, even with a therapist I trust. I'm afraid of being told to just stop thinking about it. I can't.

When I hear stories of folks with mental health conditions who have somehow managed to "overcome" (I hate that word) and do something really awesome, I feel like I am being told that I am simply not trying hard enough. Like, I should just turn on my Mental Illness Superpowers and put myself through med school or write a great novel because some guy with a similar diagnosis who I have no association with at all managed to do it.

What if things like jobs and school contribute to your craziness? What if you are literally unable to work or to attend classes? What if you have to psych yourself up for hours just to make a five-minute bike ride to the grocery store?

I used to fake sick to avoid school, ever since I was little. I used to wake up hating everything about myself and refused to leave the house. By junior high, I was intentionally showing up late to school just so I could be by myself while I gathered books from my locker, instead of surrounded by all the other girls. I left school when I was fourteen, tried several correspondence courses, gave them up quickly, stayed away from school for a few years before getting my GED. I tried going to college but gave up right away. I've had many jobs, most of which I quit in the midst of panic attacks and severe anxiety, even before I had the words to say why I was leaving. It's extremely condescending, not to mention overly simplistic, to tell me that getting a job will help me and it's also insulting to be treated as though getting an ordinary job and "contributing to society" is the ultimate goal in caring for my mental health, or that getting a job means that I am now magically stable and okay, back on track, doing what I was meant to do.

It's kind of the same thing with volunteering. It was always recommended to me to try volunteering, even though I've got a well-documented history of not being able to get along with people, of breaking down in tears in workplaces and other public places, blah blah blah. Finally, last summer, I went ahead and tried volunteering. I found a flier for the local food bank warehouse on the bulletin board at the post office, got an interview, tracked down one reference and got a friend to give me a fake reference, and got the position. On hot summer mornings, I would put on a pair of heavy borrowed steel-toed boots and ride my bike to the warehouse. I sorted and boxed thousands and thousands and thousands of items of donated foods in a small warehouse where I was the youngest person and the only girl working in a warehouse full of middle-aged men. I recognized one of them from group therapy at the hospital. The men made jokes that made me want to cry and they teased me about my bike. If boxes of cereal were deemed too damaged to donate, I'd take them home and eat them myself.

The donations came from food drives at local schools and such, but most of them were overstock from grocery stores in surrounding areas. You could always tell when the food was from a school food drive because it would be a bunch of old cans of cranberry sauce culled from the back of somebody's cupboard. When we got particularly old food, we'd announce the ridiculous expiration date; the oldest we got was a can of soup that had expired in 1999.

Anyway, with each morning that passed, I'd dread it more and more. Sometimes I'd show up late because my stomach was giving me trouble. Of course the day came along where I burst into tears and fled the building.

So my experience with volunteering was pretty much the same as all the other jobs I've had, minus the paycheque. The only job I've had that I actually liked was when I was a crossing guard; that had its drawbacks, too, of course, like being heckled by the high school kids going by everyday, and having to stand around outside during the worst weather. But it was an easy job and I got to hang out with cute kids.

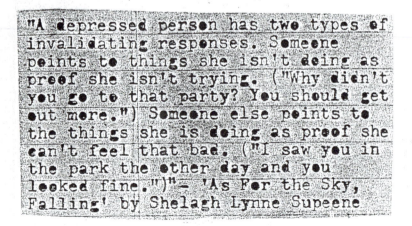

"A depressed person has two types of invalidating responses. Someone points to things she isn't doing as proof she isn't trying. ("Why didn't you go to that party? You should get out more.") Someone else points to the things she is doing as proof she can't feel that bad. ("I saw you in the park the other day and you looked fine.")"- 'As For the Sky, Falling' by Shelagh Lynne Supeene

WHAT A JAGGED LITTLE PILL

The hospital allowed me three-hour passes to go out unattended, and I used them to wander around town and hang out by the river. I'd just sit on a fallen over tree and read. Sometimes I'd go back early, feeling anxious, craving the safety of the white walls of the hospital. I felt like no matter where I went, everything was too loud. The traffic was loud, conversations were loud. In the hospital, I could hide in the quiet of my room and concentrate.

During one of my passes, I went to a used record store and found a copy of Alanis Morissette's *Jagged Little Pill*. That was one of the first cassettes I had when I was a kid. I think it was my gift for passing Grade Five. My sister and I felt pretty badass when we could finally buy albums with Parental Advisories. I'd been thinking about this album a lot lately, kept getting the songs stuck in my head but couldn't actually listen to them. Listening to this album was one of the few things I looked forward to after my discharge.

I used to get intense obsessions with musicians, start collecting all their albums and their merch, write their lyrics everywhere, read every article I could find on them and save their pictures.

But at some point, that just wasn't fun anymore. I used to have to have music playing at all times, even when I was sleeping. Now it just breaks my concentration. I don't really listen to a lot of music these days. For a while, it really seemed like all the music I was listening to was making my heart beat too fast and making me think of things I didn't want to think about, so I turned it off. Then I just kind of lost interest. I haven't paid attention to new music in years, except for when my very favourite bands put out something new. At first it was because I couldn't afford to buy all the albums I wanted to listen to or go to all the shows I wanted to see. But now I feel like there's just not much I can relate to anymore, and paying attention to what a bunch of bands are up to isn't as fun as it was when I was younger. I still look at my record collection and feel like a lot of really great albums are missing, but I no longer have a desire to track down those records, to spend wads of cash at the record store, and I am no longer concerned about needing to own certain albums as some kind of statement of who I am.

It used to be so exciting. Going to the record store on Tuesday, new release day, going straight home with the cassette or CD in my hands, ripping the plastic away, and pressing Play. The first few times I listened to a new album, I would read along with the lyrics in the booklet, read all the Thank-You's and liner notes, study all the pictures, know right away what my favourite songs were gonna be. I don't really do that anymore. I've grown content with the fact that my old favourites will probably always be my favourites, and I don't need to keep up with new stuff to feel satisfied musically. There are times when I kinda feel like I'm missing out, but it's not such a big deal anymore.

DISORDERS & DELUSIONS

Erotomania A type of delusion in which a person believes that someone else, often a stranger or celebrity, is in love with them. The person is under the impression that someone is hinting at their affection for them by sending special glances or signals their way, using telepathy, communicating via body language, and other seemingly innocuous acts, or, in the case of a celebrity, sending them messages through the media. Erotomania is sometimes referred to as the "delusion of being loved," and can be accompanied by irrational demands and jealousy.

Graphomania Also known as Scribomania, is an obsessive impulse to write. As a psychiatric diagnosis, it refers to a morbid mental condition characterized by the writing of long successions of unconnected, meaningless words. Outside of psychiatry, the word is used simply to describe the urge and need to write excessively.

Typomania An obsession with seeing one's name published; the expectation of publication.

Ecdemomania An abnormal compulsion to wander.

Planomania In psychiatry, this is defined as a morbid impulse to leave home and discard social restraints.

Delusion of Reference

A type of delusion in which a person believes that insignificant remarks, events, or objects in their environment contain special meaning for them.

Persecutory Delusions

A type of delusion in which someone believes that they are being followed, harassed, cheated, conspired against, poisoned or drugged, spied on, or attacked.

"PERSEVERENCE, PATIENCE, and POSTAGE STAMPS." – Lucy Maud Montgomery discussing the life of a writer

On Re-reading the 'Anne of Green Gables' series

Last year, I decided to re-read the *Anne of Green Gables* series by Lucy Maud Montgomery. I hadn't realized those books were going to have such an impact on me; I credit the series with keeping my spirits up throughout the year, and am not sure just how well I would have fared without them.

Anne was a staple in my childhood. Everyone in my family loved her and occasionally collected items with her likeness on them, like dolls, fancy soaps, figurines, and of course, the books. My nana still has a magnet on her fridge of a little straw hat with red braids hanging out, and my mom has a large framed picture of Anne standing in a field holding yellow flowers, a picture my sister and I gave her when we were kids. We even visited Green Gables once on an East Coast road trip when we were much younger.

While reading *Anne of Green Gables* again for the first time since childhood, I was struck by how somehow, in a way I can't really explain, the story seems to be one long metaphor for bipolar. The ups and downs and highs and lows of Anne's moods and adventures really played with the way I thought about her story as a representation of living with a mood disorder, as it had been revealed recently that LMM had.

The fascination with Anne seems to have been passed down through our family. I was recently telling my nana about how I'd been reading the latest biography (*The Gift of Wings*) of the author of the Anne series, as well as many other books. My nana was really pleased to hear that I still liked LMM and *Anne of Green Gables*. My mom loved her, my nana loved her, and her mother loved her. My nana told me about her teacher when she was a kid reading *Anne of Green Gables* out loud to her class, and said she could still hear her voice now when she thought about the books.

The biography is a heavy, 600-page epic, detailing Maud's origins and family tree; her upbringing in Prince Edward Island (the town's post office was located in her kitchen!); her struggle for an education at a time when most women were not permitted to go to college, or if they were, it was simply to pass the time while they found someone to marry; the various places she lived in after she left the Island; her family, including their struggles with depression and other mental health conditions (her husband stayed at the same mental health treatment centre as I have!); her writing habits; and her eventual suicide, which had been kept hidden so her family wouldn't have to suffer the consequences of having such stigma follow them through the rest of their lives.

Reading the Anne books throughout 2009 always brightened my spirits, no matter how low I had been feeling. Sometimes I'd read on my bedroom floor, other times I'd read down by the river, one of my favourite places to go. I hadn't realized when I began that they would have such a positive effect on me. As well as being brilliant stories in and of themselves, the books also contain the most beautiful descriptions of nature. And reading LMM's biography this spring brought back some wonderful memories of the books; I felt myself wanting to read them all over again, even though I just had. Lucy Maud Montgomery's discipline in her writing career was pretty inspiring as well; she set ambitious schedules and wrote many books within short periods of time. I wish I had the same discipline with my own writing.

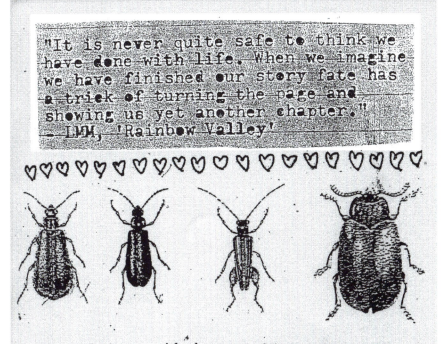

"It is never quite safe to think we have done with life. When we imagine we have finished our story fate has a trick of turning the page and showing us yet another chapter."
— LMM, 'Rainbow Valley'

(One night I met a girl who was studying psychiatry. That alone was laughable to me. I didn't talk to her much, and never saw her after that, but I overheard her conversation with someone else. She was talking about the side effects of Lithium, listing the ones she thought were the most amusing, telling them like a funny story to make her friends laugh, which they did. I was on Lithium at the time, and having a horrendous time with the side effects. The conversation was frightening to listen in on. The jokes were coming from someone who is one day going to have the power to prescribe Lithium. I want to laugh it off, but just thinking about it is infuriating.)

PAIN, PRODUCTIVITY, AND LOOKING FOR MEANING(S) IN IT ALL

I had always worried that once my depression subsided somewhat, some kind of physical pain would come along to take its place. Sure enough, something came along: Migraines were first, then an unknown condition took over, causing chronic pain in my right arm, hand, wrist, shoulder, neck, and back.

My mom always had dreadful migraines and I was afraid they'd be passed on to me. She'd alternate between sleeping it off and throwing up, and would eventually recover. I had my first migraine on January 1st, 2007. Yes, it was New Year's Day, no, I had not been drinking. I woke up in near unbearable pain and didn't know what to do. I was alone, confined to my bed. My mom called to make sure I was still alive (I was going through a rough time, to say the least), and I said yes, I was alive, but my head hurts so much I can't move. I was mad at her for calling because I just wanted to sleep. I told her about my migraine. I had no headache pills in my apartment and couldn't even think about getting out of bed and going out to buy some. So my mom came over with a bottle of ibuprofen. It was nearly a three-hour drive. She gave me the pills, stayed for a few minutes, and went home. I took the pills and went back to bed.

It was fitting that this was when my migraines would begin. It was a suitable welcome to the worst year of my life. But then that was the only migraine I had. They didn't return until last year. They would start as a throbbing pain behind my eyes, and I would see glitter and shadows, like when you press your hands hard against your eyes and see gold stars. That's always the warning sign, but I often forget. I don't realize what's coming. It gets worse and worse until I am in unbelievable pain, I am nauseas, I can't get out of bed, I am beyond irritable. I just want to be alone and hidden and asleep. I want to get out of this alive. Every time I have a migraine, I question the entire direction of my life, and feel hopeless because I am trapped in my bed. It's foolish. I shouldn't think about anything at all when I have a migraine besides making it go away, but I think about anything and everything, I make myself feel worse.

My doctor thought my birth control pills, Alesse, might be aggravating my headaches, so he switched me to Depo-Provera, a shot I get every three months. We discussed the pros and cons beforehand, the potential side effects, but I was eager to do what I could to help my head. I was tired of taking Tylenol 3's all the time, tired of migraines attacking me when I was out, when I was trying to get shit done, when I had forgotten to put a few pills in my purse. And I never liked Alesse anyway. So I got my first shot that day, and the doctor laughed when I said that I like needles. And the headaches really have subsided. I am grateful for that.

The pain on the upper right side of my body began in the winter. Suddenly I was having these shooting pains like intense pins and needles in my wrist, hand, and fingers, and eventually up my arm and across my shoulder, neck, and back; sometimes this would lead to numbness. It would get especially bad if I was writing or using the computer, and as time went on, it hurt just to hold onto a book or a utensil... pretty much anything at all, and I would also experience pain just carrying a purse., holding onto a cup, or turning a doorknob. All my doctor could do was prescribe me Tylenol 3, I saw a physiotherapist a few times while I was on inpatient, and that was helpful but only for short periods of time. I also saw a specialist who did this really neat technique that's hard to describe as it is somewhat tailored to individuals; it's kind of like massage, but also not really. Anyway, I could only see her a few times before I could no longer afford it. And it was also helpful, but again, only for short periods of time. Six months later, the pain is still persisting. There's not much I can do without hurting myself, and I have to be careful about taking medication for it because I don't want to rely on pills, nor do I want to build up an immunity and have to take more and more for it to have an effect. The weird thing is, though, that the pills have also been good for my mood; even when they don't dull physical pain, they end up giving me temporary relief from crankiness and irritability, and I find that rather than getting drowsy, I get energetic. I've also found myself taking painkillers as a preventative measure, like, sometimes I have to take a pill before sitting down to write letters; and I know that's not the healthiest thing to do, but it's pretty much what I have to do right now. I haven't got a diagnosis for this, and I'm not always able to find the time, energy, or space to do the exercises I used to do, or try yoga, etc. Sometimes I just put those things on the backburner.

Sometimes, instead of looking for ways to make the pain go away, I try to search for reasons it might be happening. Not reasons like using the computer too much and not taking good care of myself, even though those may be true, but reasons like maybe I need to quit wasting time and do things that I feel are useful and worthwhile. Maybe I need to write things that are meaningful to me, stay in touch with my close friends and not worry about everyone else. Maybe I need to learn how to stop doing things now and then and just sit down and relax; my hands need not be busy at all times.

Shortly before I went to the hospital, when I was spending my afternoons at the library, I started signing out a bunch of books on mental health. There weren't many to choose from, though there were more than I expected. Most of the books were awfully boring and stale; I've grown so accustomed to reading zines with personal experiences of mental health conditions, and examining my own, that reading statistics and descriptions of symptoms, and places you can "find help", was just not very interesting. So many books cited statistics of "lost productivity" due to mental health conditions, with no examinations of what productivity means outside of, you guessed it, having an ordinary job and contributing to society.

I have wasted so much brainspace wondering if I have been wasting my time. I feel like I have a lot of wasted years behind me. There are times when I wish I'd saved all the money I made at the jobs I had when I was a teenager, or I wish I had written more when I was younger, or I wish I hadn't wasted opportunities because I was so shy and scared. I wish I hadn't wasted so much time being crazy, being depressed, being drunk. But what's done is done. There was good stuff in the past, too, it led me to where I am today. And I haven't been "unproductive" all this time. I've just been productive in ways a lot of folks don't bother thinking about, or learning about.

MAKING CONNECTIONS AT THE HOSPITAL, AND THEN LEAVING

Leaving the hospital is always stressful for me; I don't feel ready to leave, but there's not much more they can do for me, so it's time to go. The local inpatient unit is short-term, and they like folks to leave as soon as possible. There just aren't enough beds for everyone. The psychiatrist started talking about my discharge plan on my first day there. I told him it was too soon to think about it, but he continued to bring it up each time we spoke, and I continued to burst into tears, and then laugh at myself for crying so much.

I didn't want to talk to anyone while I was at the hospital. The unit no longer had internet access, which was a relief; I didn't have visitors, I didn't write letters; I didn't make phone calls until it became necessary. I wanted no communication at all. I wanted to get away. I still do sometimes. It's a feeling I get often. I'm learning how to handle it.

When I first arrived, I kept my head down and didn't really talk to anyone; I wasn't there to socialize. If someone tried to talk to me, I'd scowl, or I'd shrug my shoulders and walk away. I spent most of my time in my room. In the past, the nurses had always tried to get me out of my room, not understanding that hanging out in the common area or diningroom was not necessarily good for me; it was stressful and tended to make me feel much worse. This time, they generally left me alone. But eventually, I started coming out of my room more often, I began eating meals with the others, and I began talking to a few people. My roommate, who annoyed me at first with her persistent question-asking, turned out to be pretty sweet, and we ended up talking more just before she left; she gave me a worry stone to hold onto when I was feeling down. I held onto it while watching traffic from the window. Watching the traffic made me feel intensely nervous and sad, especially at night.

I also met a guy who was into the same music as me, so we talked a lot about that; we had funny little things in common, like we both had the same favourite Nirvana song, and we were both at the same David Bowie concert a few years ago. We wrote down recommendations for one another. Another guy I met was fond of telling stories, and we ended up talking a lot, too. He showed up at my room one night with a little stuffed bunny he had brought up from the gift shop. It was the lone black bunny amongst all the white ones; he said he felt bad that no one came to visit me, and wanted to get me something. My next roommate looked familiar, but we didn't figure out where we knew each other from until the day I left. It turned out she had babysat my sister and I once when we were kids, and was best friends with our best friend's older sister, so we used to hang out at the same house quite a bit.

A few of us exchanged contact information, but we don't really keep in touch very well, or at all. In some cases, mental health conditions and substance abuse problems are pretty much the only things we share in common, so it can be hard to connect outside of the world of hospitals and such. But I still think about them often; I wonder what they're up to, I wonder how they're getting by. Time passes in a really strange way in the hospital. One day feels like a week. You become attached to folks so easily, you're sad when they leave, then you forget them after only a day or two.

I never feel safe with psychiatrists. I've just never met one I liked, and I think the way they work is really fucked up. When I was at the hospital, I was told absolutely nothing about my medication; I wasn't even told what I was taking until I asked. I wrote down the names of the pills so I could research them later. I know most folks probably wanna get out of that place as soon as possible, but I fought to stay a little longer; I didn't feel safe going home when they wanted me to, and I begged and pleaded to stay a few more days. At the last minute, they let me stay. But on my last day, I was kicked out early because there was someone in the emergency room who needed a bed. That messed with my head a little; I have a lot of issues with feeling unwanted and abandoned, so to be kicked out like that was really uncomfortable, even though it was of course inevitable that I had to leave. So I left. I had been there fifteen days.

When I got out, it rained for a week. All my plans to keep myself alive were spoiled, as they were all outdoor plans. The house was depressing. Everything felt the same as the day I went to the ER. I was still sad and angry. I had begun cutting myself after nearly a year of not. I'm trying not to feel guilty that it still makes me feel better. After awhile, the meds kicked in. They knocked me out at night and kept me asleep until sunrise. I began keeping a regular routine for pretty much the first time in my life, and I've been sleeping better than I have since childhood, which is obviously good for my crazy brain. I've become a morning person after a lifetime of insomnia and night owl-ism. I like waking up early, making coffee, reading a good book as the rest of the town gets started on their days. I like listening to the birds singing; I have always loved their songs, but it's nice to hear them as I'm waking up rather than when I'm going to bed. Routine and meds are basically saving me right now. It's not easy, though; of course there are times when I'd rather stay in bed, times when I have no energy, times when everything seems pointless. And there are many nights when the thought of staying up 'til sunrise working on projects, reading, writing, thinking, making plans, writing lists, seems awfully tempting. But I'm afraid that if I fall back into those old patterns, I'll lose what I have gained. So I keep getting out of bed.

I'm not anti-psychiatry, and I never was, not even when I wasn't taking meds, when I thought that was healthier for me (and it was, at the time(s), but things change). It's cool to choose to be med-free for yourself, but I just can't deal with folks who think everyone should be unmedicated; I think it's condescending and ridiculous. But I do sometimes feel like I'm anti-psychiatrist simply because I've never met one I liked. I've never met a psychiatrist who didn't leave me feeling angry and frustrated over and over again. We all have to find ways to live in a world that doesn't always seem too welcoming. Sometimes those ways involve medication, sometimes caffeine, sometimes alcohol, sometimes bike rides, sometimes being by yourself... You just gotta find a way to take care of yourself, no matter what.

♡♡ ♡ ♡ ♡♡ ♡ ♡ ♡♡ ♡ ♡♡ ♡ ♡♡ ♡ ♡ ♡♡

HOW THE BABY-SITTERS CLUB GOT ME INTO WRITING AND SNAIL MAIL

The townhouses my mom, sister, and I lived in when we were kids had a bank of mailboxes was a quick walk away, either around a corner and down the cobblestone path from our front door, or cutting through the grass from the back door. Finding mail in our little box was exciting enough even when it wasn't for me; but the best days were the days when the Big Key was in our mailbox. The Big Key was an ordinary key with a blue plastic card fastened to it, about the size of a credit card, and it had instructions on how to use the key and how to return it.

The Big Key opened one of the Big Mailboxes. If you had the Big Key, that meant you'd been delivered a package that didn't fit in the ordinary ones. The bank of mailboxes contained a few larger ones along the bottom, and you'd try the Big Key in each lock until one opened.

I've always had trouble using keys, even today. Locks either don't wanna lock or don't wanna unlock. If I couldn't get the key to open any of the mailboxes, I'd have to get my mom to give it a try.

It was in the Big Mailboxes that I got all my BSC membership swag. I'd convinced my mom to buy me a membership to the Baby-Sitters Club Fan Club. I always got really excited when the Scholastic fliers were handed out around the class and when we had book fairs downstairs in the Green Room. I'd write up a list of all the books I wanted then cross them off one-by-one until I had a manageable list that my mom could afford.

The BSC membership stuff was shipped in cardboard box with that classic red Scholastic logo. It was such a thrill every time a package arrived. I don't remember how often the packages were sent — perhaps every month or every three months, for a year or so. Each parcel came in a clear plastic bag with white plastic handles that snapped shut and the BSC logo printed in blue. There was a newsletter, also printed in blue, and even an official membership card. There were special treats in each package as well, most of which I've forgotten by now, but I do remember a pencil with the BSC logo, a large pink heart-shaped pencil-top eraser that I used for display purposes only, and some stationery, too (which I probably used to write letters to my best friend after she moved away, and to my sister, when we affixed homemade mailboxes to our bedroom doors). And there were the books, of course. Three books in each shipment. By the time my fascination with *The Baby-Sitters Club* came to an end, I had more than one hundred books.

For a long time, one of my most cherished possessions was *The Baby-Sitters Club Chain Letter Book*, a hardcover, full-colour book filled with dozens of letters, postcards, and pictures the members of the BSC sent back and forth while Kristy was in the hospital and the others were on vacation. I also had the Postcard Book, a collection of postcards to be pulled out along the dotted lines, mailed or collected.

"P.S.: I hope you know what S.W.A.K means," writes Karen in a letter to Kristy. "If you do not, DON'T ask a boy about it. I will tell you when you come home."

Everything was written in their trademark unique handwriting: i's dotted with circles and hearts, misspelled words scribbled out and written again... I don't have my copy anymore, but I think there may even have been a love letter or two from Mary Ann and Logan.

I always wondered what Ann M. Martin was like in real life, and what her house looked like. I used to imagine visiting her, just showing up on her doorstep to give her a copy of my manuscript and discuss the art of writing. In my mind, her house would of course be located on the same street as Kristy's home. I had a distinct vision of what her front entrance would look like, but could never see past it.

I wrote a lot of stories inspired by the BSC when I was a kid. Sometimes the girls from the BSC would be in my stories, but most times the stories were about similar girls that I had sort of made up. I didn't just write the stories; I drew the covers as well.

Eventually I grew out of it, shortly before the series came to an end. I hid my 100+ BSC books in a box and once I'd decided for good that I didn't want them anymore, I sold them at a yard sale. Many of my BSC books had been acquired at yard sales. My nana used to carry a list with her of all the books I was in need of, and whenever she found them at yard sales, she'd check the numbers of each book and bring back the ones I hadn't read yet. When I decided to get rid of mine, my mom and my nana tried to talk me out of it, but I was resolute; I had no more use for them.

I never finished reading the series. I stopped reading around the time Abby joined the gang, and although I don't remember much about her anymore, I do remember that I liked her enough to name characters in my own stories after her. Every time I find them in used bookstores, I consider building up my BSC collection again and re-reading them. It might be neat to read the full series and see what happens in the end.

♡ ♡ ♡ ♡ ♡ ♡ ♡ ♡ ♡ ♡ ♡ ♡ ♡ ♡ ♡ ♡ ♡

"Psychiatry demands that individuals, not society, change. If a patient is abused, poor, uneducated or exploited at work, psychiatry considers therapy to be successful when she has adjusted to her situation. She will be pronounced cured when she declares herself, or the doctor declares her, willing and able to go back to whatever situation drove her crazy in the first place." - 'As For the Sky, Falling' by Shelagh Lynne Supeene

Mental Health (and the) Concept of HOME.

Robert's Street Social Centre

5684 ROBERTS STREET

This is a flier for the workshop I held.

Maranda Elizabeth will be facilitating a discussion on the concept of home and how our mental health affects how and where we live. Questions to consider might be: Where do you feel the most at home? How do mental health and personal income dictate how you live? Do you ever feel homesick? Is the way you live accepted by conventional society; and do you want it to be? This will be an informal discussion, with hopes of creating a collaborative zine based on ideas and inspiration that may come from our conversations. Prompts will be provided as well as readings of excerpts from zines on similar topics.

FRIDAY, JULY 9th ♡ 7-9 pm

Did you experience any of the following symptoms? If yes, fill in the circle.
Anxiety
Irritability
Mood swings

MENTAL HEALTH & THE CONCEPT OF HOME (WORKSHOP)

During my residency at the Roberts
Street Social Centre, I held a workshop on mental health and the concept
of home. Just as the time of the workshop was approaching, I had the urge
to cut my hair, so I asked one of the
folks in the house if she was good at
hair-cutting, she said yeah, and I got
out my scissors. We chopped my hair off
in the backyard and I let it fly away
for theX birds to use in their nests.
(A few days later, I cut a couple more
inches off.) Folks started showing up
for the workshop as I was having my
hair cut, and we decided to stay outside since the weather was so beautiful. We brought out a table, some papers and pens, set up a few chairs, and
waited for everyone else to come over.
I felt nervous, of course. I'd never
held a workshop before and wasn't sure
what to expect. But sometimes I just
have to say to myself, Fuck Shyness,
and go for it. We had a great turn-out

especially for a Friday evening. There
were probably about twelve of us there.
I introduced myself, told everyone about my zines, why I came to the RSSC,
and why I was doing this workshop. I
talk/write about mental health and the
concept of home a lot, but I don't always hear the two being examined togeth
er, so I thought we could have some interesting conversations along these lines. Everyone else was then encouraged
to introduce themselves and share why
they came out to the workshop, what the
were hoping to talk about, etc. It was
great that everyone seemed so open and
willing to share. I told them that I am
shy and awkward and a little scatter-
brained, and definitely needed everyone
to participate in the conv ersation and
support one another.
I brought a few zines with me to show
everyone, zines I thought suited the
theme of the workshop. I thought perhaps the zines would inspire conversations and creativity; I had planned on
having us complete a little compzine by
the end of the workshop, underestimat-
ing the amount of time we had to work
on such a project. We didn't make a
zine, but had fun taking notes, drawing

ete., while we shared our stories, and I
was given a few of those creations at th
end in hopes of putting them together in
to something we can show to others and
hold onto.
Listening to everyone talk about their
homes, their lives, their worries, etc.,
was really wonderful. It seemed like so
many folks had spent a lot of time traveling, and nearly everyone had left
their hometowns. I think most of those
who attended were currently living in
Halifax, though some were just passing
through. Many stories were shared, though the conversations tended to veer
away from the topic of mental health. A
few of us tried to steer it back a litt
le bit, but it just wasn't happening. I
know mental health can be difficult to
talk about, especially amongst folks
you don't know very well, or have just
met. I don't worry too much anymore about talking about things like anxiety,
depression, meds, hospitals, living sit
uations, etc. , but I know that so many
are still struggling, still keeping it
a secret.
One topic we kept returning to was that
of community. It seemed to be at the

forefront of everyone's minds. I find it
hard to talk about community because I
have never felt a part of one, and am
quite envious of those who do. Community
seemed to be of utmost importance in the
place you feel is your home. When I thin
k of community, I think of the future.
Community seems far away to me, something I am still searching for, something
I hope to cultivate over time and finally understand what it is that other
folks mean when they speak of having a
supportive community.
We also talked about dealing with various living situations involving roommates and co-ops, reasons for choosing to
leave your hometown, comfort levels with
being near or far from your family, bein
misfits / targets of harassment, and
gentrification (especially in the North
End of Halifax). I wish I could remember
our exact words. These were all much-
needed discussions, and could have gone
on indefinitely.
Funnily enough, I felt very, very anxious throughout the workshop; certainly
more anxious than I felt throughout my
Halifax adventures up until then. I th-

ink I was just worried that everyone would be expecting certain things from me,
and I wouldn't be able to provide that;
also, I never feel like I am a good con-
versationalist. I need time to think about thingsm write them down, work through them. Otherwise, my mind goes blank.
There was a lot I wanted to discuss that
I just plain forget until the workshop
was over, even though I had brought notes with me. There were more questions I
wanted to ask, stories I wanted to hear.
But in the days after the workshop, folk
s were approaching me to tell me what a
great time they had, how much they were
glad for the opportunity to discuss these things; I was alsomtold that I appeared very confident and on top pf things, which I appreciated because I had
not really felt that way.

Halifax is a place that feels like a
home, even in the very short time that I
have been here. Although I have felt lik
e a bit of an outsider since everyone
around here has all these connections

and memories and histories together, an
I am new here and only around temporarily, I also feel welcome here, I feel
comfortable, I feel confident. I have

been seriously considering moving here a few years down the road. Later this summer, I will be moving (again), and perhaps that place will be the one that feels like a home, at least for a time.

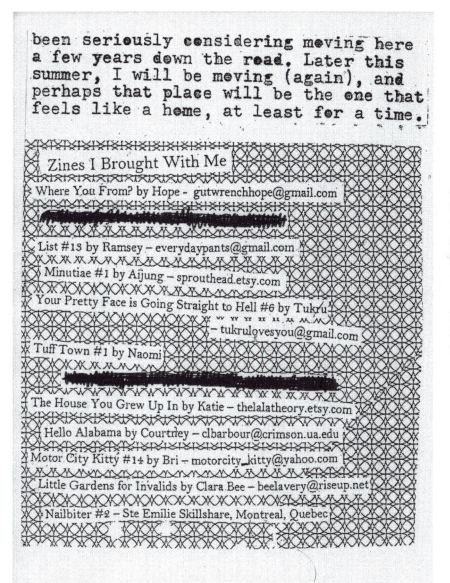

Zines I Brought With Me

Where You From? by Hope – gutwrenchhope@gmail.com

List #13 by Ramsey – everydaypants@gmail.com

Minutiae #1 by Aijung – sprouthead.etsy.com

Your Pretty Face is Going Straight to Hell #6 by Tukru – tukrulovesyou@gmail.com

Tuff Town #1 by Naomi

The House You Grew Up In by Katie – thelalatheory.etsy.com

Hello Alabama by Courtney – clbarbour@crimson.ua.edu

Motor City Kitty #14 by Bri – motorcity_kitty@yahoo.com

Little Gardens for Invalids by Clara Bee – beelavery@riseup.net

Nailbiter #2 – Ste Emilie Skillshare, Montreal, Quebec

OUTRO OUTRO OUTRO OUTRO OUTRO OUTRO

There is so much I have left out of this zine. I wanted to write about how I have been struggling with whether or not to apply the term 'disabled' to myself. I've read so much about the lack of folks with mental health conditions identifying as disabled, and I have also read a lot about folks with visible disabilities feeling like they are being erased from the discussion as examinations of invisible disabilities seem to be very prominent right now. I don't want to silence anyone, but I do need to talk about my own experiences.

I also wanted to write about language I find problematic. Like, using words such as 'crazy' when what you mean to say is 'ridiculous', 'weird', 'wonderful', 'odd', 'busy', etc. Or using the word 'lame' when what you meant to say was 'inconvenient', 'disappointing', or 'annoying'. I know it's been written about so much already, but seriously. Choose your words wisely.

Sometimes I call the hospital my second home, but I don't really want to feel that way forever. I don't want to constantly be expecting nervous breakdowns, debilitating anxiety, intense depression to take over. It's hard to make plans when you're always expecting them to fall apart, always feeling like you can't really be counted on for too long, just in case.

It's almost becoming a joke to me, going in and out of the hospital, going on and off drugs, feeling really high then feeling really low. I don't want to follow these patterns for the rest of my life. If I had some kind of stability, if I had a reason to stay away from the hospital, if I had something to lose, I might feel better. I have been so terrified of committing to anything, of making big decisions, because I've got a history of fucking up. But I'm getting to a point where maybe I need to commit to something after all. Maybe I need to make plans, maybe I need something concrete to stay well for. And when I do get down, I don't want to go as low, I want to recover quicker and quicker until it doesn't scare me anymore.

THANK YOU! I can't thank the folks at the RSSC enough. I don't want to name names because I'll leave someone out and feel bad, though I do feel the need to say special thanks to Capp, Sarah, Elise, Jess, Jake, Laura, and everyone who introduced themselves and asked about my project. Thanks for picking me up at the bus station, showing me around town, offering support & space & supplies, and allowing me to feel at home. Thank you for creating such a wonderful zine library, providing cheap photocopies, and cultivating such a rad atmosphere. I'll probably cry a little when I leave.

If you wanna learn more about the RSSC, please visit robertsstreet.org.

©

My address right now is Maranda Elizabeth Maranda Elizabeth six months, but if you're writing after that, P.O. Box 1689 Guelph, Ontario N1H 6Z9 Canada

schoolformaps@gmail.com / schoolformaps.etsy.com

46

INTRO

Hello 2011! That number sounds so futuristic.

So much happened this year. It was truly the best year I've had so far, and I am so thankful for all the good that came my way, especially after the last few years being so rough. I am trying to hold onto my sense of wonder and magic and surround myself in positive energy so 2011 will be even better. I am believing hard in the universe and my own self.

I decided to declare 2010 my Year of Change. I made resolutions and, more than one year later, have been doing my best to stand by them. I made a lot of changes in 2010, and I am continuing to do that this year as well.

One of last year's resolutions was to work on fiction daily. I really did work on fiction most days, and that was probably the biggest contributor to my overall good spirits. Fiction is where my heart is, and that is what I have been focusing on. Moving into the New Year, my goals are to continue working on fiction everyday, and to write one short story each month, as well as to complete the current draft of the novel I'm working on. These goals are attainable, I know I can do it. I'm learning how to set concrete goals, and to actually do them, rather than just writing them down and thinking about them and talking about them and hoping about them (even though I do those things as well – visualization, yeah!).

This zine is about some of the best times I had in 2010, and how the new year's been going. As always, please write letters!

Maranda ♡ ♡

TWO WEEKS IN HALIFAX

Halifax was a city I'd only been to once before, and even then, not *to* it, but *through* it. When I was seven, my mom, sister, and I went on a road trip to the East Coast for a cousin's wedding. I remember stopping at my nana and poppa's beforehand; they had purchased a few dresses and let my sister and I choose which ones we'd like to wear to the wedding. So I chose a soft, sleeveless white dress with blue floralprint, and she chose the matching dress in pink.

I remember the trip in small glimpses. Sitting in the car for long periods of time always made me feel sick. One night, we slept in the car, and I couldn't believe my neck could be so sore. Another night, we stayed in a motel, and I had nightmares about a man breaking into the room.

We took the ferry to Prince Edward Island. There was an arcade, and all the boys would spit on their hands while playing so no one else could play the games. At PEI, we slept in the car again, though this time it was parked in someone's driveway, and the seats were folded down so we could stretch our legs a little. Other folks slept in bedrooms, the livingroom, the front porch, maybe even the kitchen. I remember my sister and I tagging along with our aunt and cousin for bridesmaid dress fittings. The dresses were pink gingham. I don't remember the wedding itself, which is a little bit surprising because when I was a kid, I thought brides were celebrities.

That was the only trip I ever took growing up. Vacations were for people with money. I've never traveled much. Nova Scotia and Prince Edward Island when I was seven, a Greyhound to Pennsylvania when I was twenty, a couple trips to Ottawa and Montreal to visit my sister over the years, a trip to Kingston, and various trips to London, Ontario. Oh, and I used to visit Guelph a lot before I moved here.

Each year, the Roberts Street Social Centre, also known as the Anchor Archive, invites writers and artists to stay for a two-week residency throughout the months of June – September. In the early days of 2010, I was feeling a little hopeless. Well, not hopeless, but maybe kind of aimless, like I had no direction, no goals. My moving plans kept falling apart, I was getting annoyed with myself and my bad habits, and my faith in zines was faltering. I had to get out of my house, I had to get into a different headspace, but I didn't know where to go.

I applied for a residency at the Roberts Street Social Centre, and promised myself not to get my hopes up. I didn't even tell anyone until a friend of mine told me she had applied, and I confessed that I had, too. When we discussed our projects, I thought for sure she'd get in and I wouldn't. The reason I didn't tell anyone was not only because I didn't want to get my hopes up, but because I didn't want anyone to know how disappointed I was either.

But then I got an email.

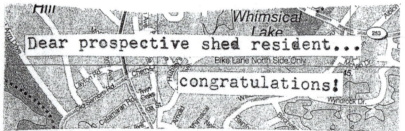

I gasped aloud, all alone in my room. I read the email at least five times, probably more. But then I started to worry that it was all a mistake, and I waited for a second message, an apology and a withdrawal of the invitation. That's how low my self-esteem was, I guess. I couldn't believe that anyone would ever choose me, that they would like my project proposal, that they would invite me to another province and put me up for two weeks to work on it. I read that email over and over again for the next few days, stunned. And I began writing a list of everything to bring with me. I didn't forget anything. I even went out and bought a bikini, even though I didn't know how to swim, because I knew I had to see the ocean. And I listened to CBC Radio Halifax: the music, the weather, the traffic, the talk, everything. I waited for months and months and months not really believing I was going until I was actually there.

I went to Montreal first. My sister lives there and any opportunity we get to hang out, we do, now that we live so far away and can't just drop in at one another's places. I sat in the car for five hours listening to Amy Winehouse and Bif Naked before we finally got there. Montreal is all about good food, pretty things, lots of wandering... I have a habit of spending a little more than I'd like to when I'm traveling because I just can't resist yummy food and thrift stores and shelves full of notebooks. It's actually a problem for me and I need to work on it.

I've always thought it would be cool to have some kind of yard sale / zine fair / crafty times in my apartment, and just invite folks on up to buy stuff and sell stuff and trade stuff and make stuff. When I was in Montreal, we found these girls who were holding a vintage clothing sale in their downtown apartment. We went upstairs and rummaged through their hangers and trunks and admired pretty dresses. I got a purple halter-top with red polkadots for $1.

My bus to Halifax was an early one. I didn't know if I should sleep a little bit or just stay up all night. I ended up passing out on the couch in my clothes for an hour or so, waking up before my alarm went off. I forgot to brush my teeth. I overpacked my bags and at the last minute, left some stuff behind at my sister's so that I'd have more room in my backpack; I knew I'd be bringing back zines and books. So I unloaded my purple Walkperson, a bunch of cassettes, the notebooks and stationery I'd purchased the day before, and some clothes I didn't think I'd need. It was still dark when we left.

My sister and I took a bus downtown, and when the transfer didn't show up, I kind of panicked. We stood around for a long time, hoping it was just late, and as the sky turned that funny shade of blue that shines just before the sun rises, we watched wedding guests file out of a building across the street, poofy dresses and so much laughter. One guy backed his car into another car, and nobody seemed to notice, so he just inched up a little and didn't say anything. It must have been a good party, to last 'til after five o' clock in the morning. I was still worried, though. I worry very easily while traveling, afraid that one minor thing will ruin the trip. *What if the bus doesn't show up? What if I miss the Greyhound? When will the next bus show up? What if every bus in the world disappears and my plans are canceled?* My body ached so much from carrying my luggage; I knew that as soon as I took off my backpack and stretched, the bus would show up, and sure enough, I set my backpack down on the sidewalk, and there was the bus chugging along. We made it to the station safely, waited in the longest line-up, hugged goodbye, and I was off.

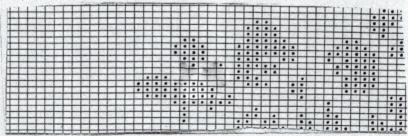

Windowseat! The last one on the bus and I got it! I seriously can't travel by bus if I don't get the windowseat, otherwise I get sick and headachey and cranky and just really gross. Montreal to Halifax, three transfers, seventeen hours. I packed Arrowroot cookies, saltine crackers, cantaloupe, strawberries, juice, and water. I might have brought an avocado sandwich, but I don't remember. Unfortunately, the man who sat beside me elbowed me the whole way and spread his legs too far so they touched mine, even though there was plenty of room for the both of us. I'm not yet assertive enough to tell people to stay out of my space, so I just sighed and passive-aggressively nudged him back and apologized not very politely. I napped on and off, the kind of sleep you get on a bus when you don't really fall asleep at all, and you have dreams while you are still aware of everyone around you, and every bump in the road wakes you up, and you hurt your neck real bad. The first transfer was in Ste. Foy. I was grateful to be away from that man, but lo and behold, on the next bus there he was, and he had actually saved a seat for me. I would have appreciated his kindness if he hadn't been all up in my personal space. He gave me the windowseat, at least. As the bus got going, he tried to strike up a conversation, and I was relieved when we realized that he only spoke French and I only spoke English. I always feel like an ignorant asshole for not knowing French when I'm in Quebec, but this time, it finally worked out in my favour. He was quiet the rest of the way and didn't sit too close.

From there, we headed to Riviére du Loup. The landscape changed, suddenly much more hills and lush trees and green everywhere. Wildflowers, rivers, people-watching. I knew nothing about the towns we were transferring in, but was curious. What is each town like? What is each town's reputation in the province? What beautiful sites am I missing by simply passing through, seeing nothing but the parking lot of a bus station? We passed through quite a few quaint little towns with pretty houses, churches, and quite a few Virgin Mary statuettes.

I brought along the *Doris* zine anthology to read on the bus, as well as *Swann* by Carol Shields, *Euphoria* by Connie Galt, and some zines from Fight Boredom distro that I got while hanging out in Montreal, including *Nothing Rhymes* and *Nailbiter*.

The man beside me got off in Ste. Foy, so I got to sit by myself from there to Moncton, then from Moncton to Halifax. I finally arrived just after midnight. It's a little disorienting to arrive in a new city in the dark, but I knew there'd be plenty of time for exploring later. I just wanted to breathe and to sleep.

Canadians in general, but East Coasters in particular, have a reputation of total politeness. It's not exactly true, at least not in my experience, but it really did seem true when I was in Nova Scotia. Little things, like, on the bus, they'd tell you when we were getting close to the station and remind you to call your friends and family to come pick you up. A couple of the stations we went to were new, and one woman was really upset when she got there and realized she'd given her friend the wrong address to pick her up, and didn't have a cell phone to contact them. It was midnight and she didn't have a ride and we were on the outskirts of some town, not close to anything. So the bus driver stayed until she was able to contact someone, and didn't continue our trip until someone had come to pick her up. In Ontario, I think they'd just leave you behind to fend for yourself.

Capp picked me up at the bus station, and we spotted one another right away, even though neither of us knew what the other one looked like. Zinesters will be zinesters, I guess. We stowed my luggage in the trunk of a borrowed car then made our way over to the Roberts Street Social Centre. I'd barely slept in the last twenty-four hours.

I left my stuff in the shed then came into the house for a tour. My first glimpse as the kitchen light was switched on was a little mouse in the cupboard scurrying into a bag of flour. Maybe not the best welcome ever, but I was so taken in by the beauty of the place and the fact that I was finally here that I just thought it was cute, and hoped it was the only one.

When I woke up on my first morning, I had no clue where I was. It was like when you've just moved and you wake up confused, but at least you're in your own bed. Nothing about the shed was familiar, and it took me a few moments to figure out where I was. When I got out of bed and went into the house, there were a bunch of excited kids rehearsing for a play. So cute.

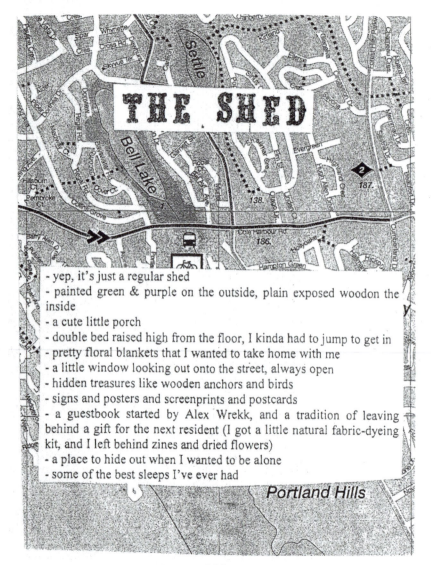

THE SHED

- yep, it's just a regular shed
- painted green & purple on the outside, plain exposed wood on the inside
- a cute little porch
- double bed raised high from the floor, I kinda had to jump to get in
- pretty floral blankets that I wanted to take home with me
- a little window looking out onto the street, always open
- hidden treasures like wooden anchors and birds
- signs and posters and screenprints and postcards
- a guestbook started by Alex Wrekk, and a tradition of leaving behind a gift for the next resident (I got a little natural fabric-dyeing kit, and I left behind zines and dried flowers)
- a place to hide out when I wanted to be alone
- some of the best sleeps I've ever had

Portland Hills

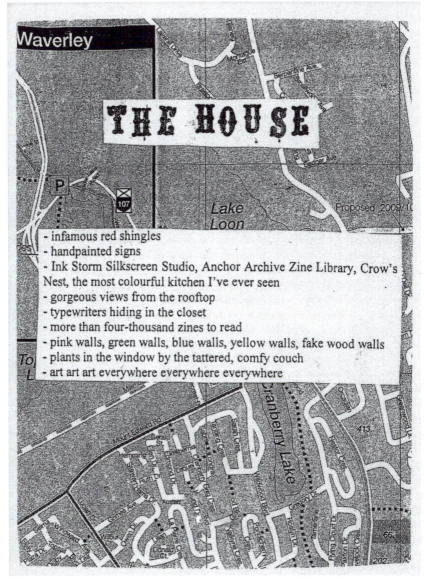

THE HOUSE

- infamous red shingles
- handpainted signs
- Ink Storm Silkscreen Studio, Anchor Archive Zine Library, Crow's Nest, the most colourful kitchen I've ever seen
- gorgeous views from the rooftop
- typewriters hiding in the closet
- more than four-thousand zines to read
- pink walls, green walls, blue walls, yellow walls, fake wood walls
- plants in the window by the tattered, comfy couch
- art art art everywhere everywhere everywhere

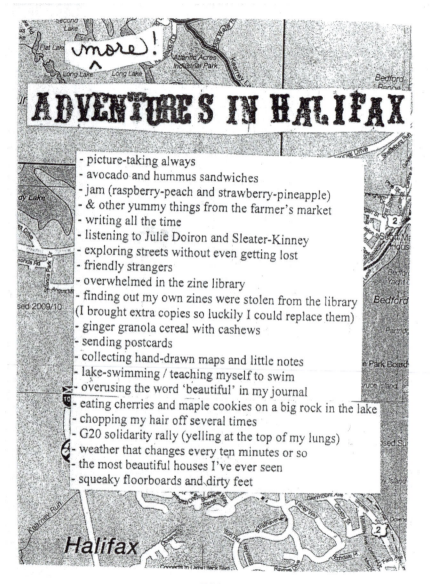

^ more!

ADVENTURES IN HALIFAX

- picture-taking always
- avocado and hummus sandwiches
- jam (raspberry-peach and strawberry-pineapple)
- & other yummy things from the farmer's market
- writing all the time
- listening to Julie Doiron and Sleater-Kinney
- exploring streets without even getting lost
- friendly strangers
- overwhelmed in the zine library
- finding out my own zines were stolen from the library
(I brought extra copies so luckily I could replace them)
- ginger granola cereal with cashews
- sending postcards
- collecting hand-drawn maps and little notes
- lake-swimming / teaching myself to swim
- overusing the word 'beautiful' in my journal
- eating cherries and maple cookies on a big rock in the lake
- chopping my hair off several times
- G20 solidarity rally (yelling at the top of my lungs)
- weather that changes every ten minutes or so
- the most beautiful houses I've ever seen
- squeaky floorboards and dirty feet

Halifax

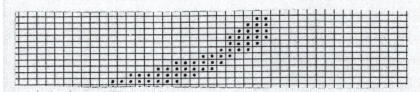

When I finished my zine, I decided to throw an Ice Cream Social Launch Party. I thought it would be cool to hang up a bunch of streamers and balloons and stuff, and was even able to borrow an ice cream maker from someone so I could make soy ice cream from scratch. What a dream! The decorations didn't work out, and neither did the ice cream, but I had a wonderful time anyway.

The ice cream maker was basically a metal container within a plastic bucket with a crank on top. I threw in the ice, soy milk, raspberries, strawberries, bananas, sugar, and salt, and started cranking away. As folks gathered for the launch, everybody took a turn at churning the ice cream. But each time we checked on it, it was still just soy milk and frozen berries. No ice cream. We kept churning. The reading went on without the ice cream... Elise read from a zine called *One Way Ticket* by Julian in Montreal, Sarah read from *Ice Cream* zine by Cindy Crabb, and I read from the zine I had just finished, of course. We held the reading out in the backyard, and I think maybe twenty or so people showed up. I got shaky when I read, as always.

The ice cream never truly came together, so I served what I called Frozen Fruit Soup instead: a messy conglomeration of cold cold soy milk, frozen fruit, and crunched up ice cream cones in a bowl. Delicious. It was a recipe adventure, rather than a recipe disaster.

The day before I left, I finally went to the ocean. We drove over the bridge and through Dartmouth to a small town called Lawrencetown. Driving along an ordinary road, then suddenly you reach the top of a hill, and as you curve down, the ocean expands before you, blue water, blue skies, blue everything, so gorgeous. I gasped and kind of freaked out a little. I couldn't wait to get out of the car.

Just the sound of the waves was amazing. That's not something I get to hear everyday. We walked along the boardwalk, up a set of stairs, then down and onto the beach. Soft, warm sand and rocks everywhere. I took my shoes off. We laid down our blankets and soaked up some sun before daring ourselves to go into the water. I put my shoes back on to protect myself from the rocks, then set them aside again when we reached the water. I dipped my toes in first, and it was so much colder than I'd expected it to be! I shivered and wrapped my arms around myself, but still trudged on, wanting to see how deep I could get. I went in up to my waist even though I still had my clothes on. My skirt got soaked. I was nearly screaming at the cold waves, desperate to swim though I knew I couldn't. So many others were in the water, kids and surfers and tourists. I went back to my red gingham blanket, collecting little rocks on the way back, one for my mom and several for myself. I took off my clothes and lounged in my bikini. Sitting on my blanket, I dug through the sand for something to do with my hands and found a lavender seashell. Along the beach, I found even more.

All day long Elsa sat by the sea, waiting for nightfall and the return of her brothers. But she was not alone, for in the form of a swan the youngest brother stayed to keep her company.

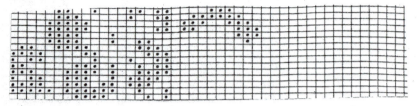

When I was feeling more confident, I went back to the water, deeper this time, letting the waves crash over me, feeling stones and seaweed against my legs, and losing my balance more than once. The strength of the waves was incredible. I don't know why I thought the ocean would be calmer. It's powerful. It's loud and it's beautiful. Jess and I held hands so that we wouldn't fall. I was afraid of the waves stealing my glasses and carrying them off to sea, but I couldn't take them off or I wouldn't be able to see. Every time another wave came, I thought, *This will be the one that sucks me under*. I could no longer balance on my feet with the waves hitting me and the rocks beneath, so I fell to my knees, and then I half-swam half-crawled back to the edge of the water, sat down, and took in the ocean from a safer distance. A wave would wash over me then go out, leaving me tangled in seaweed and picking up more rocks for my collection. If I saw a rock and missed it before the next wave, it would be gone forever. When I licked my lips, I tasted salt. I never wanted to leave.

Walking away from the water, I continued listening to the waves. I didn't want to take my eyes off the sea, but I had to look down to make sure not to hurt my feet. The ocean might have saved me a little bit, as these things sometimes do. I thought, *The waves are enough to keep me alive. How can I leave a world with such magical bodies of water?*

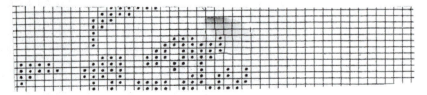

July 17th, 2010

Last night-time walk in Halifax, last night-time sleep. There is a lot to contemplate; perhaps I will have time to write while I'm on the bus, or maybe not 'til I get home. I am bursting with ideas on how I want to write and how I want to live. I've never felt as good as I've felt these last two weeks, and I need to hold on to that, be patient in Lindsay, and carry it with me to Guelph.

I thought I'd cry when it came time to leave Halifax. I knew those two weeks were going to fly right by, and I was so consumed with making sure I got the most out of every single minute that I didn't even want to sleep. I explored as many streets as possible, took hundreds of pictures, read as many zines as I could (though not as many as I wanted), had so many excellent conversations with everyone... I didn't want to leave. In fact, I very seriously considered moving there. What stopped me was the fact that I had just signed a lease in Guelph, and I thought all the paperwork and the physical act of moving to another province would just be way too complicated. So I packed my bags and said my goodbyes. My bags were very heavy. I'd gotten so many books and zines while I was there that I had to mail my clothes back to my home, unable to carry everything all at once. I did the seventeen-hour bus ride all over again, and my sister met me at the Montreal bus station. From Montreal, we rode with our mom to Toronto to catch the very end of a family reunion, then made it back to Lindsay. In thirty-six hours, I slept only two. I accidentally brought the keys to the Roberts Street Social Centre home with me and had to mail them back. Those two weeks in Halifax, I wish I could keep them in my pocket and pull them out whenever I need them.

LAST DAYS IN LINDSAY

You know what? I was really scared of going back to Lindsay. Terrified. I was afraid that after experiencing the pure wonderfulness of Halifax, going back to Lindsay, even for just a few weeks, would suffocate me. I was afraid all the good energy I'd absorbed on the East Coast would be drained. I pushed all thoughts of that town out of my head while I was away, but it was impossible to ignore on the way back. I knew where I was headed.

It was a good thing my sister came back with me. I think the transition back to life in my hometown would have been a lot more difficult without her. My friend Vincent visited, too, and shaved my head for me. The three of us had a picnic in my backyard then we went to the Old Mill for a photoshoot. Later, Amber and I rode bikes with Slushies in our hands and hung out on the old steps to the public library, hidden behind shrubs.

We also went out drinking, which is not very like me anymore, but I couldn't resist. We shared pitchers and did karaoke together, *Excuse Me Mr.* by No Doubt, during which a fight broke out and the cops showed up and we kept singing. I had to take anxiety meds before going to the bar, and was happy to have survived. Then Amber left and Vincent left and I dealt with the rest of my time in Lindsay and then I got the fuck out of there.

I believe a town is what you make of it. Whenever people complain to me about Lindsay, I tell them about all the great adventures I've had there, and I hope that they'll be imaginative enough to create their own until they can leave, if that's what they want to do. Lindsay does hold a special tiny place in my heart, even if I can't stay there too long without wanting to kill myself. Even now, when I go back to visit for a couple days, my anxiety gets turned up to eleven, and I'm happier just curling up on my mom's couch and reading a book than I am going outside and wandering and whatnot. It's like I don't want to be seen there. I want everyone to know that I have escaped, and that it is for good this time.

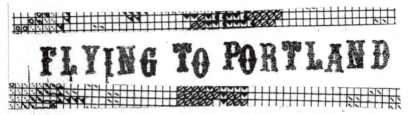

FLYING TO PORTLAND

I bought my plane ticket on a whim, spending nearly half my savings on the trip. I knew my sister was planning on going, but I wasn't really into it until she called me up and we talked about how awesome it would be to go together. My sister and I had never traveled together before, and I had never flown on a plane. So she booked our tickets the next day, and that was that.

The airport was stressful. I didn't pack much because I don't mind wearing the same t-shirt three or four times without washing it, and knew I'd need extra space in my backpack to bring home zines and books. I was nervous about flying, though. Not flying itself, but going through customs. I didn't bring toothpaste or shampoo because I thought they'd confiscate it, and I blacked out all the prices on my zines just in case.

Our flight was at 5 pm, and we got to the airport around three. It took nearly two hours to go through the whole process of customs. We told them we were going to a conference on independent publishing and staying with friends.

As the plane took off and broke through the clouds, I wished I had my very own cloud car, like on *Care Bears*. I always wanted one when I was a kid, and I still do. Amber took the windowseat and I leaned over her to watch us get further and further away from the ground. When the food and drinks carts came around, we each got a Heinekin, an in-joke and reference to one of our favourite movies, *The Weddding Singer*. Amber wrote postcards while I read a book

(*Lemon* by Cordelia Strube). When the woman in front reclined her seat without looking behind her first, the trays tipped, and she nearly spilled beer all over us. I get annoyed when people recline in their seats, especially when they don't check first t make sure there's room. We've only get so much room on planes and buses, and I think it's only fair. On a bus in Halifax, the girl in front of me asked if it was okay to recline her seat, and I was totally shocked because she was the only person who'd ever had the courtesy to ask first.

I felt strangely miserable most of the time I was in Portland, and I don't really know why. There were a lot of good times, like photobooth adventures while drinking yummy beer, taking pictures of pretty houses, scamming free rides on public transit, visiting the Independent Publishing and Resource Centre, hanging out with my zinester pals, eating delicious and cheap vegan food, blah blah blah. I don't know what I was expecting, but I felt like something was missing. It's probably because I require a lot of alone-time, quiet-time, to keep my sanity, and there's not a lot of that available when you're traveling. The one time I went out for a walk by myself in an attempt to cheer up and calm down, I was sexually harassed by some dude, so I went back to the bar from whence I came and continued staring at the floor.

On the first day of the Portland Zine Symposium, I drew directions leading up to the gymnasium in sidewalk chalk, then set up my table, which, sadly, was far away from all my friends. I felt weird and uncomfortable because everyone I wanted to hang out with was sitting together, and I was on the opposite side of the room. After a few hours, I switched to an empty table closer to my friends, and the next day, I got closer still, but I just didn't enjoy myself the way I thought I would. I was very happy to be home. The stupid thing is, if I hadn't gone, I still would've been jealous of those who did. I'm glad I went, but it'll be awhile before I go back. I want to give Portland another chance to win me over.

KINGSTON WRITERSFEST

I sold my guitar so I could go to the Kingston Writers Fest in September. Erin told me about it, and the moment I visited their website, I knew I had to be there. We went through a lot of difficulties and false starts planning the trip, but finally, right at the last minute, everything was arranged. We booked the cheapest motel room we could find, which was only a short walk from the writers fest, and we got a ride to Toronto and took the Megabus directly to Kingston (while in Toronto, I ate the most delicious yam burrito of my life). I'd never been to Kingston before, so I was excited not only for the fest, but also for the opportunity to adventure in a new-to-me city.

The sun was setting when we arrived in Kingston, and there was a full moon. I tried to take pictures, but I've done that before, attempted to take pictures of the night sky and the moon, and they almost never turn out. We only got slightly lost, but somehow managed to find our way into the town proper and locate the bus that would take us to the motel. The bus driver was the friendliest I've ever met, and he seemed to know just about all the passengers personally. It was a long ride, though, and since it was so dark, there was virtually nothing to see. And we were hungry. We'd stuffed our bags with cheap groceries, and when we got to the motel, we spent the rest of the evening wolfing down peanut butter and banana sandwiches, and looking up nearby bookstores.

There were quite a few writers we wanted to meet and workshops we wanted to attend, but the two at the top of our list were Cordelia Strube and Joyce Carol Oates. Cordelia Strube is a Canadian novelist who we had both recently discovered and fallen in love with; I'd picked up her book, *Lemon*, a few times at various bookstores, always drawn to the cover, and finally purchased my own copy after Erin recommended it to me. She did a reading at my favourite local bookstore, The Bookshelf, which I'd planned on attending, but I got nervous at the last minute, and felt intimidated by the people standing around at the door when I walked by, who looked like real-life adults. So I skipped the reading and sort of regretted it, but that's life. And I won't bother to tell you who Joyce Carol Oates is because you probably already know, and if you don't, you need to look up her name and find some of her books right now.

Cordelia Strube held a workshop titled *Writing the Teenage Mind*. We didn't know when went in that we'd be writing with prompts and reading aloud to the group. More and more, I've enjoyed working with prompts, so it didn't feel like too much of a problem for me until I actually read my piece. I shake when I'm nervous, and trip over my words like I've been drinking. So that's what I did. I shook and trembled, but read the best I could, though I couldn't finish it. What I'd written was kind of intense for me, and after hearing many of the other stories the group had worked on, mine was nothing at all like theirs (frankly, I thought my story was better than most of the others – confidence ain't no crime – but it was also remarkably darker and than theirs, and according to my diary, I was afraid I'd scare the others), and I felt a little odd. I also sort of cried – I have an annoying tendency to cry in public. It doesn't bother me so much anymore, I just worry that it might make other folks uncomfortable. The story I'd written was part of a vision I'd had for a long time, but had never been able to write down.

Erin read her story next, and although ours were different, we had a lot of strange similarities as well. It should also be noted that at least three people mentioned squirrels, my favourite animal, in their stories, which I thought was weird and wonderful. Time passed too quickly, and the workshop was over. As we packed up our things, a few women in the workshop complimented the story I had written, and one woman whispered a sweet thank-you. That was all the validation I needed to know that what I had written was worthwhile, and to be glad I had had the guts to share it.

Erin and I had both brought our copies of *Lemon* to have signed, but Cordelia grabbed her jacket and headed out faster than we could catch her. Through eavesdropping on the elevator, we knew that she was staying at the hotel the workshops were held at, so we each wrote her a quick letter thanking her for her workshop and telling her how we'd hoped she'd be able to sign our books, and left the letters at the front desk. To our surprise, she emailed us back while we were on our way home and offered to meet up with us in Toronto and sell us her books at half price, autographed. Neat! It was a few weeks before I could get back to the city, but I did end up catching up with her again, and talked with her and her daughter for awhile over delicious caffeinated drinks, and she wrote some wonderful notes in our books.

We had very few obligations the next day, so we packed a picnic of avocado sandwiches and soy chocolate pudding, and went back down to the hotel, which was on the water. We barely strayed from Princess Street the entire time we were there, which was alright with me, since there were so many beautiful sights to see and neat little bookstores and junk shops to explore. Every window display featured writers who were appearing at the festival.

Down a little hill and on the water, there was large willow tree partly on land, partly underwater, and that was where we had our picnic. There were some dirty plastic chairs, broken beer bottles, and a pair of busted up glasses. The little waves crashed to shore, sometimes splashing our legs. We collected beach glass. I had never seen beach glass before, and there was an incredible amount of it here. A lot of it was green, but there were also blue pieces, clear pieces, patterned pieces from china plates, and of course, many amber pieces. I thought it was funny to collect these gorgeous pieces of water-softened glass that once held alcohol and were likely ugly and unappreciated, smashed up somewhere and eventually ended up under this willow tree. We filled our hands with glass over and over, and collected the pieces in our coffee cups. From there, we went into the hotel to score free coffee and to write at one of the tables by a window on the sixth floor, where we had a nice view of the city. I eavesdropped some more and watched some writers I didn't recognize sign their books.

And that night turned out to be pretty much one of the best nights of my life. Joyce Carol Oates was doing a reading at the Grand Theatre, and then having a conversation with another Canadian novelist, Jane Urquhart. There were several writers whose work I had never read but whose name I was familiar with, and Jane was one of them. I had a second row seat, and the folks in front of me never showed up, so it was kind of like having a front row seat. After an outfit change (we both dressed in red), Erin and I rushed through the rain to get there on time. As we waited, I sketched the stage in my diary so I wouldn't forget what it looked like. Just some pretty chairs and stuff, nothing too fancy, but I wanted to remember it. After handing out some awards to local high school kids who'd entered writing contests, it was finally time for Joyce Carol Oates to come out. She stood behind a podium and read a story called *Pumpkinhead*, from her latest short story collection, *Sourland*. That lady is breathtakingly gorgeous. Her face is both sweet and mysterious, and she was simultaneously dark and humourous. I was hardly expecting any jokes from her, and, during her conversation with Jane Urquhart, she did admit that "I'm not usually so cheerful as I seem to be," but was feeling good after having completed another novel the night before, at one o'clock in the morning. She has published almost sixty books since the 1960's, and is certainly the most prolific writer I am aware of.

The first book of hers I ever read was *Foxfire*, and I brought that book with me just in case I had the chance to meet her. I didn't really expect to meet her, though; I mean, her name is larger than life. I could not take my eyes off her. She wore a charcoal pantsuit with a mauve blouse and the prettiest shade of red lipstick. After the reading and conversation, there was a book-signing, and I was so glad I had brought my tattered copy of *Foxfire* with me.

While we stood in line, we talked to the organizer of the fest, and once she'd heard that a) we had traveled kind of a long distance to be there, and b) we were broke, she told us to feel free to attend any workshop we wanted, and don't worry about paying for it or anything. Amazing! So we got to go to a ton more workshops that we had been interested in but couldn't afford, like *Novel Architecture* with Lisa Moore, and *Found Fiction* with Michael Winter. We took so many notes in each workshop, writing faster than anyone else, and when it was all over, we compared notes and filled in the blanks in one another's notebooks to make sure we had as much information as possible. We also attended as many free film screenings as we could, and drank as much free coffee as we could as well.

And then suddenly I was standing in front of Joyce Carol Oates. It's hard not to sound like a gushy fangirl about the whole thing. She signed my book, and she asked me what I do. I told her I'm a writer. She told me she liked my tattoos. A photographer took pictures while we talked, but I haven't been able to track them down.

This was one of the few trips I've ever been on where everything worked out, everything went as planned, there were no disasters, and in fact, everything was even better than imagined. I've taken it all as a good omen, and on my darkest days, I think about collecting beach glass under the willow tree, talking to Joyce Carol Oates, Cordelia Strube, and all the other writers we met, and I figure maybe everything is gonna work out after all. Maybe I can make it work out.

When I was a kid, my poppa gave me a red porcelain box with a cat and some flowers painted on the lid. He was always giving us trinkets he collected at yard sales, and he'd never pay more than twenty-five cents for anything. We don't take the trinkets anymore, we just joke about them taking up space, collecting dust, and just generally being ridiculous. But I loved all those things when I was a kid. I don't know why, but when I was twelve, I started hoarding pills. On days that I stayed home sick (or "sick") from school, I would secretly collect pills from the plastic containers in the cupboard, and I'd hide them in this red porcelain box. I also became obsessed with reading the medical dictionaries my mom kept on her bookshelves. I think I was planning an overdose, but I don't know what compelled me to do such a thing at that age, and I sure never wrote about it back then, so I can only wonder. I started self-injuring when I was eight, and I don't have a concrete reason for that either. Anyway, I filled up the box with pills, but I must have panicked about being caught, because at some point, I just got rid of them. I don't remember how long I kept the whole thing up. I did a lot of weird things, like writing down entries from the medical books – names and diagnoses and side effects - so I could memorize them, and "accidentally" smashing a glass on the kitchen floor so I could use the pieces to cut myself.

So that little red box, it's still on my bookshelf nearly fifteen years later, only now, it is filled with the beach glass and little stones I collected in Kingston, like good luck charms to hold onto and keep me going.

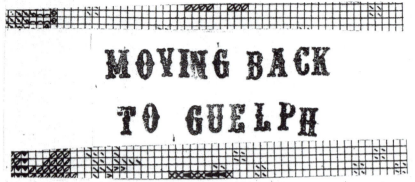

MOVING BACK TO GUELPH

There's a joke in my family that no matter where my poppa goes, he has to drive through Guelph. Always. He doesn't really leave town anymore, but on road trips before I was born, he always had to drive through Guelph. My family has lived in a lot of the surrounding cities, also before I was born, and my aunt and uncle met at the university here in the 70's. So maybe I'm indirectly connected to the city and that's why I've been so drawn to it.

I moved back this summer. I live by myself again, which is unspeakably wonderful. It feels like this space is my own, my time is my own, and like I am more in control of my life. I didn't actually see my apartment 'til Moving Day, which worried me a little, but once I got here, everything was dandy. The apartment is just about perfect. Huge windows with wide windowsills for Amélie to hang out, two big closets and a built-in shelf, natural light on three sides of the apartment, almost no shared walls with my neighbours, room to cook and bake, room for all my books, and a pink bathtub. And for the first time ever, I even have my own couch. (Actually, I had a couch the first time I moved to Guelph, a beautiful gold couch and matching chair that I found on the sidewalk, but that was so many lifetimes ago, I usually forget.). My cat has adjusted and made this place her home as well. The traintracks run by my bedroom window, and sometimes the apartment shakes when trains come by. I love it. I can write without interruption, I can walk around naked, I can do whatever I want whenever I want. Last time I lived by myself, my apartment was about the size of my current livingroom, and I was mostly too depressed to appreciate it anyway. This is so different.

When I left Lindsay, I felt like a bit of a traitor. I'm always talking about making your own fun, especially in small towns, fighting boredom, creating adventures, etc. It grates on my nerves when people complain about living in small towns without trying to do something to change their situation, and it annoys me that everyone seems to run away to the next biggest city, hoping to have their entertainment served to them. My goal was always to make my town fun. I found many ways to survive in Lindsay: bike rides, picnics, Sharpie and sidewalk chalk art, picture-taking, reading by the river, supporting independent bookstores and other indie businesses, holding my head up high no matter how bad I felt. But it wasn't easy, and it wasn't something I could sustain forever. It was especially difficult to create change in a small town where I didn't have any friends and wasn't invested in making any. Even if I did, it seemed like all anybody wanted to do was drink, and that's just not fun for me anymore. And there wasn't much point in staying after my sister left.

It gets to a point where it's just not worth staying anymore. My plan was always to move back to Guelph. The reason I went back to Lindsay a few years ago was to take care of my mental health in a place that hadn't totally broken my heart. But it took a few years to get back on track. I probably spent my first year or so drinking as much as possible, treating people like shit, and pretty much self-destructing. It wasn't pretty and I don't like to think about it. But in my last year there, things got better. I found a routine, I cut toxic people out of my life, I stopped relying on alcohol, and I started taking better care of my physical and mental health. Eventually, it wasn't me that was unhealthy anymore, it was the environment I was living in. So it was time to leave.

One of the reasons I moved back to Guelph was so I could focus on my writing. Writing has always helped to 'heal' me, as it were, but back in Lindsay, I couldn't write anymore. All I could do was think about writing, and that doesn't count for much when you're trying to get shit done. I spent a lot of time sitting on my floor, thinking about what I would be writing if I could write. Looking back, I did get quite a bit of writing done, but I knew I was capable of so much more, and that I would have to leave in order to find that spark.

The trains woke me up on my first night here, and I forgot where I was. I was so utterly confused and couldn't figure out what that strange noise was. Now I like reading the graffiti on the freight trains that go by, imagining they are the same trains that go by my sister's apartment, that we've unknowingly glimpsed the same graffiti. And I like spying on the passengers on the Via trains, wondering where they're headed and why. In nice weather, I can sit out on the little concrete porch and the train conductors wave to me.

I place a lot of value on my living space. I've always been fascinated by the structure of buildings, and feel like I've been on a constant quest to make each place I live in feel like a home, even if I haven't always succeeded, or have convinced myself a certain feels like home, then realized it was nowhere near that when I left. Although I tend to dress mostly in black, I prefer living in colourful spaces. Blank walls, and white walls especially, annoy me. Making a place a home is a process, perhaps a neverending one; it's not as easy as just unpacking and hanging stuff up and calling it home. This place feels more like home than anywhere I've lived so far, but I am still working on it.

(d) Roller skating is good fun.

OUTRO

This was an attempt to document some of the happier times I had in 2010. I've been doing a lot of hard work on becoming the person I want to be, learning how to take care of myself, and making positive changes in my life. It's not always pleasant. I still have a hard time getting out of bed sometimes, I still cancel plans because I'm feeling too anxious to leave my apartment, I still have moments where I feel like a complete and utter failure and I don't know what the hell I'm doing at all, or why. I still fall into depressions and get tricked into thinking that all the happiness I experience is fake, and that my view of the world when I'm depressed is more honest – it's not. Both aspects, and everything in between, are just as real one another. I just have to learn how to accept them and work with them.

Thanks for reading my zine. As always, feel free to write me a letter. Take good care of yourself!

THANK YOU:
Erin Schulthies, Amber Forrester, Vincent, Jess Geddes, Sarah Evans, Capp, Nicole Introvert, Alex Wrekk, the RCRG, and everyone who shared adventures with me in Halifax, Montreal, Portland, and Guelph.

telegram ma'am

SEPTEMBER 2011
ISSUE 23

+ stealing lilacs +

♡ THANK YOU ♡

Kit, Martina, Clara Bee, Erin S., Yaz, Dave, Amélie (my cat), Bif Naked

coffee, pills, plants, paper, pens, food, rollerskates, bookstores

cover design by Maranda Elizabeth
illustration by Clara Bee Lavery
littlegardens.tumblr.com
beelavery@riseup.net

♡ INTRO ♡

Autumn! For me, this is truly the beginning of the new year. This is my time for fresh beginnings, for planning birthday shenanigans (I just want cupcakes & tea & hugs), for digging out my sweaters and socks. This is the time for thinking & planning. It's still summer, but the breeze that tickles me from my windows at night is cooling down, the sun is setting just a tiny bit earlier, and I am dreaming up soup recipes. So to me, it's Fall now.

What have I done in the last year? I finished writing my first novel, I joined a roller derby league, I spent two months in ye olde mental hospital, I ignored my resolutions, I got Bif Naked to draw a tattoo for me, and I got sober. Life-changing things, really. I'm still taking it all in, I guess, still figuring shit out and looking forward to whatever's next. Mostly living in the present moment, though, because that is all I truly have.

This zine is a small document of some of these things, written down and shared so that I can move on. This zine is about fucking up and learning and letting go. Mourning my lives and creating new ones.

A note about the subtitle: I was going to change the name of my zine to *Stealing Lilacs*, but I couldn't make a decision. I've been making *Telegram Ma'am* for eight years now, and one of these days, it's gonna be time to let it go. But not just yet, I guess. Other plants I've been stealing lately are lemon balm, lavender, and chocolate mint.

♡ (POST-) HOMEWOOD ♡
/POST, NOT POSI.

This Spring, I spent two months in Homewood, an inpatient treatment centre here in Guelph, with programs devoted to depression & anxiety, PTSD, eating disorders, addictions, etc. Guess which ward I was on?! Yeah, depression & anxiety. I'd been on the waitlist for four and a half years. They called me up and told me to start packing, I was being admitted in six days. So I showed up the day after I got home from the Chicago Zinefest, headachey and lacking sleep, and spent the rest of the day answering questions and filling out forms.

While I was there, I felt like I was undergoing a kind of transformation. Maybe I still am. Maybe I always will be. I keep thinking there will be a destination, a point of arrival, when I say, 'Yep, I'm here! I'm really truly Maranda now!" But I guess that doesn't happen in real life.

TO HIDE FROM DANGER IS NOT TO ESCAPE IT.

LETTER "O"

Homewood has been in existence since the 1890's. I like the name because I like homes, woods, and words that fit as knuckle tattoos. Homewood is a series of buildings connected through hallways with black & white photos from the past all over the walls. As well as wards for various treatment programs, there's also a library, coffeeshop, gift shop, a greenhouse, art spaces, a gymnasium, exercise equipment, and so on. It's on beautiful grounds along the river with herb, vegetable, and flower gardens, lots of trees and trails, and bunnies and squirrels everywhere. Inside, it's a little more depressing. Grey walls, hospital beds, plastic bracelets, med counters, shared bathrooms, too many television sets...

I had a busy daily schedule. I got out of bed around seven in the morning, ate breakfast, attended mindfulness meditation, attended various groups in the mornings and afternoons that changed every other week, fit lunch and dinner in there somewhere, and spent most evenings reading, and writing in my journal. I spent a lot of time in my room (well, *rooms*; I changed rooms four or five times while I was there – it was upsetting to try to ground myself in a space where I was constantly being moved around, never quite able to settle or unpack). I also tried to spend a lot of time outside, but it was a rainy Spring. The season came on very slowly. There was snow on the ground when I was admitted, and then I watched all these tiny buds appear on the trees, I watched the grass turn green, watched daffodils bloom. I carried my umbrella and drank a lot of coffee. I sat on the ground surrounded in books and papers and charms and letter-writing supplies. Sometimes I would read my Tarot cards. I never went anywhere without my journal. For all that beauty, though, there were also times when I was cutting myself in the bathroom, times when I couldn't get out of bed, times when I thought I wasn't going to survive.

The first few weeks were frustrating. Actually, much of the two months I spent there were frustrating. But I also knew that I wasn't ready to go home, so there was not much I could do but stay, and try. For awhile, I felt like I was in a Depression 101 course. These are the symptoms. These are the treatments. Blah blah blah. That stuff didn't help; it was knowledge I already had. But I acknowledge that it can be important for others, who aren't magical special experts on mental health, like me.

I really don't want to write a lot about the hospital. I want to acknowledge it, I want to tell you, I want to document these things, but for the most part, I want to keep this experience to myself. So much of it is hard to put into words anyway. I do want to write about my life post-Homewood, though, and I want to share a few ideas and strategies that are helping me today, some of which planted their roots in the hospital, then bloomed and blossomed and came home with me.

Name of Deceased: _____
Date of Death: _____ Sex: _____ Age: _____
Funeral Home Staff: _____

When I came home, I felt fragile, my life felt precarious. I was not magically cured – we never will be. I was grateful to be on my own again, to sleep in my own bed and to snuggle my cat whenever I feel like it, but I was also now living outside the structure & routine of hospital-life, and that is something I have always struggled with. Frankly, I like programs that force me to wake up at a certain time, then medicate me so I can sleep at a certain time. I wish I had the self-control to be able to keep myself on a proper schedule, but it has never happened, not consistently anyway. I have never been able to take care of myself for long periods of time. Sometimes it seems like a good idea to stay up all night, to quit my meds, to hide under my blankets.

So it was scary. I was absolutely terrified. I was newly sober, but still harming myself, and I felt lonely and scared. I had grown attached to that place, but I also wanted to live a healthy life and take good fucking care of myself. These were/are hopeful days.

BORDERLINE ♡ PERSONALITY ♡ DISORDER

I was diagnosed with Borderline Personality Disorder while I was at Homewood. It was actually a relief. When I read the symptoms, I realized I had every single one. I felt like, after all these years, I finally knew what I was working with, and could make decisions along the old road of recovery. I was also incensed, though, at the fact that I had been misdiagnosed with Bipolar Disorder several years back, and had spent all this time being treated for something I didn't have. I have done a lot of work to let go of those resentments, though it does still come back to me sometimes, I still get upset. But as I am learning, I can't change the past, and my anger or regret is not useful unless I am doing something constructive and healthy with it – otherwise, they are just negative feelings I am allowing to eat away at me.

I didn't know much about BPD when I was diagnosed. What I knew was this: More women than men are diagnosed; some believe it doesn't exist; and Susanna Kaysen had it. That was the extent of my knowledge. Again, I feel like I've missed out on a lot by not having been diagnosed sooner since the symptoms are so obvious, but if you are talking to doctors for only five minutes at a time, if you are not able to clearly and coherently and honestly express what's going on with you, and if they misinterpret or just don't give a fuck, it's no big surprise that you might be misdiagnosed.

As I learned more about BPD, it felt like, pardon the cliché, coming home. This was a diagnosis I understood, it all made sense to me. My entire life was suddenly illuminated, and I had this clarity I had never experienced before.

The criteria for a diagnosis of Borderline Personality Disorder, as listed in the DSM-IV-TR (*Diagnostic and Statistical Manual – 4th Edition – Text Revision*) are:

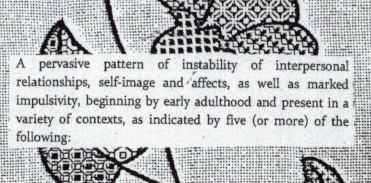

A pervasive pattern of instability of interpersonal relationships, self-image and affects, as well as marked impulsivity, beginning by early adulthood and present in a variety of contexts, as indicated by five (or more) of the following:

1. Frantic efforts to avoid real or imagined abandonment. Note: Do not include suicidal or self-injuring behavior covered in Criterion 5.

2. A pattern of unstable and intense interpersonal relationships characterized by alternating between extremes of idealization and devaluation.

3. Identity disturbance: markedly and persistently unstable self-image or sense of self.

4. Impulsivity in at least two areas that are potentially self-damaging (e.g., promiscuous sex, eating disorders, binge eating, substance abuse, reckless driving). Note: Do not include suicidal or self-injuring behavior covered in Criterion 5.

5. Recurrent suicidal behavior, gestures, threats or self-injuring behavior such as cutting, interfering with the healing of scars (excoriation) or picking at oneself.

6. Affective instability due to a marked reactivity of mood (e.g., intense episodic dysphoria, irritability or anxiety usually lasting a few hours and only rarely more than a few days).

7. Chronic feelings of emptiness.

8. Inappropriate anger or difficulty controlling anger (e.g., frequent displays of temper, constant anger, recurrent physical fights).

9. Transient, stress-related paranoid ideation, delusions or severe dissociative symptoms.

It sounds like fun, right? Well, on my better days, I do try to view it as some kind of adventure, since that seems like a moderately appropriate way to deal with it now, given my options. Other days, it is torture. I'm dealing with the same symptoms I've always had, I just have a better name for it now, and I can track down literature on the diagnosis, and navigate with a map, faded and torn as it might be.

The first question I had, and a question I am now often asked, was, "Borderline between what and what?" Borderline Personality Disorder was named in the 1930's. It originally referred to someone who appeared to be on the borderline between neurotic and psychotic: too neurotic to be neurotic, and not psychotic enough to be psychotic. Views have changed since then, as they do, but the name persists. There have been other names proposed for this diagnosis, however, such as Emotional Regulation Disorder and Emotional Intensity Disorder.

On the topic of language, I do need to say that just because I've been diagnosed with BPD, doesn't mean I'm "a borderline." Don't ever call me that. As with any other diagnonsense, if I have a cold, I do not become A Cold, and if I have cancer, I do not become A Cancer. Please take the time to be critical of language, and try to err on the side of not using de-humanizing or oppressive language.

Knowing what I have, though, knowing these tricks my brain is playing on me, doesn't make it easier. I wish I could fix everything. When I started learning about BPD, I wanted to condense this information into the format of a well-meaning letter and apologize to everyone I have harmed. I have hurt a lot of people, I know, but they've hurt me, too. Still, I know that it would only be more painful to bring it up again. It is healthier to simply let it go and move on. I fucked up. I'm trying not to anymore.

There's no end to this story. I'm living it everyday.

♡ GETTING SOBER ♡

April 20th, 2011 was Day One of Sobriety. I was still hospitalized (that is such a weird word) the last time I got drunk. I came home to take care of my cat, spent the evening alone drinking a cheap bottle of wine, went back to Homewood, and nobody noticed because I went right to bed. I slept in the next day.

Sobriety is a core aspect of my current path of healing and recovery. Sadly, it can also be kind of alienating. We live in a bar culture, obviously. Every activity, every event, is an excuse to get drunk. There are aspects of drinking that I miss, and some I hope I never experience again. I never want to be black-out-drunk again, never want to do all those terrible-regrettable things. I don't want to feel like I have to be intoxicated to have the guts to be honest with someone. But sometimes I miss bringing a bottle of wine on picnics, drinking a beer or two on a patio, that giddy-woozy feeling when you're not sober but not drunk, and the burning-throat feeling at the beginning of a night of dancing and adventuring, when your limbs start to tingle just a little. But even that feeling was always so dangerous for me, because I knew once that feeling came along, it wasn't going to be enough, I'd have to have more & more & more. And I would wake up hating myself, then do it again anyway. So now I just have to stay away. Today, I have been sober longer than I ever have been since the age of nineteen, and that is wonderful.

THEY ARE SUCH A ♡
♡ GENDERQUEERDO

"Wouldn't it be cool if we lived in a world where our identities didn't need to constantly be explained and validated? Well, I'm going to attempt to partially explain my current identity anyway, and then take a trip back to la-la land where an explanation of who I am is not necessary. I feel like I am rewriting parts of my life, scribbling in the margins, crossing stuff out and adding stuff in. It's a project that will never be complete, but certainly an adventure worth working on, worth attempting to capture moment by moment, and maybe even make some sense out of it at some point."

- written on my blog awhile back

So I recently "came out" as genderqueer (I hate the phrase "coming out" but I'm not sure what else to say). I wrote about it in my 24-hour zine, *Little Acorns* #5, and in bits and pieces on my blog (marandaelizabeth.com). And letters for my friends. It's strange. I mean, I feel really good about it, but I also feel like now, because I have this identity or whatever, and because I use gender-neutral pronouns, everybody is now expecting me to change my name and my style and everything. And I feel like I need to remind everyone that I am still the same person I was before I told you this!

'Girl' just never fit. 'Woman' certainly didn't. I feel like 'woman' is for grown-ups, and I am not one and never will be. For awhile, I used 'lady' and 'gal' tongue-in-cheek because I didn't know what other words to use. But then being referred to as 'she' bothered me. Being presumed Girl bothered me. While I was at Homewood, I was annoyed at having 'F' for Female stamped on my hospital bracelet. I also knew if I told them the F was wrong, they'd just add it to my list of Crazy. I feel more free as "genderqueer" or "genderless", but feel more bound as well. Because of the expectations maybe. But I have been having good conversations about these things, verbal & written, and maybe this is like another adventure in my life, figuring shit out. I use the pronoun 'they' now, not 'she'. It is worth noting that I still have all the privilege of continuing to be perceived as a Girl, and all the lack of privilege of continuing to be perceived as a Girl as well. Funny how that works.

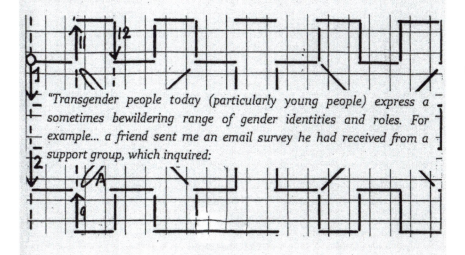

"Transgender people today (particularly young people) express a sometimes bewildering range of gender identities and roles. For example... a friend sent me an email survey he had received from a support group, which inquired:

Do you identify as transgender, transsexual, transvestite, crossdresser, transgenderist, genderqueer, FTM/F2M, MTF/M2F, transman, transwoman, transperson, third-gendered, gendertrash, gender outlaw, gender warrior, trans, transfag, transdyke, tranny, passing woman/girl, drag king, drag queen, male lesbian, girl boy, boychick, boy girl, boy dyke, gender-bender, gender blender, transqueer, androgynous, transfolk, butch dyke, nelly-fag, gender-different, gender subversive, man/boy with a vagina, chick with a dick, shape-shifter, he-she, she-male, transboy, transgirl, androgyne, gender variant, genderfucker, trannyfag, trannyqueer, trannydyke, Two Spirit, new man, new woman, she-bear, Tomboy, intersexual, female guy, tranz, bearded female, herm, hermaphrodite, MTM/M2M, FTF/F2F, ungendered, agendered, genderfree, bigendered, midgendered, polygendered, pangendered, omnigendered, crossgendered, byke, boi, pre-op, post-op, no-op, no-ho, epicene, othergendered, transkid, female impersonator, gender-atypical, ambigendered... or any other related term not on this list?"

The Riddle of Gender: Science, Activism, and Transgender Rights by Deborah Rudacille

(I'm still figuring out which words suit me best. I started with genderless, moved onto genderqueerdo (gender-queer-weirdo), but I also like misgendered, no-gender, genderfuck, and other words that haven't been created yet or at least I haven't heard them yet. I also like Maranda-gendered.)

This is a project I have been working on perhaps my entire life, but certainly much more within the last few years, and with an extreme focus in the last few months. Be Your Own Therapist means, basically, to learn how to take care of yourself, especially in situations where you have little or no supports in the mental health community, and little or no support in your daily life. In lieu of having an actual one-on-one face-to-face therapist, I became my own. I am thankful for the friends and family who are supportive of me, but when I am going through a particular kind of depression, when I am in distress, or when I am having a real crisis, I don't feel able to reach out to anyone, so it's necessary that I build a kind of network within myself and my living space to see me through.

Years ago, when I wanted to see a therapist but didn't have access to one, I began asking myself difficult questions in my journal, and then responding to them. The pages of my journals became something like conversations. I would write things that really terrified me, things I would be afraid for other people to read, though it might also have brought relief in some way. It reminded me of how, when I was a kid, I drew cartoon faces, taped them to my bedroom wall, and talked to them. I thought they could keep my secrets for me, or just keep me company.

While I am wary of methods of self-care that require spending money, one of the most important aspects of my Be Your Own Therapist project is books. Lots and lots of books! Surely there are many books on mental health available at the library, but I find that the local library lacks the selection I am looking for, and I prefer wandering amongst shelves of books and seeing what catches my eye, than going in and looking for something specific.

While I was at Homewood, I spent a lot of time in their library. It is a small space, but has plenty of books. There are a couple of shelves of fiction, and the rest of the shelves are devoted to books on subjects of mental health, self-harm, chronic pain, addictions, spirituality, etc. I would become enamoured with just about every book, and sign out far more than I could read. I would read several books at once, and keep change in my pocket to pay the overdue fines. When I was diagnosed with BPD, it was all I wanted to read about. I wanted to learn everything I could.

Lately, when I walk into the Self-Help or Psychology sections of bookstores, I stay for a long time. Sometimes I'll collect a stack of books and choose a spot to sit on the floor. I have only recently realized how comforting it is to sit on floors, at home and in bookstores. I don't know why. Maybe it's grounding, maybe it makes my inner child happy. A lot of books on mental health and self-help are fairly easy to find used, so if I'm drawn to a title but don't want to – or can't – spend the money, I'll write down the title and go down the road to the used bookstore and see if they have it.

Shortly after I was discharged from Homewood, I found out the 12-week outpatient program I'd been referred to had been canceled. It was to be my only outpatient care, so when I got the call, I had a minor freak-out. Be Your Own Therapist became more crucial then, as I realized that despite not having someone to talk my issues through with, life was going to go on, and I had to find ways to continue surviving on my own. I've left hospitals with no follow-up treatment in the past, and although I am beyond frustrated with our fucked up system, I do have to go on.

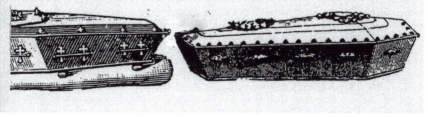

Be Your Own Therapist also involves, for me, reading plenty of books on creativity and writing, and actually following through on the exercises and prompts contained within. Unfortunately, I have a habit of not totally absorbing what I am reading, telling myself I'll read the books now and deal with everything within later, though I usually put the book back on my shelf when I am finished, move on to the next one, and forget the previous one. So right now I'm learning how to focus on what I am reading in the moment, and how to use what it is I am reading – whether it is creativity books, mental health books, spiritual books, fiction, whatever.

I've also been working on a list of things to do when I feel like harming myself, or when I am feeling unsafe, depressed, or anxious. It's a work-in-progress, and I imagine it always will be. I have made lists like these before, but don't often follow up on recommendations, whether they came from a book, a doctor, a nurse, or myself. This time, I have to. I am fucking sick of getting stuck in these depressive spirals over and over, and feeling incapable of crawling or cartwheeling out of them, or of preventing them. So the trick to these lists, it turns out, is not just writing them, but actually *doing* them.

My list is split into two parts. The first part is My Daily Self-Care Routine. Yes, I need to write down the boring, basic daily things in an effort to encourage myself to remember them, and to do them. That means taking my meds and vitamins properly, drinking lots of water, eating good food, playing with my cat, doing my stretches and exercises, going outside...

The second part of my list is called When You Feel Hopeless. This is a much longer list, and I have set a requirement for myself that, in darker situations, and they do still happen, I must do everything on this list, or at least as much as I can, before either harming myself or taking a trip to the ER. I am usually feeling better before I've had a chance to go through the whole list. When this list is somewhere near complete, my intention is to make it pretty, photocopy it, and thus have a checklist for times when I need it, which will hopefully encourage me to take a sheet out of the drawer, act out the list, and check things off, rather than my usual method of remembering the list, actively ignoring it, and engaging in self-destructive behaviour.

Although we're encouraged to go to the ER when we're feeling suicidal, it seems that when I do, I don't often find what I'm looking for. On the one hand, it can provide a very temporary respite. There are times when I have actually looked forward to hanging out in the waiting room with a book simply because it provided me with an excuse to focus on only one thing at a time, and I knew that I would eventually be able to talk to someone. It even forced me to get out of my apartment and get some fresh air, since I usually walk over. Unfortunately, I've also had some pretty negative experiences in the ER. In regards to times I've gone there feeling suicidal, but hadn't harmed myself enough to need physical treatment, even the mental health nurses didn't seem to know what to do, what to say. And then after hanging around for the hospital for a few hours and generally being treated like shit, you get to walk back home, back to whatever triggered your depression in the first place, and often without a follow-up plan. So going to the ER is always my last resort, and even though I've had more bad experiences than good, I still associate that place with some sort of comfort, though it is usually an illusion.

As for self-harm, I don't think it's the worst thing in the world. It's worked as a coping mechanism for me since the age of eight, and although I've tried, it's been difficult to quit. I've stopped for up to a year at a time, but sometimes I can barely stop for an entire week. Like the ER, and like so many other dangerous addictions, it provides comfort, in its own weird way. When I think of cutting myself, this image comes to mind of wrapping myself in a warm blanket, probably the world's most obvious symbol of comfort and safety. A razorblade is not exactly as soft and warm as a down comforter or a well-worn quilt, but sometimes it'll do just the same. I am working on combatting that false sense of comfort with actions that are healing and recovery-oriented.

- Turn off all sound
- Take deep breaths
- Drink a cup of tea
- Meditate
- Wash face & brush teeth
- Have a shower
- Read a chapter of a book
- Sit on the porch
- Write in my journal
- Play with my cat
- Tidy the apartment
- Stitch hearts onto quilt
- Take a nap
- Email a friend
- Write a letter
- Go for a walk
- Eat fruit
- Paint my nails
- Smell peppermint oil
- Light candles/incense
- Water plants
- Safety objects
- Moisturize my hands
- Go to a café
- Go to the library

Letting go might be one of the most important tasks in my recovery. Of course the past can never change, we hear that so often we don't really think about it anymore. But what if you did think about it? Like, right now? Everything that has happened up to this moment absolutely cannot be changed no matter what.

Do you know how many hours and days and weeks and years I have spent ruminating on the past? Or how many conversations I have gone back to in my mind and tried to alter, imagined different outcomes...? Still today, I imagine, what if I bumped into so-and-so who I haven't seen in five years, how would that go?

I still stress myself out thinking about conversations that happened three, five, seven years ago. This is not a valuable use of my brainspace. It is not healthy. It is said that the molecules in our body actually carry emotions from our mind, so that our cells are carrying these feelings around – guilt, sadness, hopelessness, missing someone, whatever – and transporting them to our organs and our limbs and our bones, and they live there. And so it makes sense that I can transport myself back to these situations, and suddenly have shaky legs and a churning gut. I have to press my hands against the wall to hold myself up, keep my balance, remind me where I am now.

I can't deny that certain things happened, but I can choose to attempt to move away from them, to continue my recovery without their weight on me. I didn't have the perfect parents, I didn't have healthy relationships, I got drunk and I fucked up. A lot. That much is true. But I don't want to analyze these experiences and memories to death anymore. I don't need to feel bitter forever and ever. I want to move on. I want to let go. It's about time I let go. Because if I hold onto all these things, I just don't know how I am going to live.

TELEGRAM

issue 24

February 2012

♡ ## INTRO INTRO INTRO ♡

Well, I changed the name of my zine. Slightly. I no longer feel comfortable using the title *Telegram Ma'am*, so after a lot of thinking and talking and writing and over-thinking, wondering if I wanted to begin a new title altogether or find a way to alter the current title, I decided I wanted to keep the name, sort of, but change it to reflect changes in my life and my identity; namely, that I no longer identify as female (did I ever, truly?), and writing under a gendered title felt somehow wrong and fake and weird to me; actually, potentially alienating on so many levels.

I started making this zine when I was seventeen. I'm twenty-six now, I'm the same person and I'm not the same person. I spend a lot of time thinking about identity/politics, creativity, craziness, home, the little things in my daily life that contribute to my everything, possessions and lack thereof, friendships & relationships, radical communities, the future that doesn't exist until it becomes the present, lists, decision-making, and realizing (making real!) that some things change and some things stay the same and my mind will always wander and I'll always find ways to bring it back. And I want my zine to reflect the changes and the funny little thought processes that make me the weirdo who is still writing this zine.

♡ THEY THEY THEY BLAH BLAH BLAH ♡

Okay, so, I identify as genderless. I wrote about it in *Little Acorns* #5 and *Telegram (Ma'am)* #23, and now I'm writing about it again. Because there are some things I want to get out and some things I want to clear up. In *Little Acorns* #5, I wrote that I was using the pronouns 'they' and 'she'. Really, I'm only using 'they'. I very quickly realized that using two pronouns meant people would automatically revert to 'she' because it was easier for them, because they didn't have to think about things like language and gender, and because it was less confusing. It felt like I was giving friends and strangers permission not to care, not to think, not to try to change. Not to help me destroy things and change things. I gave them permission to be lazy and careless, and I let them off the hook. And I realized other people made it more awkward than I did. Like, when they acknowledge that you're using a different pronoun, but instead of actually using it, they replace the pronoun by using your name a hundred times. Instead of saying, "Maranda sent me a letter and they told me about this event going on in their town and blah blah," they say, "Maranda wrote me a letter and Maranda told me about this event going on in the town where Maranda lives and blah blah."

Well, fuck that. My gut clenches when somebody refers to me as 'she', whether or not they know of my genderless identity and my discomfort with having my gender chosen for me by somebody else. My body tenses. I wonder if I should say anything. I don't want it to be awkward, but I'm sick of being hurt over and over and feeling unable to defend myself. Like I'm just trying to make things difficult (things are already more difficult than you realize without me trying to make them difficult!). I wilt and cringe a little inside, and sometimes outside, when I am misgendered.

When I started talking about all this, an anonymous friend sent me a custom-made necklace in the mail that says 'they' in purple glitter. Another friend sent me an embroidered wall-hanging with 'they' stitched in purple thread surrounded by lilacs. And another friend mailed me handmade pins that say, 'It's okay to call me they', and 'I am NOT a girl'. All these magical gifts I have shown off so proudly, adorning my neck and my wall and fastening them to my cardigans, and still, after seeing these words on me and having conversations with me, looking me in the eye, even some of my friends can't be bothered to remember. Can't understand how disrespectful and hurtful and gross it is to care about me and not care at the same time.

How come we can remember hundreds of names but we can't remember more than two pronouns?

I'm not a girl. Maybe my dress and my vulva are confusing you? Ask yourself why that confuses you. Ask yourself why using a different pronoun, why using more inclusive language, scares you. Ask yourself how your confusion and your assumptions and your fears might be harming those around you. I promise it's okay to ask and to not have the answers, but please, please try.

♡ IOI ♡

I had a good conversation with a friend, and I wish we could have talked longer, but the music was loud and there were things to do and other people to talk to and it's so awkward when you'd rather have this conversation on your livingroom floor than in front of the stage at a bar. But anyway, we talked about the gender thing and we talked about how we are so darn sick of feeling obligated to have the _____ 101 conversation over and over and over again. Queer 101, Disability 101, Class 101, Feminism 101, Racism 101, Gender 101, Oppression 101. How many times do the basics have to be repeated before we can move on?!

While I acknowledge and am grateful for having the privilege of access to information and resources that led me to become a feminist, a queer, a weirdo, a genderqueer, a genderqueerdo, a radical person, and a delightfully crazy person, I am also exhausted with having to explain what each of those words mean and why they are relevant and meaningful in my life. People have been writing about all of these things and more since before I was born, so why is it still so new? Even in so-called queer communities, feminist communities, safe/r spaces (no such thing), I need to give the 101 talks, I need to try to erase the assumptions about who I am or live with them quietly and ragingly.

Having this conversation with my friend helped validate the rage and frustration of the times I had to correct everyone or choose not to and the times I was criticized for not providing clear enough definitions of the words I used to people who had the ability to look it up if they cared to take the time and effort. There are gender/queer zines from the 90's and likely earlier that nobody is reading because they barely exist anymore and they weren't published as anthologies that turned into bestseller books. How are we supposed to provide access to this information? How are we supposed to get out of the 101 Beginners Classes and move onto everything else?

And this leads me to another struggle, another question. How do I have these conversations with folks who aren't involved in so-called radical circles, folks who don't have to think about these things in their daily lives? I find myself wondering how to create and participate in communities that aren't necessarily queer, or feminist, or artistical, or whatever. Or they're one but not another and maybe they care or maybe they don't, I don't know…

When I do correct somebody for using the wrong pronoun, whether it's in reference to me or to somebody else, my intention is not to make this awkward, awful thing. It's not an attack. I want this to be a casual conversation that happens in everyday lives and then you move on, like when you tell someone they got your name wrong, or that you prefer root beer to cream soda. No big deal. What if your pick-up line was something like, "Hey baby, what's your pronoun?" That might be kind of neat.

But, you know, pronouns aren't the only thing. For me, they are actually the most simple thing. When do I get to take a break from correcting messed up pronouns and move on to discussing gender and destroying the binary and really really learning how to see people without assuming their gender, describing people without prefacing the description with, "*She* looks like," or, "*He* looks like." When do I get to talk about the past and how even as a kid, even as a teenager, I sort of got the feeling I wasn't a girl, but I wasn't a boy either, and I knew nothing about gender and theory except that I liked boys who looked like girls and I had to find a way to stop my period from happening every month for the next forty years, so I had no words for what I was and no vision of who I could be.

HOW TO BE A GOOD FRIEND TO CRAZYFOLK

I'm crazy. And I'm okay with that. I'm learning how to live as a crazy person, how to take care of myself, and I'm learning what I want and need in various friendships and relationships. There are so many aspects of my craziness that I need to share (and some I'd rather keep to myself), and it's important for us – crazyfolk, and our allies and pals and potential friends – to have meaningful discussions, to have compassion and understanding, and to be open to all these things and more. I also think that those of us with mental health conditions need to seek out one another, befriend one another, get together and strategize/organize. How do we take care of ourselves? How do we take care of one another? Are there times when we need to admit that we are not always capable of those things?

Support is a really big word. And it's different for all of us. I'm writing as someone who has been diagnosed with depression, anxiety, borderline personality disorder, and chronic pain, among other things, and I'm writing as someone who grew up in and continues to live in poverty. I'm also writing as a queer, an introvert, and someone whose life has been consistently inconsistent. So that's where I'm coming from, that's part of my history. What I've written isn't going to be true for everyone, but it's what I know for myself, and I hope it will help you navigate your own conditions and boundaries, and those of your friends as well. I hope it will open discussions and I hope it will inspire you.

I'm going to begin with ideas on how to support us while we are in the hospital, and then move on to how to support us in our daily lives. And then I'll provide some self-care tips for crazyfolk as well.

♡ **When We're In the Hospital** ♡

Last Spring, I was in Homewood for two months, participating in a treatment program for those with depression and anxiety. Homewood is a treatment centre in Guelph with various inpatient and outpatient programs for people with mental health conditions, addictions, eating disorders, and so on. It's been around for more than one hundred years. Although I've always been aware that treatment is, unfortunately, a privilege, not a right, I really had that drilled into me after I was referred to their depression and anxiety program. My first suicide attempt was in November 2006. I spent a few days at Guelph General Hospital having my stomach pumped, regaining consciousness, and talking to various nurses, counsellors, and psychiatrists. From there, I was moved across the street to Homewood Health Centre, where I was admitted to inpatient for one week. I was added to the waitlist for IMAP (Integrated Mood and Anxiety Program), and told that, since I didn't have money or insurance, the waitlist would be quite long; maybe three to six months. I needed help immediately, and I freaked out. Instead, the waitlist turned out to be *four and a half years*. In the meantime, I fell apart a few times, put some of the pieces back together, and learned a hell of a lot. Nine months after being discharged, my life continues to be in a wonderful, adventurous state of transition, and my learning processes and self-care processes continue to develop. That's where I'm at right now.

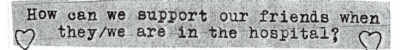

How can we support our friends when they/we are in the hospital?

1. Ask if we'd like visitors! And if we say yes, show up! When I was in Homewood, almost nobody visited me. A few people talked about visiting, asked about visiting hours, sent well wishes, but when it came right down to it, they did not show up. That's not useful; it's disappointing. You don't need to be afraid of making plans with us, of coming onto hospital grounds, of hanging out. We are still human! We can still have conversations, we can sit down and drink coffee together, talk about our days, share stories, and it doesn't have to be this weird, awkward thing. If you think it is, that's your problem, not ours. Investigate those feelings. Talk about them. Get rid of them.

2. If you're comfortable with visiting, please also understand that we will have days when we don't want to see anyone. Don't take it personally. Our days are mostly spent talking about difficult things. When I was in Homewood, a lot of my time and energy were spent on anger, depression, confusion, rage, and regret. Many of my conversations revolved around depression, anxiety, abuse, self-harm, trauma, and so on. By the end of the day, I was exhausted. I sat in my bed reading, journaling, napping, or daydreaming. The majority of our days on inpatient are spent in group therapy settings, and, for me, carving alone-time in each day was absolutely crucial.

3. Don't forget we exist! Maybe we can't participate in everything that's happening on the outside, but we are still here. We probably miss you, but we need to take a break and take care of ourselves right now. Please don't create unnecessary distances between us, or treat us like we are somehow different than we used to be. I don't want to feel like a total freak when I come back to my supposed supportive communities (at least not anymore than I already do!).

4. Remember that these lists can and will change for different people at different times. The best you can do is ask us where we're at, ask us if we'd like visitors, ask us if we want to talk about our mental health or anything but our mental health. Ask if you can share stories from your own life on the outside as well; we still care!

I feel like I would have had more visitors if I had been at the Regular Hospital instead of the Mental Hospital. Mental health conditions are obviously treated different than physical health conditions and injuries and whatnot, and while in some situations, that makes sense, I think that when we are in an institution where we are isolated from our friends and our communities and the routines of our daily lives, we need support and comfort no matter what the reasons are for us being there. If your friend was confined to a hospital bed because they'd broken their leg, you'd probably visit, and you probably wouldn't pretend that the cast on their leg was invisible. So if your friend is in the hospital because they're being treated for a mental health condition, visit. Talk to them. Don't pretend it isn't happening.

♡ ## When We're at Home ♡

For those of us dealing with mental health conditions, and many others as well, communication can be really hard. I am shy. I find it difficult to initiate plans and conversations with my friends, though I am trying and I feel like I am getting better at it. Sometimes it's easier for me to hide behind my computer screen and talk to you on the internet, or to write a zine and photocopy it and hand it to you, than it is for me to simply call you up and invite you over. I also have a difficult time making plans because my moods change rapidly and unpredictably, so I might make plans when I'm feeling super-pumped about life, then wake up the day of our get-together and feel pretty much unable to get out of bed. I don't like cancelling plans, but sometimes it's necessary. I'm learning what kinds of communications and conversations I need in my daily life, and I want to help others learn about their own needs and boundaries as well. I want to share these things, talk about these things, develop awareness about our various kinds of so-called crazy.

♡
How can we support our friends in our daily lives?
♡

1. Come visit, or invite us over to your place! I am not always comfortable in crowded places, and I'm usually broke, so while I do enjoy going out from time to time, it's not something I like to do overly often, and I am usually too broke anyway. I like meeting up and hanging out at cafés, but can't always afford a cup of coffee, so I'd rather just hang around at my place or yours, drink coffee or tea, and have good talks. You don't need to worry about keeping me entertained or being the most interesting person in the world, and hopefully neither do I. I'm into cheap hangouts and good conversations, but then again, I've never turned down a trip to the bookstore either.

2. On a broke-related note: Disability! I'm on disability, and so are many other folks with mental health conditions and/or chronic pain. Please don't judge us for a) where our income comes from, or b) what we choose to do with it. ODSP (Ontario Disability Support Program) is well-known for not providing a reasonable living wage. So I can't always go out and spend a lot of money, see all the shows I want to see and buy all the records I want to listen to and all the books I want to read and eat out at restaurants all the time and buy a latté everyday. So please don't expect me to. Let's hang out without feeling pressured to spend money!

3. Please respect our boundaries. For example, I often need to go to bed early because I take meds that make me tired and make me require more sleep than the average person to function in my daily life, and I also have histories of insomnia and mania, so encouraging me to stay up all night is not always a fantastic idea. I do like to stay up late sometimes, and I miss my past night-owl-ism now and then, but it's best for my mental and physical health if I try to maintain a fairly regular sleep schedule. Similarly, I require quite a bit of alone-time to recover from social situations, and I also require quiet-time and one-on-one time with my pals in general, so please respect that.

4. Listen to our stories. Don't imply that we are Too Crazy or Not Crazy Enough. Both of these responses are incredibly invalidating and judgemental. Treat us with respect and compassion and care.

5. Don't take the effects of our treatments personally. For example, a lot of the meds I've been on over the years have caused memory loss. I am not good at remembering names, sometimes I ask questions that were just answered five minutes ago, sometimes I forget the plans we just confirmed, and sometimes I am simply very scatter-brained or very groggy and blurry. It's got nothing to do with you, just my weird moods and the chemicals in my body and my brain and my thoughts moving too rapidly to catch up with.

6. Ask us what's going on in our lives, ask us how we're feeling today. Ask us if we'd like a hug!

7. Do not give us unsolicited advice! It's annoying and condescending. While I am totally open to listening to your stories and discussing what has helped you or what has helped your friends and family, I am absolutely not okay with the assumption that those are the things that are going to help me, too. I've tried many treatments; some have been helpful, some have not. Some of the treatments I'd like to try are entirely inaccessible to me due to my low income and lack of coverage. I don't like being recommended treatments that cost money; that goes for various therapies and "alternative" treatments, as well as diets, vitamins, and supplements as well. If I could try them, I would, but that's not where I'm at right now. If your next sentence begins with, "You should...", then maybe just keep it to yourself, please and thank you. (But if I ask you for advice, hopefully you'll be willing to share!)

8. Say and do things that let us know you value our friendship.

9. Discuss these lists with your pals. Talk about what you'd add, what you'd take away. Write your own lists. Share them.

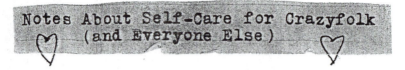

Notes About Self-Care for Crazyfolk (and Everyone Else)

Self-care is the most important of all! I can't stay sane or functional if I'm not making efforts to take good care of myself. Self-care means so many things to so many people, and it can change and evolve everyday. For example, sometimes I take care of myself by recognizing when I need alone-time, and staying home. Other times, I take care of myself by recognizing that I am using alone-time as a way of hibernating and isolating, so I instead force myself to go outside, or make plans with friends.

The following is a small list of some of my methods of self-care. The trick is not only to recognize when you need to devote some time and effort to taking care of yourself, but to *actually do it* instead of just thinking about it, writing lists, procrastinating, etc. It took me a long time to figure that out, and I feel like I am re-learning it everyday.

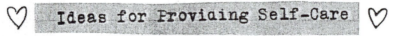

Ideas for Providing Self-Care

1. Write it down: journals, fiction, zines, letters, whatever, I need to write to get stuff out of my system, and sometimes I communicate better through writing than talking.

2. Turn off all technology: internet, radio, music, cell phones... Give yourself a break from life by creating a silent, calm atmosphere.

3. Keep up your basic daily self-care rituals, like having a shower, brushing your teeth, eating a decent breakfast, even if you're not planning on leaving the house.

4. If you have animal companions, take time to snuggle with them and talk to them.

5. Slow down. When I am rushing through my activities and my days, I start to feel really crazy and jittery and like I'm constantly running out of time. When I make the effort to simply walk slower, prepare my food slower, focus on one thing at a time, I feel more calm and safe in my own body.

6. If you are doing things that are harmful to your psyche or your body, ask yourself why. Ask yourself what you are trying to accomplish, what feelings you would like to be experiencing, and then search for less harmful ways to find those things.

7. If you need to get out of the house, but don't want to talk to anyone, go to the library. I like wandering the aisles and seeing what catches my eye, and I feel really great when I come home with my backpack filled with free books.

8. Declare a Self-Care Day! I do this sometimes when I really need to. A Self-Care Day means I get to do whatever I want all day long – within reason – and I don't allow myself to feel guilty about not running important errands, or cancelling plans so I can stay home, or ignoring my to-do list in order to drink lots of coffee and make art, or whatever. Self-Care Days, for me, usually involve staying home, daydreaming, working on writing projects, not bothering to respond to emails and whatnot, reflecting on the state of my life in my paper journal, and burning yummy-smelling candles. I especially like to declare Self-Care Days on what I call Bad Anniversaries – certain dates that roll around each year and make you feel bad because something terrible happened that day however many years ago. Those are the days that I really need to be aware and take care of myself. Your Self-Care Days might look way, way different from mine, and that is absolutely okay. Do whatever you need to do to keep yourself alive.

These lists could go on forever, and they will vary and warp and change and grow for each person. I highly encourage you to try out some of the things on these lists, to write your own lists, and to discuss them with your friends and family. It takes an incredible amount of time and energy to figure out what you want and need, and it takes even more effort and guts to share these things with people in your life. It's gonna be hard, but it's also gonna be wonderful.

CLEAN TIME VS. RECOVERY TIME
(THREE HUNDRED DAYS SOBER)

Each time we avoid self-destructive behaviour,
we choose recovery.

"Clean-time vs. recovery-time" is a concept found in twelve-step programs. The difference between clean-time and recovery-time is this: "Clean-time" is just what it sounds like; how many days you've been clean and sober. But "recovery-time" is something else; recovery time indicates the days that you are actually focusing and meditating upon and sharing and appreciating your sobriety, the days when you are taking good care of yourself and going to meetings and learning and growing.

The difference between the two has been on my mind a lot lately. I quit drinking last Spring, and I am writing this zine at three hundred days sober. I wanted to celebrate somehow, but when this day came, I sort of thought, Why bother? Today, I am feeling three hundred days clean, not three hundred days recovering.

I don't know if it's because my life has been hectic or because my moods have been wonky or because I have been sick with migraines and nausea, but I just haven't been devoting myself to the practice of being sober. I want to. I want to (re-)commit myself to living a sober life, to caring about staying sober and figuring out how that fits into the kind of life I want to live, but I am feeling confused about just how to do that, how to experience this process, how to understand it. I don't want to lie and say that I don't still now and then feel the desire to get fucked up, or at least to alter my brain a little bit and see how it goes. It's just that I can't do that without fucking up everything.

Remaining sober is a learning process. I'm in the midst of learning how to communicate honestly without alcohol to give me a certain kind of courage and fearlessness, I'm learning how human interaction works without booze, I'm learning what it's like to stay up late without having to apologize to anyone in the morning for being an awkward embarrassing jerk. And I'm learning the sillier things, like how much I love sober karaoke and sober dancing.

I want to talk to other sober folk. How are you getting along? How long have you been sober? Why did you decide to quit? How do you feel when people are drinking around you? What are you learning so far?

GET OFF THE INTERNET

Seriously. My friend Dave and I were having a lot of talks about our internet habits, which led us to making a zine called, *Real Life: A Magical Guide to Getting Off the Internet*. We've been asking questions like:

- Why do we spend so much time online?
- Why do we choose to do things that hurt us?
- How do we set realistic rules & boundaries for our internet-use?
- What you would rather be doing?
- What are your internet bad habits?
- What is your online persona like compared to your real life self?
- Do you feel like you need to check your messages *right now*? Why?
- and so on...

I feel like the internetz takes up too much time in my life and too much space in my brain. I was spending too much time online; it was necessary, but it also became excessive. There were all sorts of things I wasn't getting done because I was too busy staring at a screen.

As I was working on the zine, my internet was cut off. I hadn't paid the bills in a long time, and I'd lost count of how many threats they'd sent to cut me off, how many times a day they called to remind me that I owe them money. So that was my accidental solution. Get cut off. It's inconvenient at times, of course, but it's far from the worst thing in the world. Not having internet access at home forces me to think more about my priorities and work on them, and it means I have a lot more time to do other things; like making zines, writing letters, reading good books, and hanging out with my pals.

Lately, I've been too broke to use my five-year-old pay-as-you-go cell phone as well, meaning I can be pretty difficult to get in touch with sometimes. It's frustrating, but I like to remind everyone that friendship existed before technology, that before phones and internetz and all these gadgets and contraptions, we found ways to communicate, ways to get together. I like to encourage my local friends to simply show up at my place, throw snowballs or pebbles at my window to get my attention, and I like to encourage my long-distance pals to write letters, especially since even when I do have internet access at home, I am not so fantastic at responding to emails and stuff anyway. I am more comfortable sending more thoughtful responses in pen and ink. Not having the internet, and sometimes not having a cell phone, tricks me into learning things like patience, focus, non-urgency.

♡ **OUTRO OUTRO OUTRO** ♡

Thank you for reading my zine! I'm finishing up issues 24 and 25 of *Telegram* just on time for the NYC Feminist Zinefest in February and the Chicago Zinefest in March. Maybe I'll see you there?!

I adore snail mail and would love to hear from you. There are things I want to talk about and people I want to find. I want more genderqueer pals. I want to talk about the idea of community – creation, participation, local & long-distance... I want to talk to people I don't know yet, people who make things, people who get what I'm talking about and people who don't need me to give them the 101 talks because they're willing to learn things on their own. I want to talk to folks who are learning about sobriety. I want to talk about the things we do in our daily lives that bring us closer to our ideal lives. I want to read really good zines. I want everyday and everything to be an adventure.

Take good care of yourselves!

Maranda ♡♡

TELEGRAM

issue 25

February 2012

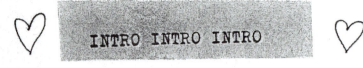

INTRO INTRO INTRO

Isn't it weird when somebody asks you how you are, you automatically say, "Good," and then you realize that you actually *are* kinda good? That things in your life are actually working out just fine right now, that you are feeling inspired and doing positive things with that feeling, that you have friends and good conversations and a nice home and all your time is spent doing these wonderful things that you actually want to do? And you scrunch up your face in confusion and say, "Like, for real, good. I am doing well."

That's where I'm at right now, I guess. And it's always hard to feel like this and not just expect things to go awfully wrong because they always do, to not expect to take to your bed for a few weeks with a sudden depression, or get seriously sick, do something foolish, ruin it all, fall apart over and over. Those things could happen. Maybe they won't. I am feeling content with the state of my current life, I like my days, I like where things are going. Maybe I'm onto something. I'm getting better at taking care of myself, and calmly accepting those moments when I can't.

I wanted to make a zine about creating magical, artistic, creative, meaningful daily lives, so this is it. I get a lot of questions about that sort of thing, and I wanted to make a space to answer those questions thoughtfully and with care. Not that I am the Magical Expert on being Crazy & Creative, but I've got experience with both, and I need to share it. I want my friends and acquaintances and strangers to learn & grow & create the lives they want instead of just daydreaming about them, feeling frustrated like it's never gonna happen. Nothing's ever gonna be exactly like I want it to be, but I do have the ability to make at least some positive changes in my life, to focus on specific goals, to live a life that is more than just survival. And I think you have it in you, too.

ASK ASK ASK

What does your ideal daily life look like? What is holding you back from living that life? What can you do to make your current life more like your ideal life? What changes do you need to make? How are you going to make those changes? What kinds of art do you make? What kind of arts do you want to try? What can you eliminate from your budget to give yourself more money for other things, or less stress about running out of money? Do you make your art at home or elsewhere? What is your home like? Could you make changes in your home to make it a more inspiring space? Do you have a whole house, a whole apartment, a whole bedroom? Do you stay in one place for long periods of time, or do you travel? Do you move a lot? Why? Why not? How stable is your living situation? How stable is your mental health? Do you want to change either of these things? What makes you want to make stuff? Do you write? Do you carry a notebook wherever you go? What does your notebook look like? Where would you like to be one year from now? Five years? What did you do today to bring yourself closer to that place? Are you a secretive person? Do you spill your guts to just about everyone? Does your home look like you live there? What do you see from your windows? Have you ever drawn that view? Written about it? Stared out your window and lost track of time? Do you make eye contact with strangers? Do you smile at strangers? Do you eavesdrop? Do you sleep well? What kinds of things do you dream about? Do you drink? Do you get fucked up? Why / why not? How do these things affect your art? How do these things affect the way you communicate? How do these affect your mental health? How do these things affect your daily life?

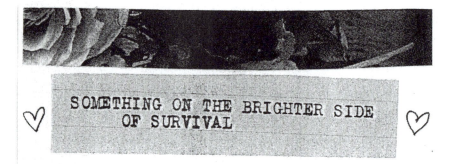

SOMETHING ON THE BRIGHTER SIDE OF SURVIVAL

I use that word a lot. Survival. For a while, that was enough, but not anymore. It began to sound depressing to me. Just surviving? I mean, yeah, sometimes that's what my life is. I'm getting by. I'm alive. But I want my life to be more than that. I didn't think it was possible; I was too crazy, too depressed, to think I could have a particularly meaningful, magical life, to think that I might do anything worthwhile, to think that I might finish anything, that I might enjoy my days, that other people might care about me, might care about the things I write.

Survival meant staying alive. That's all. Passing the time, not hurting myself too much, not killing myself. Sometimes I had to go to hospitals to survive, sometimes I had to avoid them. I wanted something else, and I feel like maybe now I'm actually making those things happen.

What do you do to allow yourself something more than just survival?

LET'S GO OUT!
WHAT'S IN YOUR BAG?

I have a hard time leaving the house without ten million books and notebooks and pens. In case of an emergency. I don't like to be stranded anywhere without something to read. And I need Notebook A in case I want to write in my journal, Notebook B in case I need to write a note for a piece of fiction, a stack of stationery in case I feel like writing a letter, my little agenda because I don't know what on earth is going on if I don't have it with me. And there is the floral zippered pouch filled with zines and fliers, the red zippered pouch that acts as my portable pharmacy, filled with pills and Rescue Remedy and I forget what else. I have my umbrella and my digital camera and a disposable camera. I have three black pens, a purple pen, a red pen, and a purple Sharpie. I have a violet pouch filled with stones and acorns. I have at least one book with me, maybe two, because when I get to where I'm going, I want to be able to choose between fiction or non-fiction, depending upon my mood and concentration levels. Oh, and my wallet. All this fits into my backpack. I can't carry bags on my shoulder anymore because of chronic pain, so backpacks are kind of saving my life right now.

Sometimes I use everything in my backpack, sometimes I don't. Sometimes I feel foolish for all the things I carry around, like I am too attached to them, like I might even be identity-less without them, but sometimes I feel like, fuck that, I am a magical artist, I am allowed to carry all these silly things around with me wherever I go, I don't care. One thing I am trying to do right now is use smaller notebooks so they don't take up much space, but at the same time, I have a bad habit of buying notebooks all the time whether or not I actually need anymore right now, so I also use large notebooks in an effort to curb my notebook purchasing bad habits because larger notebooks last longer. Like, I have been writing in one particular diary since November 2010 and I am not even halfway through that notebook, which means I can quit buying diaries all the darn time.

What do you carry with you when you leave the house? Why? What do these things say about you? What kind of bag do you carry your stuff in? Where do you bring these things? What could I learn about you by searching through your bag and what would remain hidden?

♡ MAKING LISTS OF PRIORITIES ♡

On the first day of each month, I write a small list of my priorities for that month, and I also read my Tarot cards and draw one that I leave out in a visible spot to guide me through the month and keep me on track. Some examples of the things I write on my lists are:

- finishing projects
- taking a break
- Doing Nothing
- time outdoors
- friendship
- getting rid of stuff
- breathing
- get off the internet
- self-care
- honesty
- challenge myself
- meaningful days
- something on the brighter side of "survival"

I pin these little lists up with pretty magnets so I see them everyday and I ask myself what I am doing at this moment that is helpful and positive for my current priorities. And then I will find something to do. That might mean choosing a project to work on so I am closer to finishing it, going for a walk, making plans with a friend, taking a few moments to meditate, shutting off my computer... Whatever it is I need to do, or need to feel, I try my best to find a way.

♥ DRINKING COFFEE & THINKING ABOUT ♥ DOING STUFF

Is there ever a time when I am not wondering, *What do I want to do with my life?* I find labels and I apply them to myself. Writer. Zinester. Weirdo. Genderqueer. Artist. Aspiring Life Coach (seriously). I think about who I want to be, and then I think, *Well, fuck. Why don't I just become that person right now?* So I am, because I said so.

I prepare a pot of coffee before I go to bed, so when I wake up, I just have to press a button. The coffee brews while I pee. My cats, Amélie the tuxedo cat, and Lily-Biscuit the ginger cat, follow me into the bathroom. I bring a giant mug of black coffee into my livingroom and decide what I want to do while I wake up. Is there something I need to write down? Did I have a vivid dream last night? What book do I want to read? Do I feel like fiction or non-fiction? Do I intend to leave the house today? I wish I got out of bed earlier. Can I afford a silly fancy latté, or should I make more coffee and bring it to the library? Who am I? What the fuck am I doing with my life?

In Winter, I need to have a warm drink in my hands at all times. It helps me feel safe and in control. Sometimes I overdo it on the caffeine, but whatever, it's my favourite antidepressant. Sometimes I switch to peppermint tea. Everybody knows I have endless tea in my kitchen, nearly twenty varieties to choose from.

I want to write all day long, but sometimes I just stare into space, watch squirrels from my windows, scratch at my skin, and daydream about all the things I'd like to be Writing, all the things I'd like to be Doing. Sometimes I say, *Shut up, Maranda, just get up and Make Something*, other times, I continue to daydream. I can Make Stuff tomorrow.

When I'm the most depressed, I wish somebody would actually, physically hold my hand and guide me through life because I can't do it. I need help. I need somebody to make my decisions for me and I need somebody to hold me accountable for seeing those decisions through. I need somebody to gush to about the day I woke up not wanting to kill myself, the day I finished a project, the day I didn't get angry at a stranger, the night I went to sleep at a reasonable hour looking forward to tomorrow. I need somebody to acknowledge that things are happening, that I am making things happen. I need somebody to hold me accountable.

I am trying to find that validation, that acknowledgement, within myself. I want myself to be enough. I feel like things will make more sense when I can sit with them quietly and not have to shout them out to the world, even though sometimes I like doing that, too.

I once had the thought that I would like my life to be an art project, an experiment, but I had a warped view of what that was, and it led to self-destruction. I used to not be able to focus on each moment because I was busy thinking about how I might write about it later. But I never had the wherewithal to write it just right. So I wasn't living and I wasn't writing. I don't know. My head was too messy.

I still want my life to be an art project, but a different kind. I can't name it, it's hard to explain. What if my life could be all about how to create an amazing life and all this positivity and all this meaning and whatnot, while living with depression, while living with BPD and PTSD and anxiety and all those other diagnoses and neuroses that are always adding up? What if I could create a life worth living, and what if I could help others do the same?

I joked for a while that I wanted to be a life coach, but now I sort of actually do, but I would come up with another name. Maranda Elizabeth, Creativity Coach, helping you create magical days and meaningful art and self-confidence through ridiculously honest expression, etc. I always thought I needed somebody to hold my hand and guide me through life, make my decisions for me, and now I think I'd rather *be* that person, in a positive and inspiring way, not a control freak way. I don't know if this is another one of my manic ideas, or if it's real (not that manic ideas aren't real, but that's another conversation for another zine).

♡ ALL THOSE MYTHICAL CRAZY ARTISTS ♡

So, all these cool people make all this really neat art, and they are crazy, and maybe one day they go crazy enough to kill themselves, and then their art has even more meaning, now it's really magical and inspiring. You listen to their music when you're sad, and their books line your shelves, and their paintings are reprinted on placemats and coffee mugs. You hear these stories about them, these myths, and you totally romanticize their lives, the way they created and the way they finally escaped.

I used to think affirmations were really foolish and useless until I began creating my own and actually using them. Last time I was in ye olde mental hospital, I said to myself, over and over, *I would rather be Margaret Atwood than Sylvia Plath*. I stumbled into this affirmation by mistake, during a meeting with my nurse, my psychiatrist, and the director of the inpatient program. We were talking about what on earth to do with Me, because I felt like nothing was helping, and I was risking being kicked out of the program by continually self-injuring, which, as you might guess, isn't allowed on hospital grounds. I didn't want to go home yet, but I couldn't figure out what to do, what to change, And then I said it. I said that I wanted to live and I wanted to make art, and I wanted the things I made and wrote and whatever to be appreciated and valued and shared while I was alive. I didn't want to kill myself to be a success. I mean, what a bore. It's such an old story.

Even when I'm taking my meds and taking care of myself, I am still prone to manic episodes and bouts of insomnia. I have a symptom called rapid-cycling, which means that my moods can change wildly and quickly, and those changes in my moods can lead to things like impulsivity, poor decisions, physical illness, self-injurious behaviour, jealousy, anger, and all sorts of unhealthy things that I must learn how to manage and keep under some kind of control in order to stay alive.

There are no magical cures, but there are things that help. What helps me the most is writing. And I don't want to go crazy writing. I don't want to write a novel that hits the bestseller lists after I kill myself. I would rather write all sorts of novels and zines and letters and non-fiction and short stories, and continue to create this wonderful magical life for myself, and maybe one day all my messy words will lead me to some kind of "fulfillment", maybe they'll give me the money to buy myself a little home and more tattoos and trips to visit my friends. Sometimes I imagine going back to my hometown, way in the future, when I can be an eccentric older weirdo, and there will be all these funny rumours about me, and I'll have shutters on my windows that are painted lavender, and overgrown gardens and squirrels climbing the trees, and stacks of stained glass windows that I've been collecting from junk stores, and even though people will say mean things about me sometimes, they will also be totally intrigued and fascinated by me because I have all sorts wonderful stories, real and unreal, and they wish they could be as wild and honest and carefree as me. They'll marvel at how I created all these things, and how I lived through it all.

I don't know about you, but when I'm in hospitals, I have a hard time finding the artsy ones. There have been a few. I knew a girl who made incredible paintings with all sorts of spirals and colours and patterns that you could lose yourself in. She took me to the movies once, when I was new on the ward. But for the most part, I have met a lot of ordinary people who happen to have mental health conditions and happen to have access to treatment (sometimes). Not that that's a huge terrible problem, I just feel like with that reputation of crazy people being artists and artists being crazy, you'd find more artsy crazyfolk when you're hospitalized, but for me, that hasn't been the case. Maybe I'm getting into dangerous territory here, but I feel like there are all these stories of meeting wonderful weirdos on inpatient and getting involved in unhealthy but super-romanticized friendships & relationships, and there's this fantasy of meeting that one fuck-up who's gonna change your life forever, and I'm like, Where are you?

I feel like even on psych wards, I am the lone freak because I Make Art, and people seem to know that about me right away, before I say anything. I guess I have artist vibes. And then, because I Do Stuff, I am looked at as either the Crazy Artist, or in fact I am not Crazy Enough, *because* I am actually doing things and making things, and I guess I am supposed to be totally incapable when I am depressed and anxious and have that plastic bracelet on my wrist again. (Sometimes I am incapable, but for the most part, I have gotten pretty good at forcing myself to do things because I know that's what keeps me alive.)

Anyway, this led me to the belief that the crazy artist thing is just a huge gigantic myth. It makes money, it sells art. Maybe it convinces people to make more art before they die. Maybe it convinces a few of us to stay alive. I don't know. I know that I feel more inspired by people who have survived. I do have a silly romantic fascination with The Twenty-Seven Club, but I'm going to be twenty-seven myself later this year, and I am not going to be ready to die. My brain will probably be spinning with even more ideas, and maybe some of the projects I'm planning right now will be on the go, maybe some of them will even be complete.

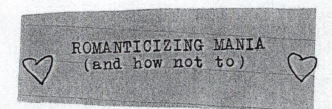

ROMANTICIZING MANIA
(and how not to)

As writers and artists, I think we need to be able to admit when we are romanticizing something, and get real, I feel like my heart and brain wander down this path too easily, and I need to catch myself. I mean, when is romanticizing something useful, and when is it harmful? Are there aspects of your life, or other peoples' lives, that you tend to romanticize? How can we unlearn this trick and find something new, find healthier ways to make our art and keep ourselves alive in the meantime?

Mania is dangerous. Obviously. Sometimes I feel it creeping up on me, but sometimes I worry that my activities, my ideas, my overwhelmedness with everything in my head, is going to trigger mania. And now I have to pay attention to the tiniest details, the itchy molecules of mania, and make a conscious decision not to let it take over. To calm, down, breathe, take a sleeping pill if I can't sleep. Sometimes I feel it coming on when I've missed my meds only once. With a long history of insomnia and mania, I need meds or I simply don't sleep. If I try, I lay in bed tip-tapping my feet quickly, daydreaming too hard, writing scribbly notes in the dark that may or may not make sense later, pacing the apartment, watching my bedroom slowly slowly slowly grow lighter. Or I stay up all night Doing Stuff. That is often an appealing possibility; let the mania take over, write write write, stories lists ideas plans letters another novel, whatever. I'll let myself do this sometimes. But I try not to romanticize this notion anymore, that I need to be crazy to be creative.

♡ FIGHT BOREDOM WRITE ANYTHING CLUB ♡

Fight Boredom is a project my twin sister began a few years back, with a focus on, well, fighting boredom. It started as a compilation zine, and evolved into manifestos, crafternoons, a distro, a blog, a letter-writing club, a mindset, and a lifestyle. Only boring people get bored, my sister says. Fight Boredom began in our hometown, Lindsay, Ontario, and now we've carried it to our current homes; Montréal, Québec for her, and Guelph, Ontario, for me. I like to think of our towns as branches and our projects as leaves.

When I moved back to Guelph, there were all sorts of little clubs I wanted to start, all sorts of projects I wanted to work on. But you know how it is with these things. Not enough time, not enough energy, and when you finally get your shit together, everybody says these are good ideas but then they don't show up because they have their own lives and stuff. Sometimes I feel like I'm really good at coming up with names for clubs and projects and stuff, and not always so great at seeing them through.

Finally, I'm realizing I just need to do stuff. Waiting around for the perfect time is no good because that day is not actually going to happen. Waiting around for the perfect venue that is free and close to everyone and accessible to everyone is no good because that place isn't gonna come around either. I know because I tried.

So now these things happen wherever I am, whenever I feel like it. The clubs I wanted to start the most were these: a) a snail mail letter-writing club, and b) a club for writers of zines and fiction and whatever. I wanted a regular time and date for these things, so I could carve out time in my schedule instead of procrastinating. For the snail mail club, I wanted however many of us to gather somewhere like the library or a café or whatever and I wanted to provide stationery and stamps and tea, and we could all just catch up with our pen pals and one another and everything would be wonderful. And for the writers club, I wanted us to meet up in similar locations, or maybe just my apartment or something, and we could work on our writing projects and share them with one another for critique and advice and encouragement and whatnot, and we could make zines and stuff if we felt like it. They'd be like work-on-stuff-dates, like you know how sometimes you're working on something, and you wish you had company, like a silent friend sitting nearby working on their own thing? So many people said they'd join me. But it just never came together. It was daydreams that I talked about with my pals but never truly organized, never truly got my shit together.

And I realized I couldn't organize everything all on my own, couldn't find the perfect times and places, so I combined these ideas into the Fight Boredom Write Anything Club, and now I call impromptu gatherings at places like the queer library where I volunteer, the public library downtown, my apartment... wherever. When warmer seasons come around, we can meet up on a picnic blanket down by the river, on my porch, in somebody's backyard... And this is just more comfortable, it makes more sense to me, to no longer wait around for permission, for the perfect time, for everybody's schedules to magically match up. Let's just write anything anywhere, everything everywhere, and hope for the best. Forget planning, let's just do stuff.

INSPIRATION

Where do you feel the most inspired? Are there specific places that just make you feel like breathing and smiling and writing? Are they indoors or outdoors? When do you feel the most creative? Morning? Daytime? Dusk? Midnight? Do you feel inspired just as you're falling asleep, or is that just me? What seasons make you feel particularly creative? Are there objects that inspire you? Emotions? Weather patterns? Dreams? Do you ever stumble on the sidewalk because you're writing while walking, or is that just me, too? Do you ever look up words in a thesaurus just for fun?

Inspiration – grasp, penetration, acuteness, perspicacity, sagacity, mother wit, understanding, comprehension, savvy, imagination, impulse, flash, sensation, feeling, predilection, emotion, revelation, manifestation...

What do you do when you experience writer's block? Have you thought about just writing random words, unconnected, no full sentences, and seeing where that leads you? (This actually might be dangerous if you are in the midst of a deep depression, but it can be helpful if you are feeling safe.)

Some of the places I feel inspired might sound cliché, but it's true. I feel inspired in cafés, especially when I find a seat in a cozy corner and feel like I am partly alone, partly surrounded. I feel inspired in bookstores, on buses, and in cities that are not my home (I also feel inspired at home, here in Guelph, and of course my twenty or so years in Lindsay creep into most all of my art). I feel inspired when I'm falling asleep and when I'm drinking coffee. I take notes wherever I go in an attempt to never lose that feeling.

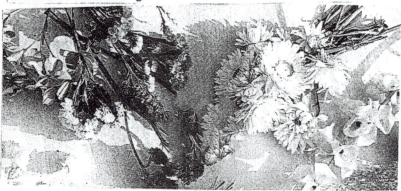

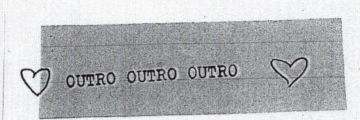

OUTRO OUTRO OUTRO

Thank you for reading my zine! I'm finishing issues twenty-four and twenty-five just on time for the NYC Feminist Zinefest in February and the Chicago Zinefest in March. Maybe I'll see you there?! My days have been hectic and wonderful, and I'm feeling pretty good about my life at this moment, feeling like good things are happening and I am changing and everything is fascinating, everything is a learning process. Please write to me! I adore snail mail. Let me know about all the creative and magical and artsy things you're up to!

NOTE: My zine used to be called *Telegram Ma'am*, but I altered the title after realizing that, as someone who does not identify as female (or male), the gendered title made me uncomfortable, and could be potentially alienating on several levels. I've been making zines for about ten years now, and changes are inevitable; I thought about beginning a new title altogether, but *Telegram (Ma'am)* is such an important part of my life and I'm not ready to give that up.

before when i would think of the city it was always a fantasy, a theory, an ideology; something about library books and a desk and long nights and working in manhattan and living in brooklyn and reading poems on stages and having interesting people for lovers and friends and drinking a lot of coffee and writing a book that i knew could be something, studying philosophy and women and men and humanity in some tiny little room all my own... and it's amazing, really, when your fantasies become totally and completely REAL...

...and if i die in new york at least i will die free

by carly houser
(rest-in-pissedoffedness, old friend)

TELEGRAM

issue 26

July 2012

♥ INTRO INTRO INTRO ♥

In search of inspiration, I asked my friends to ask me questions about anything at all, and I turned my answers into a zine. Each question, both simple & complicated, brought back so many memories and stories, and I found myself eager to write them down and share them. Thank you to my friends who asked thoughtful questions, and thank you for reading my zine. As usual, send snail mail and make your own zine!

♡ QUESTIONS ♡

♡ What is your writing process? ♡

It took me a long time to realize that if you want to be a writer, this does not mean you need to set your alarm, wake up, write for eight hours. I learned that you don't have to write everything in order. You don't have to write it down exactly as it happened, you don't have to write it in the order you want to print it (if you want to print it at all). You don't have to work on only one project at a time. I tried so hard to make Writing my "full-time job," and I felt like a total failure when I couldn't make it happen. I wasn't a failure, though; I was in the midst of a forever-long process of figuring out how to write. I don't have one simple writing process. I like hearing about others' writing processes, and then integrating parts of those into my own life.

Whenever somebody asks me about my writing process, I feel like I need to say, 'Here's step one, and this is step two...' But writing doesn't work like that, not for me. The way it goes for me, is, I think of something from the past, or somebody says something and I feel angry, or there's something I want to share. There are so many stories that need to be told. One of my fears is that all my journals, zines, letters, blog entries, are all just making up one long suicide note. But maybe they're keeping me alive, too. (I could never write a suicide note before my attempts, because there was too much to say and I knew I'd never be able to write it all.)

♡ ♡ ♡

I have two writing desks. One of them is lilac. I painted it with the same spraypaint I used to paint my bike. And my other desk is white wicker with a drawer that I painted the same shade of lavender as my livingroom. The drawers of each desk hold stationery, blank paper, writing scraps, and the lilac desk holds three copies of my first novel that my friends edited for me. There are plants and candles on my desks, and a jar full of pens (black, purple, red), and space. Space for my paper, my laptop, or piles of junk; I call them my to-do piles. They are never finished. My lilac desk looks out my bedroom window onto the traintracks and treetops and the sky, and my wicker desk faces a wall with postcards and notes and a chalk board.

I don't always write at my desks. I also write at cafés, under trees, on my porch, at libraries, on my livingroom floor... right now, I am writing in bed. I write in pieces. I take frequent breaks. I like to light candles when I write, and drink coffee or tea. I take notes. I keep little notebooks with me, and I stick post-its to my walls and notes to my fridge. I hold onto the notes until I figure out what to do with them. I have notes from a decade ago, waiting to find their place. I write when I am angry, frustrated, or sad, and also when I am feeling hopeful and optimistic. I dare myself to be as honest as I can, to write the things that scare me. I want my writing to be encouraging. I don't want to whine; I want to find solutions, I want to create magical ways of living.

♡ **What was the most frightening experience you had as a kid?** ♡

I don't remember a specific instance of being frightened, but I had recurring nightmares when I was a kid, and they terrified me. I used to have nightmares about my mom. In these nightmares, I had two moms, an evil one and a good one, and I couldn't tell them apart until it was too late. I'd dream that I was watching TV with my mom, and then I would hear a key in the lock of the front door, and it would be my mom coming home. Suddenly I had one mom on the couch and one coming in the front door, and I didn't know which one I needed to run away from. I always ran upstairs to hide, but I had to run by the front door to get to the stairs.

My sister had the same nightmares. We called the evil version of our mom "Scary Mom." I'd run upstairs and hide under the bed, and Scary Mom would chase me under and try to tickle me, but I knew she was actually going to hurt me or kill me. Then I'd wake up in my own bed, paralyzed. When I woke up from nightmares, I'd want to call out to my mom, but I couldn't do that when they were about her. I was afraid to move every time I had a nightmare, so I'd just hide as still as I could under my blankets, afraid to get up, afraid to fall asleep. I thought there was somebody else in the room and I'd stay very still to keep them away from me. My sister and I would tell each other about our dreams. "I had another Scary Mom dream last night."

I also had dreams where Scary Mom was made of deep blue velvet ribbons and had silver buttons for eyes. And I had nightmares where I would fall down the stairs, but then I would be flying. I was scared of stairs until I was in my mid-teens. I would race up them all the time because I thought somebody was chasing me. I didn't like to stand near my bed because I thought somebody would grab my ankles from underneath, so sometimes I'd race up the stairs and dive into bed to avoid the monsters. I had these nightmares from around age five through eighteen. I feel like I spent most of my childhood being scared, but it's hard to define just what it was I was so afraid of.

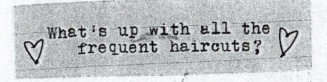

What's up with all the frequent haircuts?

My sister asked me this. I don't know if she was serious or not, but I'm answering it anyway. Haircuts can actually be kind of significant in my life, even if I pretend like, oh, it's just hair, who cares. I used to give myself haircuts at three o' clock in the morning. Now it's just whenever. Sometimes I cut my hair instead of cutting myself. I tend to cut or dye or change my hair in some way when I am feeling unspeakably sad and don't have it in me to change the circumstances of my life beyond my hair. Or when I feel like I need some kind of change in my life but I don't know what it is yet. Also, I frequently forget who I am or I want to be somebody else, and a haircut always seems like the thing to do to re-find myself or create somebody else (it never totally works; I'm always just me). My hair is all wrapped up in my weird identity issues.

♡ Can you pinpoint the best day of your life? ♡

I can pinpoint good eras of my life, but not specific days. And I can find the good moments in some of the darkest days. Like, some of my favourite times were a few summers ago when I would ride my bike down to the river at sunrise, and read under the trees, but I was going out that early because my insomnia was really bad that summer, and that was all I knew what to do. I also once spent a summer having cute dates with somebody and going to the drive-in and making out in the backseat of their parents' car, and I look back fondly at those times despite shitty things that happened later. I am a nostalgic person and I'm not afraid to admit it anymore. I used to love going to shows in my hometown and dancing with my sister, which was also sweet times amidst some darker, shittier things. My best days aren't when I'm doing really loud important exciting things, but just the quieter, simpler things that help keep me content. My best days are when I can read good books & zines on my porch and write letters with the sun shining over me, days when I can lay down my picnic blanket in the grass and call that little square my home, days when I can ride my bike and nobody runs me over, and I like days when I get tattooed, capturing more stories on my skin forever, and the way the tattoo machine needle feels. I like days when I bump into friendly people, known and unknown, and their words brighten my day and give me something to think/write about. I like days where I can get out of bed early and get all my boring errands done before noon, and I like days where I get good letters in the mail. Moving days aren't my favourite, but the next few days after moving into a new place are fun for me; unpacking, settling, creating a home and a routine and everything. I also like staying up all night writing, and nights when both my cats fall asleep against me, and days where I realize all the boring things on my to-do lists are done and all I need to do now is the fun stuff: writing, daydreaming, adventuring...

♡ What are your thoughts on gender? ♡

Confusion and bafflement. I don't like to make broad statements about gender. I can only tell you about my own experience. I've written a lot about my own gender identities in the past, and sometimes I feel like I talk about it too much, but at the same time, there is still so much left unsaid, so many conflicting feelings that I can't ignore. Like how, in one way being genderqueer can feel so freeing, and in other ways, it's this daily struggle to figure out who I am, worry about how I am being interpreted / how I am representing myself, and whether or not I want to be the same person I was yesterday. Simple things like getting dressed have always been difficult for me, and now there is this whole other side to whether I choose to wear a skirt or pants, make-up or none, what kind of shoes I wear, how I style my hair; and then that extends to what kind of bike I ride, what kind of bag I carry, what kind of glasses I wear, on and on. Sometimes I wish I could be a "girl" again, but I know that wouldn't make things as easy as I like to imagine, nor would I suddenly feel more comfortable and accepting of myself. I'd just be hiding and lying. At the same time, I don't feel like I fit in with any kind of genderqueer community either; because I don't wear the genderqueer uniform, because I get misgendered in queer spaces and feminist spaces, because I've never felt I fit in with any kind of community at all, and this hasn't been an exception.

It also seems like no matter how much I talk about gender, a lot of people just really don't get it. It took (and continues to take) even close friends too long to start using my preferred pronoun, and there are still a lot of people around who call me 'she'. Sometimes I let it go because I don't feel like having that discussion *again*, but inside, I'm feeling all stabby and gross. It's gotten to the point where there are so-called friends I've considered simply discontinuing contact with, which is hard, obviously, but I can only go through this so many times before it becomes unacceptable. While I understand not everyone knows anything about gender theory or has had to really think about how they relate or don't relate to their own assigned gender, I also think I've been really forgiving, to a point that may have caused some damage; I also think that, whether or not you know a damn thing about gender, when somebody tells you what pronoun to use, you just use it.

As I was reading my older zines and getting my anthology together, I realized that I pretty much over-identified as 'girl', trying to find a sense of belonging: girl-friendships and girl gangs and girl-romance, and I guess I've had to give that up. Although I get angry when it's assumed that I'm a girl, I also have these brief moments of... not acceptance, but like I've infiltrated some secret group and been mistaken for one of them. The feeling doesn't last long, and it's not as strong as the feelings of frustration & anger, invisibility, left-outedness, and occasional dissociation and ambivalence. For the most part, it feels like an act of violence inflicted by the sadly unaware, or simply uncaring. And it seems I might be doomed to endure these repeated injuries forever.

♡ **What were you doing between the ages of eighteen – twenty-two?** ♡

I was unspeakably shy when I was eighteen, and symptoms of my agoraphobia were at their height, so I think I spent a lot of time hiding in my bedroom and wearing pajamas all day everyday because I had no reason to get dressed. Agoraphobia got so bad that I could barely go out onto the porch to check the mailbox, or walk out to my mom's car to get a ride somewhere, and I certainly couldn't do everyday ordinary tasks like go to stores and run errands, or even go for a walk. If somebody knocked at the door, I would hide behind the furniture. I also had an eating disorder, and I would keep track of everything I had ~~written~~ eaten and drank in my diary, and try to make the lists smaller each day. I had no real goal of weight loss or anything, I just wanted to fade away and disappear, and I thought that not eating would aid me in that mission. I remember writing in a purple fabric-bound journal with beads and embroidery threads stitched into the cover, listening to Melissa Auf der Maur's first album, and dreaming of shrinking to the size of a bug and living in a forest, eating leaves and berries and drinking creek water from the tops of acorns as little cups. As you might imagine, I was also really into Francesca Lia Block. I had just gotten my own computer, and I spent most of my time on LiveJournal. My sister had started dating somebody around that time, and I was a little jealous as I was now spending more time alone than I used to, and I felt guilty and pathetic every time my sister went out and my mom would ask me why I wasn't going out with her, why I wasn't going to parties, why I wasn't interested in dating anyone. She kept asking if I was a lesbian, and I kept not having an answer.

♡ ♡ ♡

I remember my nineteenth birthday quite vividly, which was of course the first time I got legally drunk. Actually, I didn't have ID yet, so I was kicked out of the first bar, but they had already served me, and I remember chugging a pitcher of beer as I gathered my things to move on to the next bar. I remember heckling some dude with a guitar to play Pearl Jam, and he played *Black*, and I remember going to the bathroom with my sister to guard the door and watch her drink, and I drank half of it while she was peeing. That was in the fall, but I didn't start really drinking until the following summer, which I might as well admit, was mostly because I had finally started dating somebody, too, and I felt too nervous to make out or interact at all when I was sober, so whiskey saved my life, it seemed. It was always a problem, too, of course, but me and the people I was hanging out with were able to ignore it for a long time, probably because we were all drinkers and to question one person's drinking problem might lead us all to question our own, to question everyone's. That was the summer I spent at the drive-in, in the backseat, drinking a lot of whiskey. I lost my virginity that summer, after a metal show at the Trasheteria where I had dove into the moshpit determined to get the most bruises.

♡ ♡ ♡

I was prescribed antidepressants around that time, and saw a therapist who did Cognitive Behavioural Therapy, and taught me how to walk outside again. Agoraphobia had become too much, and I became especially terrified of going outside after being hit by a car the previous winter. I liked this therapist. She was the first therapist I ever liked, the first who ever said anything that made sense to me. She would take me for walks through downtown Peterborough. At first, we would walk beside one another. Then she'd walk a little bit ahead of me or a little bit behind, and I'd be learning how to walk on my own. We'd start by walking only one block, then our walks would become longer. I think I saw her for twelve weeks, and we would go for a walk during each appointment. Sometimes I'd have a panic attack, and we'd turn around and go back to her office, or we'd stop and sit down on a park bench and she'd help me re-learn how to breathe again. She also tried to teach me how to use telephones, since I had a phobia about them, too, but my ability to use phones didn't last for long, and I still avoid them today.

♡ ♡ ♡

After that summer, I got a job as a crossing guard. We'd said we were only going be together for the summer, until he left town and went back to school, but as September approached, the boy I was dating asked how I would feel about taking the Greyhound to come visit on alternating weekends. I got the job so I could pay for bus tickets, and I spent the next ten months visiting him in Guelph, and then I moved in with him in the summer. I also started cutting myself again that summer, after not cutting for maybe something like three years. I got upset at something silly, biked home, cut up my hips with a kitchen knife, and when he came home and lowered my skirt and saw the cuts, he got mad at me. I don't think I cut myself for a while after that, but a few months later, in November 2006, just after I had turned twenty-one, I had my first suicide attempt. I had a fight with my boss at a sandwich shop where I worked, stormed out during my shift, and swallowed sixty sleeping pills, some Tylenol 3's, and alcohol. I cleaned the apartment as I did this, fed my cat and played with her, and then I went back to bed, where my partner was still sleeping. It was mid-morning.

I was in the hospital for a few days, then moved to the mental health treatment centre across the street for a week, and then I came home. Things were obviously different, and very uncomfortable and strained. I wanted to forget the whole thing, and he did, too, but it was impossible to pretend it never happened. We discussed taking a break, we discussed moving to Toronto, we discussed all sorts of things, but really, we just got very sad and broken for a while, and we broke up.

♡ ♡♡

That Winter is a blur. I had no outpatient treatment after leaving the hospital, and no real home; I spent time in our shared apartment, where we were both still sort of living since we had nowhere else to go, and we alternated between fighting and fucking, fighting and fucking. My violent streak came back when we fought (and was quelled briefly when we fucked, though when I look back, I see how we always used sex to try to solve our problems, and I remember that moment of agreeing with one another: "We're just fucking and splitting the bills."). Sometimes I'd go back to Lindsay and stay in the spare room of my mom's apartment. At the time, after realizing I was no longer capable or willing to work, I was in the process of applying for welfare and disability. I remember the books I was reading at the time: *The Time Traveler's Wife* by Audrey Niffenegger and *Alice's Adventures In Wonderland & Through the Looking-Glass* by Lewis Carroll, both of which were given to me, along with a double mix CD, by a dear pen pal I have since lost touch with. But really, I spent most of my time crying & crying & crying and wishing I could actually go through with this damned suicide, wishing I had the guts. Just that debilitating kind of depression where you can't eat, can't talk, can't think, can't write. Just lie in bed. Lie in bed all day and all night and never know how much time has passed, just that it is passing far too slowly. I remember the grey carpets, the stacks of boxes and garbage bags containing my possessions, the smell of cinnamon, and the way I broke down the first time I washed the dishes at my mom's apartment, somehow totally frightened and overwhelmed that they weren't my lover's dishes and that they never would be. I used to get mad at him for leaving too much peanut butter on the knives when he put them in the sink, the smell of hot water on stale peanut butter makes me feel ill, and now here I was sad that I wasn't washing his dishes anymore. I remember buying a new blanket, one that could be mine and only mine, orange, the happiest colour.

My partner stayed in our apartment as he tried to find someone to take over the remaining six months of our lease, and I swung back and forth between my mom's place, the mental health ward at the local hospital, a shelter for homeless youth in Guelph that has since ceased to exist, and eventually I moved back to Guelph and rented a room with a 97-year old woman. I thought my life would calm down then, and I could use the room to write and take care of myself and figure shit out. It turned out to be a lousy living situation on several levels, some of which have been documented in previous zines, but I do have a few fond memories. The room came furnished, so for the month that I was there, I was able to use a dreamy, old writing desk with little compartments, so I wrote my zines and letters and diaries there, with my cat by my side.

I moved out to live with someone I had met online and known for about a week, which is to say, not at all. My drinking got truly out of control, and I was smoking pot most days, which is not like me. I can look back now and see that I was in an abusive situation with a charismatic, manipulative person. We never discussed our "relationship," and never admitted or dealt with the problems we were having; we were both jealous, passive-aggressive, avoidant, and uncommunicative. There's nothing I can say about this situation without feeling such bewilderment; my only explanation for how any of it could have happened is that I must have been a totally different person at the time. Not just that I was constantly drunk and fucked up, not just that I was heartbroken and confused, not just that I was manic and desperate, but like another personality must have taken over my body.

♡ ♡ ♡

It all fell apart pretty quickly, as these things do, and I broke down, fled the place, and stayed with my mom yet again, before returning to Guelph the following month and renting a room in an apartment by the river. It was a small room, and I mostly hibernated, except for my sunrise-insomniac-bike-rides, and busking late at night with my roommate. My cat ripped a hole in the screen door so she could go outside, and sometimes she would bring back dead mice that she had suffocated in her mouth and kept intact, and leave them on the floor as little gifts for me. I had intended to stay in this place much longer; I was sick of moving all the time, sick of constant instability, but I became extremely depressed and lonely. I had no friends; the only people I interacted with aside from my roommate were strangers I'd pick up online, have sex with, and then discard and ignore. I decided to move back to Lindsay in September, but I wasn't sure if I was moving back to save my life, or to kill myself.

When I moved back to Lindsay, my sister gave me a porcelain doll with a little note tucked inside: *You and I are gonna take over this town!* She had moved back a few months earlier after getting back together with an ex-partner, and we were determined to live creative and adventurous lives in our small, hopeless hometown. We made plans for crafternoons and graffiti nights, and we promised we wouldn't have to get drunk to have fun (we were still drinking, but were trying not to let alcohol be the necessary ingredient in all of our activities). Our plans were filled with letdowns, though. Fight Boredom, the name we attempted to organize under, was one of those things where people would say it was a good idea, but then they wouldn't show up. Or they'd insist on drinking when we said we wanted to have a sober afternoon. My sister and I wanted to learn how to communicate with~~out~~ alcohol, how to have fun, how be social, and how to create. I remember watching her make zines while sitting on the floor, cutting up paper and banging on her typewriter, laying out the pages. I guess sometimes I'd read or I'd work on something, but sometimes we'd give up on doing stuff and just waste time on the internet and dance on her bed to mix tapes from her pen pals. And sometimes we'd give up on the sober adventures and drink a bottle or two of wine.

I rode my bike a lot, and vacillated between trying to live healthier, and just giving up. I was still making zines, but my friends were scattered all over the place and I didn't have any close friends in Lindsay, so I was feeling isolated from the communities I would rather have been participating in. I quit drinking a dozen times, not for much longer than a few weeks at a time. I remember going to open jams at a certain bar on Thursday nights, and going to shows, and being a drunk, obnoxious jerk. Once, I rode my bike home drunk, left my lock in the parking lot of a bar, crashed, and lost my glasses. I retraced my steps the next day, thinking they must have fallen off when I crashed and that I'd been too drunk to care, but they weren't there; three days later, I found them under my pillow. I continued the drunken sluttery thing for a while (no shame! just stories!), my insomnia got really bad, and I seemed to be trying a hundred different psych med combinations at once, unable to differentiate the effects and side effects of any of them, just knowing that I felt totally dead. The meds seemed to shut down my brain, make me incapable of all the writing I wanted to do and adventures I wanted to live. I was in and out of the hospital and started seeing a therapist. Seeing her was helpful in some ways; she was an encouraging person, she helped me deal with some of my anxieties, helped me make sense of some of my patterns & habits and try to break them, blah blah... But there was also something missing. I'd been unknowingly misdiagnosed at the time, and when I look back, I see that I was very clearly acting out every symptom of borderline personality disorder, but no one else had figured it out yet, so I was being treated for bipolar disorder, which is must different from BPD, though the two can often be mistaken for one another. I also had a lot of shit going on that I felt totally unable to talk about, and it was important stuff that I should have been dealing with back then but didn't know how. I had another lonely summer, and I stopped seeing my therapist when she took time off to be with her family. I attempted going back to school but dropped out after three weeks, got myself deeper in debt, had another drunk birthday with my sister. I had another pathetic depressive Winter, trudging back and forth in the snow for group therapy and during the day and spending nights with someone I was weirdly involved with in a way that lacked communication or respect or anything at all (not to say there wasn't anything good in it – I was inspired to start working on my first novel for real during that mess, and was able to work on a few issues that I don't feel like writing about right now) and I still feel sad/confused about it sometimes, but also figure I must have been a different person back then and had to live through that experience to get to where I am today. You know how it goes.

And then it was New Year's Eve and I met YOU (my friend Dave, who asked this question)! And we drank a lot, too, and had good adventures, and then we started changing our lives together and oh my gosh. So there's four or five years in a few pages.

Should I seriously, seriously buy a house?

You already bought a house, but let's talk about it anyway! I'm totally stoked on you buying a home, and so excited to see what you do with it. I dream of owning my own home someday, and it makes me really happy that a good friend of mine has found a way to make that happen for themself.

♡ How did you learn to become so honest?

I taught myself out of necessity. (Actually, *I am continually teaching myself out of necessity.*) I think my honesty comes from a place of acceptance of my craziness and a need for everyone to know about my craziness because pretending to be sane, or even functional sometimes, can actually be debilitatingly awful for me, and also, I just felt so trapped in my early-20's, and naïve in my teens, and I needed to find ways to move through those feelings and create something different for myself. I also learned how to be honest through zines, telling stories because I didn't know what else to do, and just daring myself to say scary things because it helps me get through them. And each time I said something that scared me, I'd find others who had similar feelings, similar stories, I'd find others who felt validated and encouraged and less alone, so I just kept on going. (And while of course those connections are so damn important, I also need to say that I sort of do this more for myself than anyone else; it's how I keep myself alive.)

♡ ♡ ♡

I'm still more honest in my writing than I am when I am having a conversation with someone, but I've been working on it, and I'm getting better with being honest out loud. It's a process, as everything always is. I've always been much better at communicating through writing than speaking, and for a long time, that really bothered me, I struggled with it and felt totally helpless and apologetic about it, but I'm learning now that it's okay; if it's easier for me to write a letter to someone than it is to talk to them, then that doesn't need to be a problem in my life; it simply is what it is. Right now, I find that when I am speaking honestly with people, I tend to be self-deprecating, so that's something I'm trying to change, because I feel I am minimizing my own experiences if I can't tell a story ~~while~~ without making fun of myself in the process. Also, I've had that lifelong habit of knowing just what to say a day after a conversation or whatever, so I'm learning to accept that, and other things, and just knowing that it's okay if that's how I communicate.

I guess I just think that pretending to be okay, or sane, or normal, or even pretending to be the same kind of weird as the other weirdos around me, is really boring and soul-destroying, so if I just keep daring myself to be as honest as possible, I'll become more me, and I'll find a way.

♡ How did you learn to see others' work as inspiration & encourage- ♡ ment instead of feeling jealous & incapable?

Have you ever felt so jealous you thought you might puke? I still feel like that sometimes, but it's not as bad as it used to be. I was jealous in many areas of my life. I remember how when I was a kid, I'd be jealous of my friends for getting cool birthday presents that I knew my family couldn't afford, and I've been a jealous person in my relationships, but hardly ever able to discuss it. And of course, these jealousies extend to the realms of creativity, art, writing, zines, all those things. Let's talk about it.

The journey to even begin trying to understand my feelings of jealousy started with this:

♡ ♡ ♡

1. Riot grrrl politics, especially these two parts of the riot grrrl manifesto: *BECAUSE we are interested in creating non-hierarchical ways of being AND making music, friends, and scenes based on communication + understanding, instead of competition + good/bad categorizations* and *BECAUSE we are unwilling to let our real and valid anger be diffused and/or turned against us via the internalization of sexism as witnessed in girl/girl jealousism and self defeating girltype behaviours.*

2. Realizing I was quietly & secretly jealous in my relationships and that my jealousy was destroying my self-esteem and mental health (and my crummy self-esteem was creating more jealousy / feelings of I'm not good enough, etc.).

3. Knowing that if I don't create, I can't live, and that I am writing to take care of myself and tell stories and become the person I want to be, and that this is not a competition (and that, in fact, competition is boring & destructive & embarrassing).

♡ ♡ ♡

Sometimes it wasn't the art I was jealous of, but the fact that somebody seemed to be having more success than me.

The thing is, I hadn't figured out what "success" meant to me yet (hint: it doesn't always mean money & fame & adoration and all your dreams magically coming true at once), and I hadn't yet learned that the way I perceive somebody else's life is not necessarily the way it really is. I was really good at projecting all my fears and insecurities onto other people, and letting it wreck me. It's important to remember that a lot of artists choose to document publicly only the more positive things going on with their lives and their art, and it's easy for us to forget that they're also going through a lot of shitty days, times when their self-confidence has disappeared, days when they are feeling stuck and unable to create, days when they are too broke to eat and too sad to make things, etc.

♡ ♡ ♡

I actually remember the exact moment I realized my jealousy wasn't killing me anymore. It was last March, looking at so many zines & books on the shelves at Quimby's in Chicago when I was there for the Chicago Zinefest, and just knowing that all those wonderful things people were writing & doing, I could do those things, too (or different things), and I didn't feel like they were better than me, ahead of me, more interesting than me, cooler than me, blah blah... I reached a point where I realized my life was finally coming together the way I wanted it to, and I suddenly felt inspired, capable, and determined.

♥ Creativity & Jealousy: How to Deal ♥

1. Write down what your jealousy feels like, why you feel jealous, who or what you feel jealous of. Be disgustingly honest. Nobody else has to read it.

2. Write down ways you feel inadequate in your art. Now write down the opposite.

3. Allow yourself to feel jealous and make art anyway.

4. Learn how to be inspired without emulating somebody else's style. Be more like yourself, not more like somebody else.

5. Ask yourself why you are making what you're making. Find reasons to keep on going regardless of jealousy, envy, frustration, etc.

6. Know that there is no limit to your own creativity, and that there is more than enough room in the world for all of our art.

7. Know that you have your own voice, and that your voice is valuable and necessary.

8. Understand that creativity is more about process than outcome. Learn to love the process at least as much as the result.

9. Know that somebody else (a friend, an acquaintance, a stranger) succeeding does not mean that you are failing. What you do might seem less visible or less popular than what somebody else is doing right now, but that doesn't mean that it isn't worthwhile or valuable.

10. Talk to artists/writers/musicians/whoever you're really into. Talk about how you're feeling, ask them how they deal, ask them about their processes, tell them about yours. Maybe some of them are actually jealous of you! Share stories and encouragement, work together, organize together.

♥ Questions ♥

Do you ever feel jealous of other zinesters, bloggers, writers, musicians, illustrators, and artists? What is it that you feel jealous of, and what do you do when your feelings of jealousy get particularly bad? Have you found ways to move through your jealousies and make art anyway? How do you react to your friends' & acquaintances' perceived successes? What are your current strategies for dealing with jealousy & envy? Would you like to change those strategies? How did you come to believe that the things you make/write/draw/play/sing aren't good enough? Are you willing to do the hard work necessary to unlearn those beliefs? What books and zines and websites and artists inspire you? What art are you going to make today?!

TELEGRAM

issue 27

August 2012

INTRO INTRO INTRO

This zine branched off from another project. I asked my friends to ask me questions, and I used the questions as inspiration for my last zine, letting each one bring back memories and stories, and then sharing/purging them. But when I was asked, "What is your experience with institutionalized education," all I could think of was violence & rage & bitterness & revenge, and I knew I'd have to dedicate a whole zine, at least, to telling this story.

Despite how hard I try to be honest and open, there are many stories I've never told. Some I will keep forever, some will be told through fiction, and some will eventually find a way outta me. I feel like there are lots of different Marandas, and only parts of them are known; different parts are known to different people. My pals in Guelph don't know the Maranda(s) I was when I was living in Lindsay, the people I left behind in Lindsay don't know who I've become in Guelph, and the people who read my zines only know what I choose to tell and how I choose to tell it. These various Marandas barely begin to tell the story of who I am, and what I've lived through so far to get here.

This is maybe the scariest, most necessary, story I need to tell.

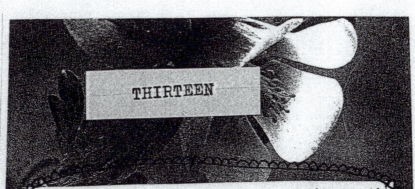

THIRTEEN

I've been having these moments where my past is catching up with me, and I'm trying to figure out what that means, trying to figure out what to do with it all. Getting stuck asking myself unanswerable questions, like, "Am I a good person?" and "What do all these things I've done actually mean?" My thoughts are spinning off in branches and vines and veins and roots, and it's hard to follow it all, but I want to. I want to trace each tiny piece and see where it leads me.

Sometimes I wonder how my thirteen year old self would feel about the person I am today. When I see people who remind me of myself at that age, I want to befriend them, I want to hear their stories. I wonder about where they're gonna end up. I think my thirteen year old self would be at least a little bit surprised that I am not dead, or that I am not in prison for murder. I think they'd be impressed at everything I've written over the years, they'd be impressed that I have my own apartment, and that I've found some truly magical ways to survive through all the craziness. I think they'd be really happy that I am still a total weirdo. I think they'd be proud of me?

What has been your experience with institutionalized education?

Sigh. I don't know where to begin with this one. It's just more nightmares. I felt homesick all the time. I faked sick all the time. I hated myself and sometimes I would fight with my mom to let me stay home from school because I felt too ugly to be seen. I'd stay in bed or watch bad TV.

I remember wearing my mom's t-shirts to school when I was in Grade Six. They were too big for me, of course. I don't think I realized at the time that I was wearing them to hide my body. I remember being in a group for kids with divorced parents; we'd be pulled out of class one afternoon a week to do different schoolwork in a different room with a different teacher. I don't remember the work we did or what we talked about. Some of us thought the woman who taught our group was also having an affair with our teacher. Our teacher had a tattoo of a mermaid on his arm, and once told me, in front of the entire class, that my mom was a lesbian. He liked to tease the kids in class, but usually took it too far. I fought with him a lot and was sent to the office a lot. When I got to junior high, there were rumours that I had thrown a desk at him.

In junior high, I was bullied and harassed daily. I was an awkward, quiet tomboy, and I wore my hair in my face, always trying to hide. I was obsessed with Kurt Cobain (um, actually, I still am), who had just died three or four years previous. I was prescribed antidepressants when I was eleven, and years later, when I got copies of my medical records, I saw that the psychiatrist had written a list of why she was giving me drugs, and among the reasons were that I "fought with my mom" and "disrespected authority."

My goth phase came along just as I turned thirteen. I dyed my hair black and tried to make my wardrobe black. But, of course, my mom had to approve my clothes, and we didn't really have the money to make my clothes match my personality, so I had to make do with what I had (I don't mean to complain about this, but to emphasize how uncomfortable it is to already feel strange & out-of-place, and then be unable to express your personality through your appearance in a way that might be helpful). We still fought a lot. Although I was dressing differently from everyone else at my school, I think the real reason I was dressing in black clothes black hair black make-up was that I wanted to hide. I hated my body, I hated my life, I hated myself, and I guess I wanted to disappear. I wore baggy jeans, extra large band t-shirts, and heavy make-up. I used to draw eyes and knives on my schoolwork, and scribble Nirvana and Marilyn Manson lyrics. I would get sent to the office for drawing pictures of bodies hanging from nooses. I started cutting myself more and more. The kids in my class would ask to see my scars, then act all grossed out and confused, and then their friends would come up to me and ask to see my scars again. "Have you seen the cuts all over Maranda's arms?" "Show me!"

I had three friends in Grade Eight. We decided to become witches. A girl I knew gave me a book called *The Practice of Witchcraft: An Introduction to Beliefs and Rituals of the Old Religion.* An aunt had given it to her because there were spells to help her with her headaches, but she didn't want it anymore. I still have that book, worn out and ripped and stained. I don't know what happened to those girls.

The first spell I cast was a spell to silence my bullies. I ended up losing my voice. There was a store downtown that sold things like stones, Tarot cards, incense, witchy things, and we would go there during lunch breaks and after school. I wanted it to be like that store in *The Craft*, but nobody ever took me to the back to tell me that they knew I was a Real Witch. The store is still there, but they mostly sell children's toys now. I had a job interview there a long time ago but never heard back. Even now, when I go in there, I feel like a cranky teenager and like the staff are watching me to make sure I'm not stealing.

I was still in Grade Eight when the Columbine shootings happened. Everyone seemed to get more nervous around me then. But not nervous enough to stop. When they yelled, "Freak!" and "Manson!" and "Witch!", they also started yelling "Columbine." No one ever got in trouble for harassing me, but if I retaliated, I'd be punished. So I was bitter. I ran away from home and lived with my then-boyfriend's family for a little while, along with my sister, who was best friends with his sister. I started skipping school and hanging out on the rooftop of the drugstore instead.

Sometimes the cops would bring me home. I remember standing in the livingroom with my mom and a cop, as he tried to convince her that I was high. My pupils were dilated, which was proof enough for him. I'd never done any drugs. I was thirteen and naïve. I'd been around pot and beer but was probably just scared of them, honestly. I think my mom believed the cop, but I don't talk about it anymore.

Then I was arrested. After I'd run away, I went back to my mom's place one night to pick up some clothes. She wasn't home, the doors were locked, and I didn't have my keys anymore, so it seemed natural to simply break down the door to get inside. I was with my boyfriend. We kicked a hole in the door, unlocked it, and went in. I went upstairs and saw that my cat had peed all over my floor and my bed and the mess I had left behind. I didn't know back then that cats pee on your things when they miss you. I found some t-shirts that weren't peed on, and came back downstairs. There was a bottle of wine in the fridge. We took it and left. Got drunk, made out, got mortified at the blood from my cunt. When I went back to school, the kids in my class said the cops were looking for me. I was arrested for break & enter and theft and I spent two months in a detention centre. The cops confiscated my favourite knife. When I told them I used it to cut myself, they asked me if I thought I was a vampire. A lot of those times are blurry. I was back at school in time to attend class for the last week. Our graduation photos arrived and my mom refused to buy any copies. I think everyone there just thought I was even weirder than before.

That summer, I shaved my head for the first time, just the back. My friend helped me out with a pink Bic razor and a bottle of water while I sat on a bench on a corner downtown. I don't remember a lot from that summer, except for hanging out with my then-best-friend, whose life was also getting weird, and hanging out with guys who were way too old for me to be hanging out with. The kind of people where you feel cool for hanging out with them, but also nervous, and you realize later that most of them were creeps. My sister moved into an apartment with some older friends downtown, still running away from home. I remember running into her downtown once, and she looked so different, wearing her friend's corduroy pants and an old t-shirt. Her hair was longer and the dye had faded. She was also arrested, for different things, shortly after I'd been released, I think. I was on probation and was arrested again for talking to my then-boyfriend, who was on my list of People It Is Now Illegal to Talk To. My uncle saw us hanging out together downtown. I asked him not tell my mom, and we started to walk away, but he called her anyway, and she found us on the way to the house I had once run away to, forced me into the car, and drove me to the cop shop. More jail time, more court dates, more blurry memories.

Each time I was arrested, they brought me to the cell they showed us a couple years back, when our Grade Six class was taken on a tour of the police station. This was the same time we were learning about drugs and How To Say No. The cops brought fake drugs to school to show us what they looked like. I thought it was so funny at the time, being brought to this cold, grey cell I'd seen when I was a kid, but it was also a nightmare. No sleep. No knowing what time or day it was. Nothing in the cell but a chrome toilet & sink, a concrete bed, and a surveillance camera.

The basement cells at court were more colourful. Orange, yellow, and brown. Tuesdays were Youth Day at court, so I'd be brought over first thing in the morning, even if they weren't calling me up to court 'til late in the afternoon. A few of us would be picked up from various detention centres in the area and brought to court in an unmarked white van, handcuffed. The cops would bring us burgers from Harvey's for lunch, sometimes a salad for me since I was vegetarian back then. I met other people from other detention centres. Boys and girls were separated. I shared cells with girls from Vanier, and talked to invisible boys in the cells beside me. As we were brought past one another's cells by security guards who handcuffed us to bring us up and downstairs & to and from the courtroom, we'd peek into each other's cells and smile or try to wave. Inevitably, we'd be packed up into cop cars again and brought back to the detention centres with more court dates to show up for. It took them so long to deal with me, I'd usually get out on time served.

Don't freak out, but I tried to kill somebody at school today.

The following year, my sister and I were arrested together. We were fourteen and had just tried to stab somebody at school. It was all over the news and in the papers, but they weren't allowed to name us since we were under eighteen. Do you know what it feels like to be arrested?

It feels like being underwater. It feels like being in one of those dreams where you're trying so hard to run but you're not getting anywhere. It feels like weights pinning your body to the sidewalk. As I was being arrested, I just started blinking really hard, trying to wake myself up.

I ran away from the school, but the cops caught up with me. My sister was a few blocks ahead. We were handcuffed and arrested separately, brought to the station in separate cars, locked up in separate cells. When we got to the station and the cop opened the back door of the car, he threatened to take me down and smash my face into the pavement. I thought we were being arrested for attempted murder. Because that's what it was. I think we always knew this would happen. I cried and cried and cried in my cell. Have you ever had to call your mom to say, "Hey, I've been arrested. Again. Don't freak out, but I tried to kill somebody at school today."

I guess I didn't try to kill her. My sister did. The knife was mine, though. What happened was this: We got sick of everything. We fought with a bunch of girls by the entrance to the school, and finally, fed up, I said, "I'm going home and I'm coming back with a knife and I am either going to kill you, or myself, or both." We lived a couple blocks from the school. I don't remember if my sister came with me or if I walked alone, but I came back with the sharpest knife I could find in the kitchen. When I got back to school, all I wanted to do was stab myself in the guts, over and over. It was all I could see. I kept the knife in my hand, and when things got really bad, after more mean words and more girls and boys ganging up on me and blowing smoke in my face and spilling their drinks on me and threatening to burn me with lit cigarettes, my sister said, "Give me the knife," so I passed it to her, and she went for the girl's throat. I have really never seen somebody's face turn so pale and so scared so fast. My sister seemed to fly at her. The knife was pressing down on her throat, but there were so many people suddenly jumping on my sister and holding her back. All I did was watch. My sister must have gotten angry with all those hands on her body, dropped the knife, and ran away. I watched her leave, and then I left, too. I don't know where we thought we were going. I thought maybe I'd just disappear. I can still see us so clearly, walking away, Amber a block ahead of me, but then my memory gets fades out.

There were opinion pieces in the paper after it happened. You know when they ask an over-simplified question to regular folk on the street, then print a photo of them with their one sentence answer? "Have you ever bullied anyone?" "How do you feel about violence in schools?"

Earlier in the school year, after having garbage thrown at me in the cafeteria, I screamed and freaked out and threatened to blow up the school. The next day, we were all sent home because not enough students had shown up to make going to class worthwhile. I was brought to the office and told that, because of my threats, less than 50% of the school population had come to school. The vice principal was the only member of staff who had any sympathy for me. I remember her telling me, "I don't know why they make fun of you just for dressing in black. I'd get it of they made fun of you for dressing in lime green, but not black." I was proud of myself for scaring them away.

The so-called "most intelligent" students had their IQ's tested. My sister and I took this test, which took a few days, and our IQ's were ranked among the top five in the school, when we had only just turned fourteen. I found out later that the people who organized the testing had fought to have us excluded, but the vice principal insisted we be tested. I'm not sure what the point of the whole thing was, I just think it's weird and funny and a giant fuck you to both the students and the teachers who thought we were worthless. I think we were bullied and harassed by teachers just as much as we were by the other kids.

I guess that's my roundabout way of saying that conventional education systems don't work. My "experience with institutionalized education" is just being treated like shit, growing bitter and resentful, knowing that I need to find a way out to save my life. If I had been forced to stay in school, I am absolutely 100% sure that I would have committed suicide. That was the only alternative I could see back then. Kill everybody else, kill myself.

My sister and I didn't return to school after serving time. The charges ended up being something like Uttering Death Threats, Concealing a Weapon, Aggravated Assault... I don't remember what else. We served two months in separate detention centres, another two months in a group home (although youth who are arrested together are typically not allowed to serve time in the same group home, they made an exception for us since we are family), and five years on probation; the first year of probation involved a curfew and reporting to a probation officer once a month and all the other usual stuff, with all the rules lifted after one year, except we weren't allowed to be near knives until we turned nineteen. We spent the rest of our teenage years hanging out at the library, making VHS mix tapes, becoming obsessed with *Velvet Goldmine*, getting soul-killing cashier jobs, and eventually getting involved with zines, the local music scene, and found other weirdos to fall in love with and leave behind.

TODAY

I still feel that strange, sullen, fearful weirdo inside me. I worry that everyone will hate me for what I did, and I worry that I will do it again. I have such conflicting feelings when I tell these stories. Thirteen-year-old Me seems to be within me all the time. I remember being so quiet and afraid all the time, and yet I was also a violent, destructive, antagonistic person. I have a hard time reconciling my various identities, making sense of things. I see this strange dichotomy and I don't know what to do with it. What am I looking for?

And why am I telling these stories to everyone?

I want to purge it all. Like actually vomit the stories all over everyone, and they can deal with it now because it's outta me. I want to take another step toward integrating the me of my early teen years to the me of today. I want to acknowledge that I still feel this violence and anger inside of me and that I'm scared of what could happen if I ever truly lose control again. Sometimes it seems like no matter how crazy I get, I am still keeping something to myself. I'm not always sure what it is. I know that I have constant visions of blood and screams; of bodies-arms-wrists banged against walls and pavement and rugburn floors. And I don't know if it's something I'm going to inflict upon myself, someone else, or both. I don't know when it will happen, or if it will happen at all; maybe I'll take it to my grave. It's come out in small bursts since then. I've screamed and slammed doors, I've hit people and choked people, and I've thrown myself against walls and floors because I didn't know what else to do. I've also collected flowers and squirrel trinkets and photobooth strips, and I've been the nicest-kindest-sweetest person in the world. So what does it all mean? How many parts of myself are split and how can I bring them together and tell their/our stories, and have that process be recovery, not destruction?

Just being willing and able to put some of it into words is sometimes enough, for now. To have the guts to tell somebody else. You. Maybe you won't like me anymore. I don't know. But the day me and my twin tried to kill someone marks the moment we finally escaped and began to learn how to walk-stomp-wander-dance our own path, the day that became integral to us really really really learning how to be ourselves, and fuck it if you don't like us.

Dear Diary,

I got a tattoo of a columbine flower today. It wasn't one of those tattoos I thought about for years and planned and pined for. At the library one day, I was in the plant section looking for books about lavender, and happened to stumble into a book about columbines instead. I knew immediately that I'd be putting the lavender tattoo on hold, yet again, and getting a columbine as soon as possible.

Whenever I hear of school stabbings, school shootings, I identify with the killer. I lack any capacity to feel sympathy for anybody else involved; before I know the story (and I think they are stories hardly any of us will ever truly *know*, you know?), I simply assume that the "victims" did something to bring this upon themselves, and I'm glad the weirdo who brought a knife to school had the guts to do something with it. Sometimes I even envy them. I mean, I think it's bullshit that they had to go through whatever they went through that made a violent response necessary, but I know the kinds of things that can bring someone to this point.

I know I may have doomed myself to forever be asked, "Why did you get a tattoo of a columbine?" The word *columbine* has grown to become associated more with school violence than pretty flowers, and I wonder if anyone will have a little inkling and make that connection. I wonder if they'll ask about it. And I wonder what I'll tell them.

Maranda ♥♡

OUTRO

Dear _____,

I've been tempted to write disclaimers for this zine, like: I was young, I was naïve, I was crazy, I didn't know. But that would be another book altogether. So I guess what I want to say is this: I hope you understand. I hope you don't hate me. I hope you can find yourself in my stories, and learn how to tell your own. I hope we can be friends.

These are only some of my stories: pieces, glimpses. My story continues beyond these pages. Secrets, adventures, survival, revenge. Each day, I am learning more about myself, more about how to create the life I want. I'm still learning how to live well with depression, anxiety, and BPD, and how to stay sober. How about you? What have you been learning lately? What are your survival strategies? Have you had any good adventures lately? Are you keeping any secrets? Do you want to share them? Write to me! Make a zine! Tell me your own stories. Take good care of yourself, and stay wonderful.

maranda ♡♡

Maranda Elizabeth
P.O. Box 1689
Guelph, Ontario
N1H 6Z9 Canada

marandaelizabeth.com

About the author:

Maranda is a zinester, writer, and daydreamer, and self-identified weirdo and genderqueer. Maranda began writing their zine, Telegram, as a way to connect with others when they were feeling shy and isolated in their hometown of Lindsay, Ontario. They wrote messages of encouragement alongside tales of depression and anxiety, and traded zines through snail mail. With each zine Maranda made, they learned to become more honest and open, began making friends by photocopying thoughts and feelings and confessions, and found that writing and sharing would be crucial to their survival. Maranda especially loves writing about mental health, self-care, and creativity, sending letters to friends and strangers, and sharing ridiculously personal stories. They currently reside in Guelph, Ontario.